T0208837

CITIZEN MILITIA

REAR ADMIRAL JOSEPH H. MILLER
MRS. CATHY MILLER, R.N.,
CNRN, CO-AUTHOR

authorHOUSE®

AuthorHouse™
1663 Liberty Drive
Bloomington, IN 47403
www.authorhouse.com
Phone: 1 (800) 839-8640

Published by AuthorHouse 02/26/2019

ISBN: 978-1-7283-0075-7 (sc)
ISBN: 978-1-7283-0076-4 (hc)
ISBN: 978-1-7283-0074-0 (e)

Library of Congress Control Number: 2019902011

Print information available on the last page.

This book is printed on acid-free paper.

Contents

Book One

CITIZEN MILITIA
11 February 2019

The United States has been at war 93.5% of the time from 1775-2018. The Global War on Terrorism was declared in 2001 and has cost us 1.9 trillion dollars.

Only a tiny fraction of the United States population knows that it is Our Military that is fighting this War. We are fighting the War in 80 Nations, Six Continents, and in 40% of the world's countries.

We need to eliminate the criminals! The only answer to the extensive crime in America is being able to identify the criminals and where indicated kill them. This can only be done with a Citizen Militia; with one militia member armed on every block in America. The criminals have never been identified and this is the only way to do it. History reveals that <u>citizen militias</u> have always been of the highest service to all governments and have kept them free and incorrupt longer than they would have been without the militia.

We are on your side which is the side of America. - *"America First Always"*

(Additions have been added to the manuscript that was sent to the President.)

I. Militia

"And ye shall hear of wars and rumours of wars: see that ye be not troubled: for all these things must come to pass, but the end is not yet. For nation shall rise against nation, and kingdom against kingdom: and there shall be famines, and pestilences, and earthquakes, in divers places. (**Matt 24 6, 7**)

"And when ye shall hear of wars and rumours of wars, be ye not troubled: for such things must needs be; but the end shall not be yet. For nation shall rise against nation, and kingdom against kingdom: and there shall be earthquakes in divers places, and there shall be famines and troubles: these are the beginnings of sorrows." (**Mark 13:7, 8**)

"Only the dead have seen the end of war." (Plato)

A **Militia** is a military organization composed of citizens enrolled in training for service in times of national emergency. (1, p.1840) My research suggests a national **militia** was first developed by Philip II, King of Macedonia, as a defense against Anglo-Saxons. (382-336 BC). (1, p. 2209) He was the father of Alexander the Great and was murdered. Alexander the Great was also king of Macedon (356-323 B.C.) (1, p.63)

Men of the militia are usually between 17 and 40 years old, but in time of need all ages maybe recruited. (3, p. 27) History reveals that **citizen militias** have always been of the highest service to all governments and have kept them free and incorrupt longer than they would have been without the militia. Rome remained free for 400 years and Sparta for 800 years as **their citizens were armed all that time**. Many states without militia have lasted less than 40 years. **No state can support itself without an army**. (3, p. 30)

Moses: "From 20 years old and upward all that are able to go forth to war (**militia**) in Israel: you and Aaron shall number them by their armies." (Num. 1:3) (4, p.780) This is repeated in fifteen verses of the same chapter and refers to the biblical date 1404 B.C. (4, p. 766) This is the concept of militia.

They also report Solomon's large professional soldiery as the first in Israel's history. (1 Kings 10:26)

1 Chronicles 12: refers to mighty men of valor as helpers in time of war. (Militia) (1 Chronicles 12: 1,4, 8, 10-16, 21-25, 28, 30, 35, 38)

Tactics of War Were Simple: Surprise, ambush, pretend flight, and surrounding the enemy. (Genesis 14:15; Joshua 8:2,3; 2 Samuel 5:23) (4, p. 1092) Also noted were men of valor as helpers (**militia**) in times of war. (2:1, 4, 8, 14–16, 21–25, 28, 30, 36, 38)

We must wait upon the Lord. "But they that wait upon the LORD shall renew *their* strength; they shall mount up with wings as eagles; they shall run, and not be weary; *and* they shall walk, and not faint." (Isa. 40:31) "Who satisfieth thy mouth with good *things; so that* thy youth is renewed like the eagle's." (Psa. 103:5)

The **militia ordinance**, of the **citizen's militia** is instituted by the ordinance. Machiavelli's **militia ordinances** were dated in 1506. (3, p. 28) **No troops can be of more service than those chosen from one's own subjects. One sees this in the history of all nations.** With experience comes courage. "No man has ever founded a monarchy or a republic without being well assured that if his subjects were armed, they would always be ready and willing to defend their country."

In the **citizen's militia** there can be no better method devised to form an army or to introduce good order and discipline among soldiers. The first kings of Rome noted that the **citizen's militia** could be quickly raised in a sudden emergency for the defense of the state.

The **militia** prefers plowman, smiths (metal workers) farriers (blacksmiths) carpenters, stonecutters (wild bird hunters) butchers, hunters etc. Less desirable are fisherman, cooks, bawdyhouse keepers, sport, or pleasure occupations. (3, p. 33)

Recruits should be selected for **moral uprightness** rather than for military skill alone. (3, p. 33) (Vegetius and Machiavelli) **These soldiers can turn their hands to more service than one.** (3, p. 34)

Rome kept legions. One consisted of Roman citizens only. (3, p. 36)

The **militia** could be a large number depending on volunteers. Machiavelli "thinks that a **citizen's militia** is an important instrument of civic education where unruly people may be disciplined, imbued with a respect for law and authority, and given a sense of dedication to the common good." (3, p. 40) Many became warlike and courageous against an enemy or country or its society. (3, p. 41)

Much of the expense of a militia is personal. Certain small arms are needed for battle with another armed group. There is an expense for training, depending on the attendees. The modern concept of the **militia** as a defense organization against invaders grew out of the defense of Anglo-Saxon group. **Militias** persisted through the Middle Ages (450-700 A.D.) in England, Italy, and Germany. With the development of large standing armies, the **militia** declined. (1, p.1840)

II. Militia (1075) (2, p. 207)

The term **militia** was first used against the Normans in 1075. The courts developed the first step in the **evaluation of the Common Law as an independent force in 1075.** The citizens were required to do military service in 1075.

III. The Art of War

The *Art of War* by Niccolò Machiavelli is a military classic of military and political war theory. Machiavelli's lifelong preoccupation was with military affairs. (3, p. ix)

"Niccolò Machiavelli, born in 1469, is surely one of the great political theorists and literary artists of our civilization." (3, p. ix) **Citizens' militia** drove out the foreign barbarians that ended their ambitions to take Rome. (3, p. xi) He served Florence fourteen years (1498-1512) devoted to the problems of war (3, p. xi) and defense as Secretary of Military and Foreign Affairs. (3, p. xii) His first official mission was the Pisan War in 1498. He wrote the famous *Discourse on the War with Pisa*. He reported to the Pope on the defense of Florence. (3, p. xiii)

He fought politics all his life concerning the citizen militia. Leonardo da Vinci consulted with him and he was **authorized to raise a militia.** (3, p. xlii) Other medieval city-states depended upon a **citizen army**. The condottieri were the first modern military specialists. (3, p. xiii) It seemed that the conscription of a **combat militia** was the only viable course for Greece and Rome. (3, p. xiv) By 1506, Machiavelli, had recruited more than 5000 men. The famous **militia ordinance** was drafted by Machiavelli and was approved in 1506. By 1507 there were 10,000 infantries. His long and arduous toil was the victory at Pisa. This gave glory to the victorious **militia**. The **militia** had 12,000 militiamen for the city's defense. (3, p. xv) A new force of **militia** was recruited just as Machiavelli died on June 21, 1527. (3, p. xvi)

The military ideas of Machiavelli were the thought of the ancients and is noted in the standard classical military treatises by Sextus, Julius, Frontinus, Publius, Cornelius, Tacitus, Vegetius, and Modestus. (3, p. xvii) They were with Latin and Italian translations.

"Xenophon related that a military model is apparently crucial for a theory of politics." (3, p. xviii) **The relationship between military and civic affairs is noted by Machiavelli.** (3, p. xvii)

Machiavelli joined the society of intellectuals in 1515 and wrote his famous *Discourses.* He continued to develop a **citizen's militia** with proper training and organization. (3, p. xix)

The Art of War is the first full-scale modern attempt to popularize classical military thought. He brought out the ancient sources of Vegetius, Frontinus, Polybius, Livy, Caesar, Josephus, and Plutarch. (3, p. xx)

In the fourth century of the Christian Era, a compendium of Roman military practice was developed. The primary source is divided into five books. (3, p. xx)

1. Organization
2. Tactics
3. Siege and Fortifications
4. Naval Warfare
5. Not completed

He further notes the nature of men to be selected for military service. (3, p. xxi) His model battle is unprecedented in military literature. (3, p. xxi) Lessons in the Art of War are included in the Persian wars. (3, p. xxi)

Machiavelli returned to the more ancient Roman Republic institution of a **citizen's militia**. He produces a critical synthesis of ancient military wisdom. (3, p. xxi) Machiavelli and Vegetius debated about recruitment, promotion, weapons, combat methods, the ordering of troops, and encampment.

The codes of military laws were lacking. (3, p. xxiv) Regular training and discipline were almost unknown. If the king was not ready to fight, he would retire to a well-fortified stronghold. **The basic strategic principle was to give immediate battle with a mass charge.**

In the *Art of War* (pp. lix, lx, lxi) Machiavelli lists 43 categories of war strategy. I am listing only a few of them:

1. Concealing one's plans

2. Find out the enemy's plans

3. On determining the character of the war

13. Choosing the time for battle

14. Choosing the place for battle

15. Disposition of troops for battle

20. Restoring morale by firmness

21. Bring war to a close after a successful engagement

29. How may the enemy be reduced to want

35. Setting traps to draw out the besieged

36. Pretended retirements

41. How to meet treason and desertion

43. Concerning the steadfastness of the besieged

As listed military leaders during 4 B.C. to 4 A.D. approached the military situation with the above perspective. **This translates the solution into action that will defeat the enemy.** (3, p. lxi) These have become the **Principles of War. Leadership is the key to victory.** (3, p. lxii) Willing obedience can be exacted, and hatred avoided. **Hatred is the prime evil that jeopardizes all leadership.** (3, p. lxiv) At the heart of leadership is the problem of obedience. (3, p. lxviii) Leaders must avoid all pride and arrogance. (3, p. lxix)

There must be good health in the camp with an adequate medical staff. (3, p. lxxi)

In ancient times the only alternative to victory was death. (3, p. lxxii) The state possesses **neither a life, nor soul, nor a personality, nor an interest in of its own.** An inner peace and spiritual life are common to all men. Civil mechanisms must be designed, constructed, maintained, and adapted to changing conditions by the conscious and purposeful efforts of men. (3, p. lxxv)

Laws should arise from the human need for social unity and protection. Each law must apply equally to all under the law. (3, p. lxxvi)

The rational military mechanism should never be confounded with the rational civic mechanism. (3, p. lxxviii) An army is an instrument of the state and should always be subordinate to it. (3, p. lxxviii) Belief must be to the common good. (3, p. lxxviii) The lack of human nature is found only in the dead. (3, p. lxxix)

"People look upon a soldier as a creature different from all other men". (3, p. 3) They are a military force that lives "in fear of God and in obedience to human laws. (3, p. 4) Ancient soldiers were picked because of their fidelity, love of peace, and a fear of God. Who ought to be more faithful than a man **entrusted with the safety of his country** and sworn to defend it with the last drop of his blood." (3, p. 4)

In the art of war, "human life is conceived in terms of a struggle between fortune and virtue. (3, p. 7) Machiavelli believes that the quality of people depends upon education and conditioning rather than nature (inborn traits). "Man is raw material to be molded." (3, p. 25)

Machiavelli on War

Machiavelli's idea was "War is war" (3, p. xxv) with no holds barred. The battlefield was not subject to common moral considerations where trickery and violence was legitimate when against an enemy. **Anything to overpower the enemy**. We used the atomic bomb on two cities with civilians where thousands were killed – War is war! Politics and war were a fundamental unity with war serving as an instrument of politics. (3, p. xxvi)

The modern enemy of our day does not obey any of the modern rules of war. Neither should we when fighting against them.

Machiavelli is "the first secular writer to attempt to allot to the practice of arms, its place among the collective activities of mankind, to define its aims, and to regard it as a means to an end." (3, p. xxvi) This political doctrine had its influence on the German philosophic historians. This idea was carried in the modern world.

National **citizen's militias** will have a vital role in the defense of a country. Machiavelli believed in the "true prophetic spirit" of the modern **citizen militia** army. (3, p. xxvi)

Machiavelli's Calculations

1. The **armed citizenry** (**militia**) would be a very definite obstacle to anyone who wanted to seize power.
2. A **militia** will always serve as the fundamental instrument of civic educators giving people a respect for authority and a sense of common purpose.
3. A **militia** is less costly than a standing army. (3, p. xxvii)

Therefore, a **citizen militia** is an instrument and a bulwark of republicanism. Military ineffectiveness of the **militia** was caused by **political restrictions**. (3, p. xxvi) The fortitude of the **armed citizenry** in 1530 was noted. (3, p. xxviii) Machiavelli stated that the infantry was the "nerve of the army." (3, p. xxviii) (Small-arms in modern warfare can be greatly underestimated.)

Machiavelli was the first modern writer on the subject of fortifications. (3, p. xxix) Machiavelli's prestige as a military thinker continued to grow all his life. The **citizen militia** was the nucleus of the Crown's infantry during the **wars of religion in the 17th century**. (3, p. xxxi)

The Dutch army under Maurice of the House of Orange was one of the first modern **civilian disciplined armies**. (3, p. xxxiv) Gunpowder and discipline became very significant. The whole of modern warfare presupposes discipline. (3, p. xxxiv)

The development of the military in the 16th century recharged **citizen militia** discipline for military justice and law. Military experience was required. The knowledge of mathematics was required for artillery. (3, p. xxxv) (3, p. xxxvi)

"Morality and ideology became factors involving the duty of the **citizen militia**, self-control, temperance, life-giving energy, and **strength of soul**." (3, p. xxxviii)

"Military discipline required: virtue, knowledge, prudence, authority, and success. Virtue consists of uprightness of life, zeal in enterprise, diligence in service, valor in danger, hardness in action, and swiftness in execution." (3, p. xxxviii)

IV. Militias Survived in America

The first **citizen militia** in America was The Military Company of Massachusetts. After this some colonies developed **militias**. (1, p. 1840)

- In the American Revolution they were very valuable. (1, p. 1840) In the book *1776,* militias are mentioned twenty-eight times. (10, p.10)
  General George Washington's famous quote:
  "Perseverance and spirit, perseverance and patience, perseverance and courage have done wonders in all ages. (10, pp. 41, 293)
  "When Boston fell it was melancholy, disease, and death." (10 p. 8)
  "Bribery, favoritism, and corruption was rampant not only in politics, but all levels of society." (10, p. 9) "Difficulties must be overcome, not yielded to." (10, p. 14)
  "A leader must have courage without this all other values including intelligence, and health are useless." (10, p. 23)
  The Americans said, "Let us stand our ground, if we die, let us die here." (10, p. 27)
  "In war man will see others die." (10, p. 34)
  "They had difficulties dealing with Congress, and Americans dedicated to the British king. If the majority had had their way America would not be America today." (10, p. 40)
  "Leaders must know the ways of politics and politicians." (10, p. 50)
  "Truth, freedom, and religion go together." (10, p.110)
  "Do what is right." (10, p. 110)
  "Those who opposed the Americans were shot dead on the spot. (10, pp. 125, 160)

"The American Revolution took the lives of 25,000 Americans." (10, p. 294)

The leaders in America who fought and died for independence with their few victories "sustained suffering, disease, hunger, desertion, cowardice, disillusionment, defeat, terrible discouragement and fear. We must never forget their phenomenal courage and bedrock devotion to country and that they too, will never forget."

Without Washington's leadership and unrelenting perseverance, the revolution would certainly have failed." (10, p. 294)

"The victory and follow-up in America is a "little short of a miracle". (10, p. 294)

- They were further developed during the Civil War as both sides used them. (1, p. 1840)
- During the 19th century various states in United States had their own **citizen militia**.
- **Militias** have served in all the American wars. (1, p. 1840)
- After World War I they became the National Guard. (1, p. 1840) This has distanced itself from the citizen.

Americanization in early 20th century was where the immigrant in the United States was induced to assimilate American speech, ideals, traditions, and ways of life. As a result, there was a great emigration from Europe, between 1880 to World War I. **Americanization was made an official part of the war effort**. Many states passed legislation providing for the education and Americanization for the foreign born. By **1921 virtually every state had a substantial foreign-born population**. The passage of this legislation and the quota system of immigration caused the Americanization movement to be disbanded. (A great weakening for America.) (1, p. 87)

A. Keep in Our Memory America's History

"The word, Paleolithic is used to describe a stage of human culture, the earliest of which we have sure evidence." (2, p. 7)

In America the earliest carbon-14 date so far recovered is 16,374 to 400 B.C. (2, p.10) There is much guess work here.

The earliest Post-Paleolithic cultures are dated 4500 B.C. (2, P. 16)

(There are hundreds. These are selected.) **(6, Paraphrased)**

1492   Christopher Columbus discovered America.

1513   Juan Ponce de Leon explored the Florida coast.

1524   Giovanni da Verrazano entered New York Harbor.

1539   Hernando DeSoto landed in Florida and crossed the Mississippi River in 1541.

1565   Saint Augustine, Florida, the oldest continuously occupied European settlement in the United States, was founded by Pedro Menendez. It became in the United States in 1821.

1607   Captain John Smith and 105 cavaliers in three ships landed on the Virginia coast and started Jamestown, the first permanent English settlement in the New World.

1619   The first representative assembly in the New World, was on July 30 at Jamestown, Virginia. The first black laborers were indentured servants. (A contract binding one person who agreed to work for a given period.) Chattel (tangible property) other than real estate such as a slave or bondsman. Slavery was not recognized until 1650.

1620   Pilgrims left, Plymouth, England September 16th on the ship *Mayflower* and reached Cape Cod November 19th. One hundred three passengers agreed on self-government. Half of them died the first winter.

1630   John Winthrop settled in Boston, Massachusetts. The history *Chronicle* newspaper was begun in 1856.

1635   The oldest continuous public school in United States on April 23.

1636 Roger Williams founded Providence, Rhode Island, in June. He democratically ruled the colony with separation of church and state. Harvard College was founded in 1644 and is the oldest institution of higher learning in the United States.

1640 Bay Psalm Book was the first book printed in America.

1661 Missionary John Elliott translated the New Testament to become the first Bible printed in North America.

1673 Regular mail service on horseback was initiated on January 1 between New York and Boston.

1676 A bloody Indian war in New England ended August 12. Wampanoag, chief of the Narragansett Indians was killed. Nathaniel Bacon led planters against the autocratic British government. Sir William Berkeley, burned Jamestown, Virginia, on September 19th. Bacon died, and 23 followers were executed.

1681 John Bunyan's *The Pilgrim's Progress* was published in America and became a bestseller.

1682 Spanish colonists became the first Europeans to settle Texas at present-day El Paso.

1683 William Penn signed a treaty with the Delaware Indians April 23 in payment for Pennsylvania lands.

1690 The first colonial newspaper, was ***Public Occurrences***. Benjamin Harris also published ***New England Primer*** for use as an elementary school textbook.

1692 Witchcraft in Salem Village where 14 women and six men were executed by Special Court.

1699 Captain William Kidd hanged for piracy. French settlements were begun in Mississippi and Louisiana.

1712 Slaves revolted in New York City, April 6. Twenty-one were executed. In 1741 there was a second uprising; 13 slaves were hanged, 13 burned, 71 deported.

1716 The first theater in the colonies opened in Williamsburg, Virginia.

1726   *Great Awakening*, the general revival of evangelical religion began in the colonies.

1732   Benjamin Franklin published the first *Poor Richard's Almanac* which continued until 1758. Georgia was the last of the 13 colonies chartered.

1739   A series of slave uprisings were put down in South Carolina.

1741   Jonathan Edwards' famous sermon, *Sinners in the Hands of an Angry God*, was important in the **Great Awakening.**

1752   The Liberty Bell was cast in England and delivered to Pennsylvania.

1757   The first streetlights were in Philadelphia.

1764   Sugar Act April 5, 1765; The Stamp Act; Quartering Act 1767; Townsend Acts, all heavy taxes on the colonists.

1770   Boston Massacre, the British fired into a Boston mob.

1773   Boston Tea Party and East India Company tea ships were burned, and the cargo was thrown overboard to protest a tea tax by Britain.

1775 - 1783 American Revolutionary War

1775   Patrick Henry addressed Virginians on March 23. "Give me liberty or give me death!" Paul Revere's ride occurred April 18th to alert Patriots that the British were on their way to Concord, Massachusetts, to destroy arms. The British sustained 273 casualties. The Minutemen lost 8. Fort Ticonderoga in New York was captured by the Colonist. Bunker Hill fought twice before retreating.

George Washington was named the Commander-in-Chief of the Continental Army by the Continental Congress on June 17.

The postal system was established July 26th and Benjamin Franklin became the first Postmaster General.

1776   Thomas Paine's pamphlet, *Common Sense,* advocating independence from Great Britain began.

1777   Washington defeated Lord Charles Cornwallis at Princeton, New Jersey.

1776   <u>**Declaration of Independence July 4**</u>

The Destiny of The Signers of The Declaration of Independence. When the 56 Signers of The Declaration of Independence attached their signatures to that document, each knew they were committing treason against the British Crowne. If caught and captured, they risked death. But death would not be swift. It would be by hanging to the point of unconsciousness, then being revived, disemboweled, their body parts boiled in oil and their ashes scattered into the wind. Our Founding Fathers valued freedom, for themselves and their posterity, to the extent that they found this fate worth the risk.

The story below tells what happened to the men who signed the **Declaration of Independence:**

Five signers were captured by the British and brutally tortured as traitors.

Nine fought in the War for Independence and died from wounds or from hardships they suffered.

Two lost their sons in the Continental Army.

Another two had sons captured.

At least a dozen of the fifty-six had their homes pillaged and burned.

What kind of men were they?

Twenty-five were lawyers or jurists.

Eleven were merchants.

Nine were farmers or large plantation owners.

One was a teacher.

One a musician.

One a printer.

These were men of means and education, yet they signed the Declaration of Independence, knowing full well that the penalty could be death if they were captured.

The American flag, Stars and Stripes, was authorized June 14, 1777.

1779   John Paul Jones on the USS *Bonhomme Richard* defeated HMS *Serapis* in the British North Sea waters on September 23.

1781 Bank of North America, first commercial bank incorporated on May 26

1789 George Washington was chosen as the first President of United States.

United States State Department established July 27

United States War Department established August 7

United States Supreme Court established September 24

1791 Bill of Rights went into effect December 15.

1795 United States paid one million dollars ransom for 115 Seamen September 5th.

The University of North Carolina became the first operating state university.

1802 United States Military Academy at West Point, New York, was established.

1804 Meriwether Lewis and William Clark explored the Northwest.

1805 United States Marines captured Tripolitania, Port of Derma, on April 27. This was the inspiration for "to the shores of Tripoli" in the Marine Corps hymn.

1812 The **War of 1812** - Britain seized 4,000 United States sailors.

1814 The British burn the Capitol and the White House. Their attack on Baltimore failed and inspired, *"The Star-Spangled Banner"* by Francis Scott Key. The United States won the Naval Battle of Lake Champlain, September 11, and Great Britain signed treaty on December 24.

1815 In New Orleans, 5,300 British, unaware of the peace treaty, attacked the United States sustaining 2000 casualties. The Americans lost 71.

1819 Spain ceded Florida to the United States, February 23.

1826 *The Last of the Mohicans* was written by James Fenimore Cooper.

1828 First United States passenger railroad the Baltimore & Ohio.

1835 The Liberty Bell cracked July 8.

1836 Texas was besieged at the Alamo by Mexican General Santa Anna. Sam Houston and Texas defeated the Mexicans at San Jacinto, April 21.

1836 "Trail of Tears", Cherokee Indians were marched from their home in Southeast United States to Oklahoma.

1841 The first immigrant wagons bound for California reached there on November 4.

Edgar Allan Poe published one of the first American detective stories, *The Murders in the Rue Morgue.*

1843 1000 settlers left Independence, Missouri, by way of the Oregon Trail.

1844 The first live telegraph was sent May 24 from Washington to Baltimore, "What hath God wrought?"

1845 Texas was admitted to the union.

"The Raven" poem by Edgar Allan Poe.

1846 Mexican War, 12,000 United States troops took Vera Cruz, March 27, 1847, Mexico City, September 14. Mexico ceded claims to Texas, California, and other territories. The term "manifest destiny" coined by journalist in 1845.

The sewing machine was invented.

1848 Gold was discovered in California on January 24. 80,000 prospectors immigrated in 1849.

Women's Rights Convention, July 19-20

1850 **The Compromise of 1850** admitted California as the 31st state on September 9.

Fugitive Slave Law forbidding slavery.

The Scarlet Letter by Nathaniel Hawthorne

Moby Dick by Herman Melville

1852 Elmwood Cemetery, Memphis, Tennessee, established. (We have had our Miller plots there over 50 years.)

Uncle Tom's Cabin by Harriett Beecher Stowe.

1854   **The Republican Party was formed, February 28**.

1855   The first train crossed the Mississippi River.

Leaves of Grass by Walt Whitman.

1858   The first Atlantic cable.

1859   The first commercially productive oil well was near Titusville, Pennsylvania, 27ᵗʰ August.

1860   The first Pony Express ride between Sacramento, California, and St. Joseph, Missouri.

1861-1865 The American Civil War

The first tra The Civil War began as Confederates fired on Fort Sumter, Charleston, South Carolina. nscontinental telegraph line in operation.

1863   Confederate forces surrender at Vicksburg, Mississippi.

President Lincoln issued the ***Emancipation Proclamation*** freeing all slaves.

Lincoln gave the Gettysburg Address.

Lincoln declared Thanksgiving a holiday.

1865   General Robert E. Lee surrendered 27,000 Confederate troops to General Grant at Appomattox Courthouse Virginia, on April 9.

J.E. Johnson surrendered 31,000 to General Sherman at Dunbar Station, North Carolina, on April 18.

President Lincoln was assassinated April 14.

1867   The United States bought Alaska from Russia for $7.2 million on March 30.

Ragged Dick by Horatio Alger.

1868   The 14ᵗʰ amendment providing citizenship for all persons born or naturalized in the United States.

The *World Almanac* began.

1869   Transcontinental railroad completed.

1870   The 15ᵗʰ Amendment making race no bar to voting rights.

1871   The Great Chicago fire, October 8-11.

National Rifle Association founded.

1873   **The first U. S. Post card.**

Jesse James robbed his first passenger train on July 21.

New York's Bellevue Hospital started the first nursing school.

1876   Colonel George H. Custer was defeated in the "last stand".

The Battle of Little Big Horn, Montana in the Sioux Indian War.

1881   Clara Barton founded the American Red Cross May 21.

The battle at O. K. Corral, Tombstone, Arizona.

1884   Mark Twain's, *The Adventures of Huckleberry Finn.*

1885   Washington Monument dedicated February 21.

1886   The Haymarket riot and bombing on May 4 in Chicago over labor battle for an eight-hour work day. Seven police and four workers died. Eight anarchists were tried and hanged on November 11.

Coca-Cola first sold May 8 in Atlanta, Georgia.

American Federation of labor (AFL) formed.

1890   The Massacre at Wounded Knee, South Dakota, December 29.

This was the last major conflict between Indians and United States troops. 200 Indians were killed, and 29 soldiers killed.

1895   *"America the Beautiful"* was sung for the first time on July 4.

The Red Badge of Courage by Stephen Crane.

1896   *"Cross of Gold"* speech by William Jennings Bryan.

"Stars and Stripes Forever" by John Philip Sousa, December 25.

1897   The first Boston Marathon April 9.

First subway service opens to the public in Boston on September 1.

1898   **1898 – Spanish-American War**

The United States declared war on Spain, April 24, to liberate Cuba from Spanish rule. They destroyed the Spanish fleet and took Guam and Puerto Rico on July 25-August 12.

Spain ceded the Philippines, Puerto Rico, and Guam, and approved independence for Cuba.

Hawaii was annexed July 7.

1902 **The Immigration Restriction Act** (federal) provided that an immigrant, on- demand, must demonstrate their ability to pass a test in a European language. In 1905 this was changed to a "prescribed language". (2, p. 932)

May 19, 1921: Immigration Act limiting the number from a given country to 3% of the number of foreign-born persons of such nationality resident in the United States according to the U.S. census of 1910. (2, p.1047)

May 26, 1924: An Immigration Bill was signed limiting annual immigration from a given country to 2% of the nationals of the country in the United States in 1890. The annual immigration should be limited to 150,000, to be apportioned among the different countries in proportion to the relative strength of the various foreign elements represented in the American population in 1920. (This excluded the Japanese) (2, p. 1048)

1903 Treaty between United States and Columbia to have the United States dig the Panama Canal, January 22.

The first successful flight December 17, Orville Wright near Kitty Hawk, North Carolina.

That same day Wilbur Wright flew an improved airplane.

The Iroquois Theater fire in Chicago killed 600 of the 1900 audience.

1907 President Roosevelt sent the "Great White Fleet" of 16 U.S. battleships around the world to show power.

1909 Admiral Robert E. Perry reached the North Pole April 6.

National Association for the Advancement of Colored People was founded. (NAACP)

1910 The Boy Scouts of America was founded February 8.

1911 **The first transcontinental airplane flight.**

1913 The 16th Amendment - started Federal Income Tax.

The Federal Reserve System began.

1914 **1914 – 1918 World War I**

1915 The first transcontinental telephone call from New York to San Francisco was January 25.

The British ship RMS *Lusitania* was sunk by the Germans on May 7. 1,198 passengers died.

1916 General John J. Perishing entered Mexico to pursue Francisco "Poncho" Villa who raided U.S. border areas. Lasted from March 1916 to February 5, 1917.

Jeannette Rankin, a Republican from Montana was elected the first female member of Congress.

1918 Influenza pandemic killed 548,000 in the United States and 20 million worldwide

1919 18th Amendment prohibited the sale of alcoholic beverages.

The first transatlantic flight for a United States Navy seaplane, the NC-4, left Rockaway, New York, and arrived in Lisbon, Portugal, in 19 days on May 27.

1921 **Congress sharply curbed immigration with a quota system May 19.**

An Armaments Conference, Washington, D.C., agreed to curtail Naval construction, outlawed poison gas, restrict submarine attacks on merchant vessels, and respect China's integrity.

1924 *"Rhapsody in Blue"* by George Gershwin.

1926 The first liquid - fuel rocket Dr. Robert H. Goddard, Army Air Corps, established.

The Sun Also Rises by Ernest Hemingway

1926 The first New York to Paris nonstop flight alone was done by Charles A. Lindbergh in the **Spirit of St. Louis**. (3,610 miles in 33 1/2 hours.)

1929 Gangsters killed several rivals in Chicago's St. Valentine's Day Massacre, which won Al Capone control of Chicago's underworld.

The Sound and Fury by William Faulkner.

1929 **The Great Depression**, worst years 1933-1934, ended in 1939 at the beginning of World War II.

1930 *The Maltese Falcon* by Dashiell Hammett.

The first neurosurgeon United States Naval Medical Reserve Rear Admiral, Joseph H. Miller was born.

Sinclair Lewis, the first American to win the Nobel prize in literature.

1931 The Empire State building, the world's tallest, opened on May 1.

Al Capone was convicted on tax evasion October 7.

1937 Amelia Earhart disappeared July 2, near Howland Island in the pacific.

1939 – 1945 World War II

1940 The first peacetime military draft in United States history.

1941 **Four Freedoms termed essential by President Roosevelt: <u>Freedom of speech</u> and <u>religion</u>, <u>freedom from want and fear</u>.**

Japan attacked Pearl Harbor, Hawaii, at 7:55 AM on December 7. 19 ships were sunk or damaged, 2,403 dead.

"A date which will live in infamy", a speech delivered by United States President Franklin D. Roosevelt to a Joint Session of the US Congress on December 8, 1941, one day after the Empire of Japan's attack

The United States declared war on Japan on December 8, and on Germany and Italy December 11.

Japan invaded the Philippines December 22. Wake Island fell on December 23.

Citizen Kane, by Orson Wells released.

1942 Japanese-Americans were placed in detention camps lasting three years.

Bataan fell on April 8, Corregidor on May 6.

The Battle of Midway June 4-7 was Japan's first major defeat.

Marines landed on Guadalcanal August 7.

The United States and Britain invaded North Africa on November 8.

1944 Allied forces invaded Europe at Normandy, France. (D-Day June 6)

Nazi counteroffensive failed December 6 to January 28, 1945.

1945 Marines landed at Iwo Jima, February 19 to March 16 with heavy casualties.

Okinawa April 1 captured June 21.

Germany surrendered May 7.

May 8 proclaimed V-E Day.

The first Atom bomb dropped on Hiroshima, Japan August 6. 75,000 killed

The second Atom bomb dropped on Nagasaki, Japan August 6. 40,000 killed

Japan agreed to surrender August 14 and formally surrendered September 2.

The first nuclear chain reaction December 2, 1942 (Fission of uranium isotope U-235) was produced at the University of Chicago under physicists Arthur Compton, Enrico Fermi, and others.

1950 President Truman authorized production of an H-bomb on January 31.

Special Senate committee appointed to investigate organized crime May 3.

1950 – 1953 Korean War

North Korea forces invade South Korea June 25.

President Truman ordered the Air Force and Navy to Korea on June 27. He approved ground and airstrikes against North Korea on June 30. United States forces landed at Incheon, South Korea, on September 15. United Nations Forces took Pyongyang, North Korea, October 20, and reached the China border November 26.

The United States banned shipments December 8 to Communist China and to Asiatic ports trading with them.

1952 First hydrogen device explodes November 1 in the Pacific.

1954 USS *Nautilus* the first operational nuclear-powered submarine launched at Groton, Connecticut, on January 21.

Four Puerto Rican independent supporters fired upon members of Congress from the spectator gallery injuring five members on March 1.

1959 **(1959 – 1975 Vietnam War)**

1962 President John F. Kennedy on February 14th said that the United States military advisers in Vietnam would fire if fired upon.

A Soviet offensive missile buildup in Cuba was revealed. President Kennedy and Soviet Premier Khrushchev agreed October 28 that the Cuban base would be dismantled.

1963 **<u>President Kennedy was shot and killed November 22.</u>**

1965 United States forces began firing into Cambodia May 1.

The Hanoi area of North Vietnam was bombed by United States planes on June 29.

By December 31, 385,000 United States troops were stationed in South Vietnam plus 60,000 offshore and 33,000 in Thailand.

1968 The Tet Offensive. Communist troops attacked several provincial capitals, including Saigon on January 30, but suffered heavy casualties. Peace talks began, and all bombing of North Vietnam halted on October 31.

North Korea released the 82 men crew of the USS *Pueblo* on December 22, eleven months after seizing the ship in the Sea of Japan. One member was killed.

1968 Vietnam peace talks began in Paris but deteriorated after 34 days.

1969 North Vietnamese forces launched the biggest attack in four years to the demilitarized zone March 30.

United States forces resume bombing of Hanoi and Haiphong on April 15.

Mining of North Vietnam May 8.

Bombing of North Vietnam resumed after the Paris peace talks fail December 18.

1973 The end to the military draft announced March 29.

Vietnam Peace Pact signed in Paris on January 27.

1975 The United States launched evacuations from Saigon of Americans and some South Vietnamese on April 29 as Communist forces completed the takeover of South Vietnam. South Vietnam officially surrendered on April 30.

Congress voted to provide $405 million for South Vietnam refugees May 16.

140,000 were flown to the United States.

1990 **(1990 – 1991 First Gulf War)**

Hussein invaded Kuwait. He withdrew in 1991.

Operation Desert Storm, Operation Desert Sabre

1993 The World Trade Center in New York City was bombed February 26, killing 6.

July 2nd, President Clinton, approved recommendations that 33 major United States military bases be closed.

On July 19, President Clinton announced, "Don't ask, don't tell, don't pursue" policy for homosexuals in the military.

The Brady Bill, a major gun-control measure, was signed into law by President Clinton November 30.

1998 The United States embassies in Nairobi, Kenya and Dares Salaam, Tanzania were bombed killing at least 257 on August 7.

The United States launch retaliatory strikes August 20 against targets in Afghanistan and the Sudan.

2001 – Present War in Afghanistan

September 11, 2001, Nineteen Al Qaeda operatives carried out the most devastating terrorist attack ever on American soil. Using four hijacked commercial planes they flew two into the World Trade Center in New York City, one into the Pentagon, and one was flown into a field in Pennsylvania after four passengers captured the hijackers.

3,000 people were killed including **2,750** at the World Trade Center. (In World War II **at Pearl Harbor 2,403 Americans were killed**.)

The United States invasion of Afghanistan occurred after the September 11 attacks in late 2001, supported by allies including the United Kingdom.

The office of Homeland security established October 8.

The United States Patriot Act October 26 amid terrorism.

2002   President Bush called Iran, Iraq, and North Korea part of the *"Axis of Evil"* January 29.

1200 United States troops used against forces in Afghanistan.

North Korea acknowledge developing nuclear arms. (Note that this was in 2002.)

2003 – 2014 Second Gulf War

Operation Iraqi Freedom

2003   The Iraq War was a protracted armed conflict that began in 2003 with the invasion of Iraq by a United States-led coalition that toppled the government of Saddam Hussein. The conflict continued for much of the next decade as an insurgency emerged to oppose the occupying forces and the post-invasion Iraqi government.

United States forces report control over much of Baghdad. President Bush declared an end of major combat operations in Iraq. Insurgents continue to mount attacks.

The Senate approved $87.5 billion on November 3 for the United States military forces in Iraq to help in rebuilding the country.

2004 The United States led coalition transferred power to interim Iraqi government June 28.

2005 **President Bush signed anti-torture legislation December 30.**

2006 <u>**President Bush signed a bill on October 26 authorizing a 700-mile fence along the United States Mexico border.**</u>

2007 A troop "surge" in Iraq January 10.

Bill approved Iraq and Afghanistan funding.

National Security Agency to monitor communications without court warrant if believed related to terrorism August 4

2008 United States airstrike in Afghanistan village killed up to 90 civilians.

2009 President, Obama called for "new beginning" in relation with Muslim world June 4.

2011 Withdrawal of U.S. troops from Iraq

The withdrawal of U.S. military forces from Iraq began in December 2007 with the end of the Iraq War troop surge of 2007 and was completed by December 2011, bringing an end to the Iraq War. President Obama signed measures extending key provisions of the USA Patriot Act May 26.

The United States stepped up drone attacks against jihadists in Yemen June 3.

On May 1, 2011, al-Qaeda leader **Osama bin Laden, responsible for the 9/11 attacks in New York and Washington, was killed by U.S. forces in Pakistan.**

A United States citizen and Muslim cleric linked to terrorist attacks in the United States was killed in September by a drone attack in Yemen.

December 12-15 marked what was to be the end of the United States military mission in Iraq.

United States convoy left December 18.

Since 2003, 4,500 United States servicemembers have been killed and 32,000 wounded.

2011   **Obama endorsed same-sex marriage on May 9.**

The United States Embassy in Benghazi Libya was attacked by terrorists September 11, 12.

Ambassador Chris Stevens and three other Americans were killed. A report released December 18th blamed the State Department for "grossly inadequate" security.

Serious flaws found in the Justice Department's gun buying **Operation Fast and Furious,** September 19.

Colorado and Washington became the first to vote to allow recreational use of marijuana.

2013   Two bombs in the Boston Marathon April 15 killed three spectators and injured 264.

2014   **(2014–present) American-led intervention in Iraq**

Operation Inherent Resolve (OIR)

Operation Inherent Resolve (OIR) is the U.S. military's operational name for the military intervention <u>against the Islamic State of Iraq and Syria (ISIS) 15 June</u>

Three Americans were videoed being beheaded for the world to see: American journalist James Foley was videoed being beheaded August 19, 2014.

American journalist, Stephen Soltoff beheaded August.

Aid worker U.S, citizen Peter Kassig, November 16.

United States officials agreed to leave 9,800 Americans and 2000 NATO troops to remain in Afghanistan September 19.

'A U.S. led operation and multinational NATO alliance formally ended combat missions in Afghanistan, December 28, after over 18 years.

2,215 Americans killed and 20,000 wounded since 2001.

The Islamic State of Iraq and Syria (ISIS) expanded their territory in Iraq in Syria declaring a "caliphate" June 29.

Airstrikes authorized, August 7, to disrupt ISIS operations there. End this brief review 28 December 2014. (8, pp. 53-67)

Americans Killed in Battle

There were thousands of casualties!

American Revolution (1775-1783)	4,435
War of 1812 (1812-1815)	2,260
Mexican-American War (1846-1848)	1,733
Civil War (1861-1865	
(Union)	140,414
(Confederate)	74,524
Spanish-American War (1898)	385
World War I (1917-1918)	53,402
World War II (1941 –1945)	**291,557**
Korean War (1950-1953)	33,739
Vietnam War (1964-1975)	47,434
Persian Gulf War	148
(Desert Shield/Desert Storm) (1990-1991)	
Iraq War (2003-2014)	4,491
Afghanistan total as of April 2017 - 3	
Syria – U.S. Deaths as of August 2107	<u>**331, 765**</u>

(**<u>More killed in Syria than in WWII</u>**

July 2017 Total is	
U.N. and Arab League Envoy to Syria, April 2016	400,000

July 2017 Syrian Observatory of Human Rights:

Children:	18,420 died	
Women	11,427 died	(8, pp. 67, 69)

B. Patriotism (8, pp. 147-150)

Leaders Come and Go

Chronologically from the fourth century B.C. to the fourth century of the Christian Era (A.D.) Leaders included: Aeneas Tacitus, Xenophon,

Polybius, Asclepiodotus, Onasander, Frontinus, Arrian, Modestus, and Vegetius were also political theorists. (3, p. lix)

(No one even knows them now, much less what they did. The same is true of the early and some of the recent U.S. Presidents.)

A national military leader must have a fervent patriotism. This connects the military and civic life. **Inaction** or **corrupt** civic order defeats the whole process. (3, p. xliii)

Noah Webster in his *American Dictionary of 1828* defines patriotism, "The compassion which aims to serve one's country, either in defending it from invasion, or protecting its rights and maintaining its laws and institutions in vigor and purity. **Patriotism** is the characteristic of a good citizen, the noblest passion that animates a man in the character of a citizen". (67, p. XIV) Includes passion and service, ideas and action. "Be of good courage, and let us play the men for our people, and for the cities of our God: and the LORD do that which seemeth him good. And Joab drew nigh, and the people that *were* with him, unto the battle against the Syrians: and they fled before him." (2 Sam. 10:12,13) Courage is an essential character of a good soldier. In April of 1775, the "shot heard around the world" was fired in Lexington, Massachusetts, beginning the American Revolution.

The patriots called, "Those liberties and rights are of which we have been deprived."

John Warren one of the brightest lights of the American Revolution, active in the political club of Boston and friend to high and low, died in the battle of Bunker Hill.

He wrote the poem *"Free America"* in 1774. Here are a few selected lines:

"Then guard your Rights, Americans! nor stoop to lawless Sway. (Also, appropriate today.)

To Picts, to Danes, to Normans, and many master's more;

But we can boast Americans, we never fell a Prey;

If we have a false standard, we explode patriotism altogether.

On July 3, 1776, John Adams wrote his wife, Abigail, about the Continental Congress's vote to declare independence. The Declaration was dated **July 4, 1776. This is the most memorable epoch in the history of America**. It will be celebrated succeeding generations as the great anniversary festival. It was the day of deliverance by solemn acts of devotion to God Almighty. To be solemnized with pomp and parade, games, sports, guns, bells, bonfires and illuminations from one end of this continent to the other from this time forward, forevermore.

John Jay, "*Federalist No. 2*", 1787
One people; each individual citizen everywhere enjoying the same national rights, privileges, and protection. As a nation, we have made peace and war; as a nation, we have vanquished our common enemies; as a nation we have formed alliances, made treaties, and entered various compacts and conventions with foreign states. We formed a wise and well-balanced government for a free people. The Constitutional Convention (1787), composed of men who had become highly distinguished by their **patriotism, virtue, and wisdom**. American virtues have included: **Patriotism, charity, courage, diligence, frugality, humanity, humility, justice, and patience. <u>A country with patriotism and love of justice will be least likely to sacrifice it.</u>**

The great Constitutional Charter was assembled in place of a recommendation of particular measures, the tribute that is due to the talents, the rectitude, and the patriotism which adores the characters selected to devise and adopt them.

Benjamin Rush on education, "The principle of patriotism stands in need of the reinforcement of prejudice, and it is well-known that our strongest prejudices in favor of our country are formed in the first one and twenty years of our lives. One sees the advantage to the community from the early attachment of youth to the laws and constitution of their country." "Young men who have trodden the paths of science together or have joined in the same sports generally feel, thro' life, such ties to each other, as add greatly to the obligations of mutual benevolence." **The youth looks to his country, the citizens look to the world**.

We must beware with great pretensions to patriotism with falsehoods, fair promises, and insidious arts. The hypocritical pretender to patriotism acquires, if in the confidence of the people, is a force against American.

"Patriotism means more than love for your country. It means love for what makes your country your country! History reveals the American soul which is more than a mere political mechanism. **America is a divine blessing from God, not man! (8, pp. 147-150)**

War as a political instrument needed to defeat the enemy is required by both thinker and soldier. "One is theory, the other is practice." There were far-reaching changes in the art of war in the 19th and 20th centuries. (3, p. xlv)

Clausewitz is the greatest military theorists of the west. His doctrines of unlimited war and of war as an extension of politics is found in Machiavelli. (3, p. xlvi) Clausewitz hails Machiavelli as having "a very sound judgment in military matters". Clausewitz for the first time gives treatment of the **moral factors** in war which parallels Machiavelli's concept. (3, p. xlvi)

An emotional force, the source of energy, bravery, and spiritual strength are noted in moral courage. Its foremost characteristics are boldness, the dynamic creative power, obedience, and for leaders, great intellect." (3, p. xlvii)

"The Relation of the Political and the Military Arts" (3, p. xlvii)
Machiavelli evidently believes that the basic relationships between the arts of war and the politics are as follows:

1. Military power is the foundation of civil society
2. A well-ordered military establishment is an essential unifying element in civil society.

3. A policy of **military aggrandizement** contributes to the **stability and longevity of civil society**.
4. The military art and the political art possess a common style
5. A military establishment tends to reflect the qualities of the civil society of which it is a part.

"Machiavelli believes the serious decline of parental, religious, and civic authority in Italy is the lack of good military organization." (3, p. 1) "Machiavelli notes a clear close tie between military power and the civil order." (3, p. xlviii) "All that men cherish, art, science, religion, and civic order, **depends** upon the security provided by military might."

"Laws, **no matter how well-designed, are of little value** in safeguarding internal order unless the military establishment is sufficient to protect the community from foreign aggression." (3, p. xlviii)

"With family upbringing and religion, **the military training received by the citizen who actively participates in a militia is fundamental to civic education**." (3, p. xlix)

"Machiavelli suggests what might be called a general theory of **human 'salvation' through the military**." (3, p. l)

"All that man can hope for, before the inevitable decay as death of the body by politic occur, is a long prosperous civic life free from the worst of the more common afflictions." (3, p. li)

"Delay of the inevitable fall is the only hope of **early salvation**. The military can be crucial in postponement of doom, but nothing will prevent the ultimate fall." (3, p. li)

A basic pattern of social behavior is egoism. Corrupt conflict among men is aggrandizement and domination without authority of law or religion. There is no concern for the common good. (3, p. li)

Political corruption means factionalism, violence and conspiracy which is between anarchy and tyrannical rule. (3, p. li)

Religious beliefs sometimes prevail in a good society. Honesty is the rule in private and public affairs. (3, p. li)

The force of the **citizen militia** fighting for their own freedom, honor, and glory may be a temporary salvation. (3, p. liii) The inevitable will come. In the political and the military arts with its founders and reformers, military commanders come together with religions and men of letters. (3, p. liii)

True virtue provides the greatest discipline and training. Training must be done in the proper way. (3, p. lv)

Leaders must prevent control by indolence, inaction, a lack of energy, faintheartedness, irresolution, and **hesitancy**. A great military always produces hero-founders. Selfishness with intelligence destroys the objection of common good. Selfishness is the heart of human relations. (3, p. lvi)

The **citizen militia** usually are a community of friends. (Fellow citizens are fellow soldiers.) (3, p. lviii)

There are ways of peace and many ways of war. **War is always present or on the horizon**. A country must always be ready for **war because it is coming**. (3, p. lix)

V. Women in Combat

For thousands of years women have served in many positions in the military. Note that this review is for those who were part of action in combat. There are many undocumented notes on this subject.

Leigh Ann Hester is the first female soldier since World War II to receive the Silver Star medal for valor in combat. She enlisted in the National Guard in 2001. In July 2004, she was ordered to Iraq where she was assigned to a military police unit. The job was to protect critical supply routes. According to the Pentagon's policy, women are not allowed to be assigned to units where their primary mission is to "engage in direct combat on the ground."

It was a Sunday morning around 9 a.m. on a road east of Baghdad. The vehicle in front of hers took a direct hit with a rocket propelled grenade.

Three members of her team were shot and wounded. Dozens of insurgents were firing on them. Her squad leader, **Staff Sgt. Timothy Nein**, grabbed her arm and told her to follow him. They ran toward the insurgents' trench line, took up position and started firing. It lasted about 45 minutes. Hester killed three of the 50 insurgent fighters. When it was over, everyone in her unit had survived.

Hester and Nein were both awarded Silver Stars for their actions that day. Hester is the first woman to win the award and the only woman to get it for engaging in direct combat with the enemy. (7)

The Silver Star is the third-highest decoration in the U.S. military for valor. (The Medal of Honor is the highest, followed by the Distinguished Service Cross.)

The military has open thousands of jobs to women in units that are closer to the front lines than ever before. However, the rules still ban women from serving in the most dangerous combat jobs such as infantry, armor, and special operations forces.

Famous Sayings of Russian Women in Combat in World War II
A million women fought in the Soviet Army. They mastered all military specialties including: "Tank driver, "infantryman", and "machine gunner". (4, Paraphrased)

- "War is an all too intimate experience".
- "A human being is greater than war".
- "There is a tremor of eternity in humans at all times in war".
- "The soul of the event is the feeling of reality".
- "It is not possible to explain War to a six-year-old".
- "War is first of all murder, and then hard work".
- "We listen to the sound of our own soul".
- "In the face of death all ideas pale. We still live in history. Words have more than once lead us away from the truth".

- "The truth is what we dream about. It's what we want to be.
- "Ten men violated one girl".
- "There were no prisoners in war, there were only traitors".
- "War is war. It's not some kind of theater".
- "After war, some human lives are worthless".
- "To kill is more terrible than to die".
- "War is also life with many roads".
- "There were two women snipers with 75 killings".
- "Destiny is something beyond words".
- "In war, our minds make records in the soul and a history of the soul".
- "In school, they taught us that there was no God, but many people prayed".
- "I saw a crying young man shot in the head which turned me into an adult at once."
- "In war, you are half man and half beast".
- "Our women pilots flew and shot down aces".
- "I was happy that I wasn't able to hate".
- "The gift of tears is a woman's gift".
- "After fighting for two years bullets were "afraid of us".
- "There were two truths in war; one's own truth is driven underground, and the common one is filled with the spirit of time".
- "When things live in the house for a long time, they acquire a soul".
- "There were many that died at the hands of a class enemy".
- "You can't shoot unless you hate. It's a war".
- "War is known as a "meat grinder".
- "The Germans didn't take women prisoners they shot them at once".
- "They came to my land and there was much hatred in my soul".
- "Death can't be tamed. You can't get used to it".
- "They amputated his legs and his right arm".

VI. The Second World War (1939-1945)

World War II (1939-1945) saw the greatest population movement in European history. The war created millions of refugees who fled the bombings of their homes and they became homeless. Quota numbers had also forced migration by the Nazi and Soviet regimes and by border changes of the war. **Nazi Germany transported 6 million Jews to concentration camps in Germany and Poland**. Most of them were **killed or died** of maltreatment. (8, p. 140)

The Soviet Union organized forced migration on a mass scale. After the Bolshevik Revolution millions of counter revolutionaries were deported to Gulags in Siberia. Millions more were forced to migrate from rural areas to industrial cities. In 1939, Estonians, Latvians, and Lithuanians were deported to Siberia. In September 1939, Russia deported 750,000 Poles to labor camps. Estimates of forced migrations exceeded twenty million.

Millions of Cossack, Ukrainian, Latvian, Estonian, and Lithuanian anti-Soviet collaborators were forced to flee west. The Red Army advanced into Germany in the final months of the war. Millions of Germans from East Prussia, Pomerania, Silcsea, and the Reichsgau fled afraid of the Soviet group's atrocities. Around **12.5 million German** refugees had to be resettled into a shrunken Germany.

Europe had been reversed in a matter of months. The most important result of the war was the division of Europe into an eastern Communist bloc, and a western democratic bloc allied by the United States. Germany was divided into American, British, French, and Soviet occupation zones. The division of Germany lasted until 1989. By 1951, 218,000 west Indians were workers in Britain. The mixing into a homogenous society with rising race tensions lead to **restrictions on immigration in the 1960's**. (8, p. 140)

1902. The Immigration Restriction Act (federal) provided that an immigrant, on-demand, must demonstrate their ability to pass a test in a

European language. In 1905 this was changed to a "prescribed language". (2, p. 932)

1921. May 19 Immigration Act limiting the number from a given country to 3% of the number of foreign-born persons of such nationality resident in the United States according to the U.S. census of 1910. (2, p.1047)

1924. May 26. An Immigration Bill was signed limiting annual immigration from a given country to 2% of the nationals of the country in the United States in 1890. The annual immigration should be limited to 150,000, to be apportioned among the different countries in proportion to the relative strength of the various foreign elements represented in the American population in 1920. (This excluded the Japanese) (2, p. 1048)

By 1972, Britain had been forced to accept over **100,000 Asians** expelled from its former colonies in Kenya, Tanzania, and Uganda. **The great age of migration is now**. More than 3 million people every year migrate to another country. Worldwide, there are over **150 million people** who have permanently left the country where they were born. The nature of migration has not changed. The reason being **fleeing war, and political oppression, but the majority have economic motives just as throughout history. There are 37 million foreign-born U. S. citizens.**

In Russia during WWII everyone in war had a "Death Passport" somewhere on their body. This helped solve the problem of the identity of a dead person. There were 20 million deaths in Russia in WWII. (8, p. 14)

Old Anglo-Saxon, a national non-feudal **militia** was loyal to the crown. (2, p. 207) (A **national feuda** (political or social system) group of 5000 knights.) (2, p. 207)

Knighthood (1278) inspired that all men had a given income. A **militia** under royal control. (2, p. 215) Second statue of Westminster (1285) the **militia** provided care for the roads. (2, p. 215)

In the American Civil War both sides used **militias**. In the 19th century some states in United States had their own **militia** that served in all of America's wars. After World War I the **militias** were established as the National Guard. (1, p.1840) The national Guard has become more government controlled than people controlled as in the **citizen's militia**.

In 1995 there were the beginning of self-appointed "**hate militias**" who called themselves "Patriots" and a mix of survivalists, white supremacists' gun-control opponents, "Christian Identity" adherents. Noted in the FBI siege at Ruby Ridge, Idaho, in 1992. Branch Davidian, Waco, Texas, 1993. Brady Bill hand gun control (1993) a further growth of these groups in 1990's. (**Politics of Hate**). (1, p.1840)

World War II

In World War II there were 20 Americans who lost three extremities. I saw one and visited a special hospital for them. Another one was a marine General's son. His words, "I was doing the best I could do Dad!" (My patient)

- "To earth we came and to earth we return. What is the color of war? It is the color of the earth".
- "All the women soldiers wanted to study the art of war".
- "Love is the only personal event in wartime".
- "A wounded man was waiting to die, a woman's smile brought him back to life".
- "He lost one leg, but he was happy to be alive".
- "The nurses would sing and the severely wounded would fall asleep".
- "It was not an enemy fighting-divisions, battalions, companies-but people, partisans, and underground fighters: men young and old, women, children.
- **Tolstoy called this many-faced surge "the cudgel of the people's war" and "the hidden warmth of patriotism".**
- "Hatred was stronger than fear".
- "The Germans shot children and had fun doing it".
- "War was woe. There's nothing to remember only the war".
- "My mother believed in God she prayed all through the war". "There was a partisan blockade on all the roads".

- "War-it's always funerals".
- To her dead son a mother said, "You promised you would bring a young wife home! But you are marrying the earth..."
- "When I got home, I kissed my mother. I kissed the ground. I had so much love in my heart and so much hatred".
- "I was arrested and taken to jail. They beat me. I learned what a "fascist manicure" was. A machine was used to stick needles under your fingernails. It was hellish pain and I lost consciousness".
- "I was naked and one of the torturers grabbed me by the breast and I spat in his face. They sat me on an electric chair, and I felt electric current running through my whole body".
- "At home after the war, after learning to hate they had to learn to love again".
- "A German woman had been raped all night long. They then tied a grenade between her legs".
- "The Germans were hated throughout the war".
- I was afraid of growing old more than of the war".
- "German tanks drove over our children".
- **"Out of 300 girls on the front line only <u>10</u> were left at the end of the day"**.
- "All of our fields had been mined".
- "Human life is a great gift, but man is not the owner of that gift".
- "There can't be one heart for hatred and another for love. We only have one, and I always thought about how to save my heart." (8, pp. 9-12)

Death, death, pain, pain-In war it's never over!

VII. The Rage of Isis

ISIS has a strong, modern-equipped army force. They establish their territory by military conquests. As they conquer territory, they control populations. ISIS is the world's richest terror group with a budget in 2015 of 2 billion dollars.

They have a propaganda machine. They have smashed Iraqi history with a sledgehammer. They posted a video in February 2015, showing their destruction of many antiquities in a museum in Mosul, Iraq. They also showed a video of a Jordanian pilot being burned to death in a cage!

They use emigration for worldwide affect by infiltrating the world with their secret warriors. They carry out massive looting and destruction of statues belonging to antiquity and old manuscripts are burned or sold in underground markets. **ISIS has no limit to crimes against humanity**. Churches and monasteries are looted and blasted to bits. All of this is done in the name of Allah. (8, p.79)

Islam means *"surrender"* (submission in *Webster*), not peace. The Ottoman dynasty killed 1.5 million Armenians during the last Islamic Caliphate in 1915. Armenian Christians were killed reducing the population from million to 387,000. In 1400 years, jihad has killed more than 260 million innocent people. Many lived by converting to Islam. (8, p.80)

There are more than 100 verses in the Quran (Koran) enjoining Muslims to "fight, kill, torture, rape, pillage, and conquer in the name of Allah."

God has no need for another name. God is the "One who Is". He is the only one who exists. Wealth is not proof of righteousness and poverty is not proof of unrighteousness. The bodily resurrection of Jesus Christ is at the heart of the Christian faith. The resurrection of Jesus is so well evidenced that it is beyond reasonable doubt. If we cannot be sure of Jesus' death by crucifixion and His resurrection, we cannot be sure of anything in history. Jesus was seen by 500 people at one time. His promise is that the best is yet to come. Jesus forgave sinful women.

Islamic wars are creating 10,000 refugees per day - a million Syrians fled for their lives in the past year. In 2013, there were 120,000 active jihadists in the world. More than **200 European women have joined ISIS** to marry a jihadist. They are provided with free houses, they pay no electric or water bills each month, they are given monthly groceries, monthly allowance for husband and wife or wives, allowance for each child, free medical checkup, and free medications. Every language is spoken, they pay no tax, and no business is conducted during prayer times. There is no racism because mixed race marriages and mixed-race children are normal.

The Hadith (Muslim writings) promises that Muslims will conquer the world. "We will conquer your home, break your crosses, and enslave your women and kill all unbelievers. If we do not our children and grandchildren will." (8, p. 83)

According to the Center for the Study of Political Islam under Sharia Law:

- There is no freedom of religion.
- There is no freedom of speech.
- There is no freedom of thought.
- There is no freedom of expression.
- There is no freedom of the press.
- There is no inequality of peoples. All people are equal.
- There is no equal protection of people. Muslim males have different laws than women and non-Muslims.
- There are no equal rights for women. Women can be beaten. A non-Muslim cannot bear arms.
- There is no democracy They say that our Constitution is a man-made document of ignorance that must submit to Sharia. All governments must be ruled by Sharia law. Sharia is not interpretive, nor can it be changed. There is no golden rule." Radical Islam hopes to capture the world for Islam and will use any means necessary to achieve their goal. (8, p. 83)

The wars of the kings began, and we have been in the presence of wars since. *"That these* made war with Bera king of Sodom, and with Birsha king of Gomorrah, Shinab king of Admah, and Shemeber king of Zeboiim, and the king of Bela, which is Zoar. All these were joined together in the vale of Siddim, which is the salt sea." (Gen. 14:2,3)

We must call our nation to appropriate action and kill the known enemy. As President Trump seems to know there is tremendous value in enlisting Muslim allies against jihad.

ISIS views all five groups: Christians, Jews, Yazidis, Shias, and liberal Muslims as "infidels without human rights." ISIS tweets: **"We will kill your people and transform America to a river of blood"**. Every American is a target.

The Obama Administration: (8, p. 95)
1. Obama, in Egypt, delivered a now-infamous speech that signaled America's massive shift in policy. "The United States pulled entirely out of Iraq despite the pleas of all the major Iraqi parties".
2. In Egypt, the United States backed the Muslim Brotherhood and gave them F-16 fighters and M1 Abrams main battle tanks.
3. The Muslim Brotherhood persecuted Egypt's ancient Coptic Christians.
4. The Obama administration continued supporting the Brotherhood even when it stood aside and allowed jihadists to storm the American embassy raising the black flag of Jihad over an American diplomatic facility.
5. Libyan jihadists attacked the diplomatic compound in Benghazi, September 11, 2012, killing the American ambassador and three more brave Americans. He refused to reinforce the American security presence despite a need, afraid it would anger the local population. This administration's decision cost American lives.

The Obama administration rebuffed both Israel and Egypt preferring to advanced proposals that empowered Hamas's allies - Qatar and Turkey. He rewarded Hamas for terrorist acts. Obama said, "This is not the authorization of a broad-based counter terrorism campaign against ISIS."

We must commit to destroying ISIS. President Trump has done this! It is imperative that jihadists face strong Muslim opposition. We are not to send money to anyone with ties to Hamas. We must investigate U.N. ties to terrorists. **We must oppose, not appease the enemy**! (8, p. 96)

America, with Obama, shows itself to be a faithless friend with a weak will. President Trump is changing this image!

To win the war against ISIS will require American courage, lives, and American will. Courage and will to kill or die is our only hope.

It is time for America to lead!

The Resurgence of Islam (8, p. 106)
There has been a resurgence of Islam in personal and in public life. In the public sphere, new Islamic governments or republics have been established in Iran, Sudan, and Afghanistan. Mainstream Islamic activists head governments, and serve in cabinets, and elected parliaments. They serve as senior officials of professional associations of doctors, lawyers, engineers, and professors. At the same time radical, Islamic organizations have engaged in violence and terrorism to topple governments or to achieve related goals.

In Egypt, Iran, Syria, Malaysia, and Indonesia Muslim states were created because most of the population was Muslim. A most significant event was the 1967 Arab – Israeli War - Six-Day War when Islam lost Jerusalem. This was traumatic to Muslims and Christians alike. Jerusalem is revered worldwide as a site of central religious significance.

Extremists were convicted in America and Europe in the bombing of New York's World Trade Center in 1993, the American barracks in Saudi Arabia in 1995, and American embassies in Africa in 1998. This activity identified Islamic fundamentalism as a major threat to global stability.

The huge numbers of Muslim refugees and the migration of many Muslims to Europe and America make minority rights and duties an even greater concern for Islamic jurisprudence. **They are invading America by politics and violence**. Keep in mind the Five Pillars of Islam are unchanged. They will take over America unless we change the system of obedience to our country.

Secularism is killing America. We are no longer a Christian nation. Muslims in America and Europe have emerged as a major religious presence.

Muslims are incompatible with democracy. They have no country to fight for. They will have peace only when all the world is Muslim. Muslims are guided by their belief in one true God, the Quran, and the Prophet Muhammed. (8, p. 109)

"And thus, have We, by Our Command, sent Revelation to you (O Prophet): you did not know (before) what was Revelation, and what was Faith; but We have made the (Quran, a (Divine) Light, with this We guide such of Our servants as We will; and surely, you (O Prophet) do guide (men) to the Straight Path-The (Straight) Way of Allah, to Whom belongs all that is in the heavens and all that is in the earth. Surely how all things (and events) return back to Allah. (for Judgment) towards Allah." (Quran, Surah 42. 52, 53)

Jesus came and spoke unto them, saying, ***"All power is given unto me in heaven and in earth. Go ye therefore, and teach all nations, baptizing them in the name of the Father, and of the Son, and of the Holy Ghost: Teaching them to observe all things whatsoever I have commanded you: and, lo, I am with you alway, even unto the end of the world."*** (Matt. 28: 18-20)

The U. S. Postal Service issued a stamp commemorating Muslim holidays. Islam found a place in America.

Wake up America!
On September 11, 2001, Islamic terrorist launched successful attacks on the World Trade Center in New York City and the Pentagon in Washington, D.C. The twin towers collapsed by 10:30 AM. Four airline airplanes were hijacked and used as bombs. 3,000 people was killed by Al Qaeda, an extremist Islamic terrorist network, with bases in Afghanistan led by Osama bin Laden. (6, p. 411)

Attackers destroyed the World Trade Center and part of the Pentagon as terrorists in the name of Islam killed more people than at Pearl Harbor in 1944 that marked the entrance of the United States into WWII in 1941.

One step that we need for many local problems can be corrected by **citizen militia**.

The attack on the World Trade Center's twin towers occurred on Sept. 11, 2001. The attack was carried out by 19 members of the terrorist group al-Qaeda and involved the hijacking of four airline planes. Two of the planes were then deliberately crashed into the towers in a suicide attack. American Airlines Boeing 767 hit the north tower at 8:45 a.m. near the 80th floor. United Airlines Flight 175, another Boeing 767, hit the south tower 18 minutes later near the 60th floor. Due to the excessive heat of the fire generated by the jet fuel, the south tower's structural integrity was compromised, and it collapsed just before 10 a.m. The north tower followed, collapsing at 10:30 a.m.

A total of 3,000 people died during New York City attack, including all the passengers on the planes. Among the rescue personnel who died were 343 firemen and paramedics. Additionally, 37 Port Authority police officers and 23 New York City police officers perished. During the attack on New York City, American Airlines Flight 77, a Boeing 757, headed towards Washington, D.C. and crashed into the west walls of the Pentagon killing 124 people. All 64 passengers on the plane died. A fourth hijacked plane, United Flight 93, crashed in western Pennsylvania after its passengers attempted to retake control from the hijackers. All 45 of the passengers died in the crash.

What Are Some Facts About the Twin Towers Attack in 2001?
https://www.reference.com/history/twin-towers-attack-2001-9e955f54027dae0 (Accessed January 29, 2019)

<u>Wake up America!</u>
The "7 C's of History"
1. **Creation:** In six normal days 6,000 years ago, God created the heavens and the earth and all that is in them. (See Genesis 1:1-31)
2. **Corruption:** The Tree of the Knowledge of Good and Evil was not to be touched. Adam and Eve ate fruit from the tree after being tempted by the devil. (The fall of man: Genesis 3:1-7)
3. **Catastrophe:** Because of global sin God sent a global flood. (See Genesis 6:1-21; 7: 1-24)

4. **Confusion:** Confusion through a multiplicity of languages instead of their common shared language causing them to spread out over the earth. The Tower of Babel (God named it) (See Genesis 11: 1-10)

5. **Christ:** God sends a savior. (see Romans 5:12-21)

6. **Cross:** But Jesus turning unto them said, **"Daughters of Jerusalem, weep not for me, but weep for yourselves, and for your children. For, behold, the days are coming, in the which they shall say, Blessed are the barren, and the wombs that never bare, and the paps which never gave suck. Then shall they begin to say to the mountains, Fall on us; and to the hills, Cover us. For if they do these things in a green tree, what shall be done in the dry?"** (Luke 23:28-31) **They put a sign on his cross in Greek, Latin and Hebrew. "This is the King of the Jews."** (Luke 23:38) The man on the cross next to Him said, "Lord, remember me when thou comest into thy kingdom". And Jesus said unto him, *"Verily I say unto thee, Today shalt thou be with me in paradise."* (Luke 23: 42, 43) Note: Jesus called Heaven paradise. *"And the Father Himself, which hath sent Me, hath borne witness of Me... Ye have neither heard His voice at any time, nor seen His shape...Search the scriptures; for in them ye think ye have eternal life: and they are they which testify of Me."* (John 5:37, 39)

   Death has no power over Jesus. "The last enemy that shall be destroyed is death." (1 Cor. 15:26) Those in Christ will pass from death unto life. (John 5:24) Their names are written in the Book of Life. (See Revelation 13: 8, 17, 18)

7. **Consummation:** God has promised to do away with the corruption that Adam brought into the world.

   "Nevertheless we, according to his promise, look for new heavens and a new earth, wherein dwelleth righteousness." (2 Peter 3:13) In the new phase, there will be no death, crying, or pain. "And God shall wipe away all tears from their eyes; and there shall be no more death, neither sorrow, nor crying, neither shall there be any more pain: for the former things are passed away." (Rev. 21:4)

Our knowledge is based on faith and the history of the world, as revealed in the Bible. Evolution is only mental propaganda.

There is much study as to what is a legal target by the International Law of Armed Conflict. **ISIS violates every single principle of the law of war**. **Suicide bombing in Iraq rose above five hundred in 2012.**

500 years ago, Luther recognized Islamic expansion as a threat to all of Europe and also to Christians. In 1530, he related that Christians must be "warned" and they must "learn" about the religion of Muhammed in order to counteract it. **Their battleground was the world**. They have exploited our political and national impotence with political, religious, and civilian targets. (8, p. 86)

VIII. Immigration

Migrations have occurred throughout history. 1970-1980's <u>12 million people migrated to the United States</u>. (1, p. 1838) Motives for immigration generally included economic, political, religious factors, personal freedom from a country, or asylum. Women and their daughters from third world countries were granted asylum to avoid forced genital mutilation. (1, p. 1364)

Immigration: New Faces in Florida (*Tampa Bay Times*, December 2, 2018, p. 1-4 E)
There are many immigrants in Florida working in agriculture, construction, and hospitality.

- 20% of Florida's population are foreign-born
- Foreign immigrants account for 50% of Florida's growth
- 57% of the foreign-born are Hispanic
- Of the 21% immigrants, 26% are working
- 55% of the state's population have some college compared to 50% of the immigrants

- The Optional Practical Training Program in Florida has 5000 foreign-born. (Pew Research, 2004 – 2016) Most of the students are from India, China, and Venezuela.
- Most of the foreign students to come to Gainesville left to work in Silicon Valley, New York, Miami, Seattle, and San Francisco.
- 78% of the Cuban immigrant population is living in Florida
- 28% of the Cubans were 65 years or older compared to 15% of the foreign native-born population.
- The total population of the 44% Haitians are in United States 78% are living in Florida and New York
- Puerto Rico is a U.S. commonwealth and its citizens are U.S. citizens.
- Since Hurricane Maria (2017) there are probably 40,000 Puerto Ricans in the United States in Florida
- 1632 people move to Florida **each day** from elsewhere in United States. 654 people arrive **each day** from abroad.

Demographics of Growth in Florida, 2017 – 2030

- **Florida's white population of 55% is expected to decrease to 49%.**
- The Hispanic population is expected to rise from 25.3 to 30.1%
- Black population from 16.2% to 17.1%
- The population in Florida is expected to rise 14% over a decade to 21.5 million in 2020.
- By 2045 there will be 27.4 million or about 7 million more than today.

The Great Migrations that Made our World Today:

The Great Migrations, (James Haywood, Quercus, 21 Bloomberg Square, London. WC 1A2NS, 2008.) **The history of the world is related to the Great Migrations. Without this knowledge, one is ignorant before they start.**

Illegal Immigrants (12 -20 Million in the United States) (8, p. 120)

Immigration is like an ocean wave. It cannot be stopped. A legal method of immigration must be developed and learn to control the flow. According to the United Nations Refugee Agency 65.6 million people have been displaced world-wide since 2016. (*Time,* July 3, 2017, p. 10)

The great age of migration is now. Over 3 million people every year emigrate to another country. More than 150 million people have migrated to make new lives abroad. Throughout history, **the majority have economic motives for migration, but they are also fleeing war, or political oppression.** (8, p. 120)

The United States has 37 million foreign-born citizens. Illegal immigrants face many problems, including dying from drowning when crossing the seas. Even though they know the chances of getting legal presence in Europe or the United States is small they still face terrifying risks. They also die from dehydration in crossing deserts or suffocation where being transported by tight enclosed trucks. Once they enter the intended country as being illegal, they faced much exploitation such as: lack of payment for their work, money loans that produce "debt slavery", false job offers, and young women are held captive and forced into prostitution. They are constantly being, and are severely afraid of being deported, including some who have been in America for many years.

The United States hosted more international migrants in 2015, with 46.6 million. The number two nation was Germany with 12 million migrants. Estimates of illegal immigrants is between 12 to 20 million. The United States is planning to build **a 5.7-billion-dollar wall along the Mexican border. India has a similar wall along their border with Bangladesh.** (8, p. 121)

Worldwide Migration from the countryside to the cities averages 160,000 people each day. 40 million Europeans immigrated between 1800 and 1914)

Major US Immigration Laws, 1790-Present
https://www.migrationpolicy.org/research/timeline-1790 (accessed 11 February 2019)

1790   The *1790 Naturalization Act* (1 Stat. 103) establishes the country's first uniform rule for naturalization

1882   Congress enacts the *Immigration Act of 1882* (22 Stat. 214), constituting one of the first attempts at broad federal oversight of immigration.

1921   The *1921 Emergency Quota Act* constitutes Congress' first attempt to regulate immigration by setting admission "quotas" based on nationality.

1948   The *Displaced Persons act of 1948* (62, 1009) allows over 200,000 individuals displaced from their homelands by Nazi persecution to immigrate to the United states.

1952   The *Immigration and Nationality Act* (182 Stat.66) consolidates several immigration laws into one statute and preserves the national origins quota system (though the law updates the way in which the quota is calculated.)

1953   The *Refugee Act of 1953* (94 Stat. 102) authorizes the admission of up to put 205,000 non-quota immigrants who are freeing persecution or have been expelled from their homes in Europe.

1965   The *1965 Immigration and Nationality Act* (79 Stat. 911) abolishes the national - origins quota system and replaces it with a system whereby immigrants are admitted based on their relationship to a US citizen or lawful permanent resident family member or US employer.

1980   The *Refugee Act of 1980* (94 Stat. 102) establishes a new statutory system for processing and admitting refugees from overseas as well as asylum-seekers physically present at US borders or in the country.

1986   The *Immigration Reform and Control Act* (IRCA) (100 Stat 3359) provides for a 50% increase in border patrol staffing and imposes sanctions on employers who knowingly hire or recruit unauthorized immigrants.

1988   The Anti-Drug Abuse Act (ADAA) (102 Stat..4181) adds "aggravated felony" as a new, but limited ground for deportation.

Initially this category is limited to serious crimes (e.g., murder and drug and weapons trafficking) regardless of the sentence imposed and the longevity of the alien's residence in the United States.

1994 The Violent Crime Control and Law Enforcement Act (VCCLEA) (108 Stat. 1791) gives the United States Attorney General the option to bypass deportation proceedings for certain alien aggravated felons, enhances penalties for alien smuggling and reentry after deportation, and increased appropriations for the Border Patrol.

1996 Illegal Immigration Reform and Immigrant Responsibility Act (IIRIRA) (110 Stat. 3009) adds new grounds of inadmissibility and deportability, expands the list of crimes constituting an aggravated felony, creates expedited removal procedures, and reduces the scope of judicial review of immigration decisions.

2001 The *US Patriot Act* (115 Stat. 272) broadens the terrorism grounds for excluding aliens from entering the United States and increases monitoring of foreign students.

2002 The *Enhanced Border Security and Visa Entry Reform Act* (116 Stat. 543) requires the development of an interoperable electronic data system to be used to share information relevant to alien admissibility and removability.

2002 The Homeland Security Act (116 Stat. 2135) creates the Department of Homeland Security (DHS). In 2003, nearly all of the functions of the US Immigration and Naturalization Service (INS) are transferred to DHS and restructured to become three new agencies: US Customs and Border Protection (CBP), US Immigration and Customs Enforcement (ICE) and US Citizenship and Immigration Services (USCIS).

2006 Congress enacts the *Secure Fence Act* after the Senate fails to adopt immigration reform legislation that had passed the house in 2005. The law mandates the construction of more than 700 miles of double-reinforced fence to be built along the border with Mexico, through the US states of California, Arizona, New Mexico, and Texas in areas that experience illegal drug trafficking and illegal immigration. It authorizes more lighting, vehicle barriers, and border checkpoints and requires the installation of more advanced equipment such as sensors, cameras, satellites, and unmanned aerial vehicles in an attempt to increase control of illegal immigration into the United States.

February 2019

All the immigration laws and actions have failed. The only answer is a Citizens Militia. The failed actions have been one group emphasizing illegal immigrants and the other emphasizing legal and good immigrants. This will always be a failure.

One must study all immigrants and separate out the illegal ones from the legal. In any review when the illegal immigrants are known the legal immigrants will also be known.

Compassion must be eliminated. Take note. What is our response when the enemy makes public to America the beheading video of James Foley and Stephen Saltoff for the world to see? The only solution is to eliminate the enemy.

Look at the Numbers (FACTS)

The numbers increase each day.

In January 2019, 20,439 illegal aliens entered the United States.

There are 26 million illegal aliens in the United States now (January 2019). (Note: The population of Florida is 21.6 million...5 million less than the number of illegals.)

Cost: (FACTS)

$313 million each day as of January 2019

$30 billion is the cost each year.

IX. Crime:

Criminal law is the branch of law that defines crimes, threats of their nature, and provides for their punishment. (1, p. 712) A misdemeanor is an offense for which punishment is other than death or imprisonment. Crimes may be divided according to their nature into crimes whose acts are thought to be immoral or wrong in themselves such as murder, rape, arson, burglary, larceny, etc. Other crime refers to those that infringe on the rights of others. (1, p. 712)

Where does terrorism begin?

In Islamic countries students spend six hours per day memorizing the Koran. The Koran is "all they need to know" to understand the universe. There are two forces on earth. Muslims and Infidels. The fight will go on until Judgment Day. (In other words, for them it will never end.) The holy cities of Islam are Mecca and Medina and are the focal points of Islam for 1.6 billion people. (4.4 million in the United States.) Saudi leaders control the **71,000 mosques** and the educational system in Saudi Arabia.

The war on terrorism has no meaning in law. The enemy is not a state, terrorists are not military combatants; they are merely international and national criminals. **We call them <u>terrorists</u>, they call themselves "Warriors of God". <u>How do you fight someone whose address is unknown</u>**?

Criminals think different than soldiers.

"Terror-us" is a new word I created related to the fear of criminal activity in the U.S. In 2000 there were 15,517 murders in the U.S. This is 42.5 per day. In over 2 months that **will be more** than those killed at Pearl Harbor.

There are **44 known terrorists' organizations** already in every country in the world (including the US). (8, p. 265)

There are **11,593,860 serious crimes committed in the U.S. each year** or **31,764 per day. <u>There are 400,000 illegal immigrants in our prisons at a cost to us of 20 billion dollars per year.</u>** (We could build 5 walls in one year with this money.) **There are 600,000 prisoners released each year in the U.S. This is 6 million in 10 years and <u>represents a persistent criminal base.</u>**

The police and the F.B.I. have lost control of crime - They just react! A murderer is a murderer whether he is mentally defective or not!

Recently there have been crimes on military bases. How are these thieves in the military going to be loyal to America? It won't happen!

Obesity is quickly becoming a national security issue. Are our troops too fat to fight? Forty-three percent of women and eighteen percent of men of recruiting age exceed weight limits. In 2003, three thousand people were 'kicked out' of the military for excessive weight. **If Islam continues to grow at the present rate by 2020 there will be more Muslims in the US cities than Christians**.

Religious beliefs do not predispose nations to peace. Even during periods of great faith Christians fought Christians and Muslims fought Muslims far more than they fought each other. Islam begin 600 years after Christ.

Ahmad Khan Rahimi, (Afghan born US citizen) "Chelsea bomber", was convicted of eight counts, including the use of a weapon of mass destruction and bombing a public place. His first bombing was when he detonated a pipe bomb at a Marine Corps charity race on 17 November 2016, at Seaside Heights, New Jersey. He detonated two bombs in Manhattan, New York, where he killed 30 people. He was sent to life in prison. He began his terrorist activities in 2012. He wrote to prosecutors "The many already drenched in Muslim blood and how will they understand our struggle?" His father reported him to the FBI in 2014, calling him a terrorist in an interview with NBC news. His sentence of multiple life terms means he is likely never to leave jail. He has tried to radicalize his fellow inmates since arriving in prison to support the Islamic State. **He has no remorse and continues his war against America even in prison.**

X. Genocide

Genocide: "The deliberate and systematic destruction of a racial, political, or cultural group." (**Webster**) As the United Nation (U.N.) convention against genocide turns 70, its failures are tragically apparent. (5, p. 59)

Those fleeing from genocide make up the world's refugee camps in Bangladesh. Genocide is a crime passed by the U.N. December 9, 1948. There are now 900,000 refugees from genocide in 27 camps. (Cox's Bazar)

The world still fails to prevent genocide, let alone punish those responsible. Men are beheaded, and women are raped and made to be sex slaves.

Genocide occurred in Rwanda in 1994. The Hutu majority attacked the Tutsi minority and 500,000 Tutsi were killed with machetes and 700,000 fled the country. The Tutsi's then overthrew the Hutu's fearing retribution. 1.75 million Hutu's fled to the Democratic Republic of the Congo (Zaire), Tanzania, and Burundi.

In 2004, in the Darfur, Sudan, **Arab militants began genocide attacks on black Africans**. Three million people were displaced, and an unknown number were killed. 200,000 fled to Chad, one of the world's poorest countries. Some "asylum-seekers" fled to Western countries. They have become economic refugees and fear being imprisoned, beaten, tortured, or killed by security forces (1924). (8, p. 122)

In September 1998 Jean – Paul Akayesu, a politician in Rwanda, became the first person ever to be convicted of genocide. November 18, 2018, the former Khmer Rouge leaders Khieu Samphan, age 87 and Nuon Chea, age 92, at a hearing in Phnom Penh, were convicted of genocide.

There are many groups, some even have their own **militias**. There are so many countries divided or denying the issue of genocide that there has been little progress. Some groups do not even bother to hide what they are doing. "**The Islamic State in Syria and Iraq published explicit rules about the duty to the pious to exterminate infidel men and rape infidel women**". (5, p.60) **Bashar Assad, President of Syria, flaunts his continued liberty by moving from country to country.** (5, p.60) It has been said, "**Democracy cannot be built on the bones of those who are butchered**".

XI. Gangs - Mobs

Gangs (1, p. 1083) are a major ongoing problem. The County and City of **Los Angeles** are the "gang capital" of the nation. There are more than 450 active **gangs** in the City of **Los Angeles. Many** of these **gangs** have been in existence for over 50 years. These **gangs** have a combined membership of over 45,000 individuals. One of the major factors contributing to increased gangs, gang membership, and violence has been the lucrative narcotics trade, with rival gangs vying for the greatest market share. (Los Angeles Police Department) http://www.lapdonline.org/get_informed/content_basic_view/1396 (accessed January 29, 2019)

This is only one city. The literature on **gangs** is massive. Factors related to gangs include: blighted communities, dropping out of school, unemployment, family disorganization, neighborhood, traditions of gang delinquency, psychopathology, and ethnic status. (1, p.1083)

Massive labor **gangs** funded and controlled directly from the imperial center toiled for centuries to ensure the wealth of Mesopotamia. (224 - 627 A.D.) (7, p. 97)

Gangs and mobs have been around for hundreds of years in countries that tolerate them as America does. They need to be eliminated as one of the features to save our country. Gangs that call themselves militia were reported active as of 26 January 2019.

Gang warfare occurred in the Hippodrome of Hephthalites and was suppressed. Two rival teams of charioteers were supported by rival gangs of racing fans. Two rival gang members were to be executed, but the gallows snapped. They escaped and led the **gangs** on a collective rampage that fanned out across the most exclusive quarters in the world. Beautiful monuments were burned. Justinian sent a squadron of crack troops and attacked both ends of the Hippodrome where an unarmed mob was calling for Justinian to be deposed. The crowd was systematically hacked and trampled underfoot. It was not noted to be a battle, but a calculated atrocity. 50,000 people were killed and one tenth of the city's population had been wiped out in a single day. In truth, the lesson taught the Roman people by the unleashing in their capital of such carnage was a destruction of an evil created in the state. **"Power without the sanction of violence barely right ranked as power at all."** (7, p. 149)

In 391 A.D. a **mob** of Christians attempted to storm the Serapeum at Alexandria. The pagans fought back. They nailed the Christian prisoners to crosses on its walls. The Christians were stimulated to destroy the pagan statue of Sarapes and its libraries. Some buildings were converted to Christian worship. Alexandria over a powerhouse of paganism had been re-consecrated to the most glorious and Christ loving city of Alexandria. (7, p. 266) One hundred years later another Patriarch, Pope Dioscorus, rarefied theology with the tactics of a **gangland boss**. The bishops who were shocked to find themselves howled down every time they opened their mouths, termed the summit in outrage, the "Robber Council". Dioscorus thugs were called black-robed enforcers that demonstrated their devotion to Christ through spectacular displays of violence. "Pagans, Jews, heretics: all felt their fists." (7, p. 267) In 457 A.D. the distant emperor ousted the disgraced Dioscorus and foisted a replacement on the Alexandrians. A **mob** hacked down the wretched new patriarch in one of his own churches and paraded his mangled corpse in triumph through the streets. "No **mob** like an Alexandrian mob for combining intellectual snobbery with a taste for atrocities". (7, p. 268)

XII. Right of Self-Defense - Guns

Every accused has a right to any and all defenses the law recognizes and permits self-defense. (1, p. 712) The legal presumption of innocence puts the burden of proving guilt beyond a reasonable doubt on the prosecution. (1, p. 712) (This has been law at least since the year 2000.) (Passed again in 2017.)

Gun ownership in America. (Study by the **Pew Research Center** - 22 June 2017)

America has a complex relationship with guns.

Three in 10 Americans currently own a gun. (30%, 46% in rural areas)

44% of Republicans own guns versus 20% of Democrats.

Protection 67% of the time is listed as the **reason for owning a gun** and tops the list as to why guns are owned.

69% of the population can see a gun in their future.

Those with one gun:

- 62% is a handgun
- 22% a rifle
- 16% a shotgun

Those with and without an education beyond high school are about the same number that own guns.

<u>**89% of gun owners see it as important. 85% of gun owners say they have a right to own a gun and it is essential to their sense of freedom.**</u>

Gunowners in a community that is not safe: 74% own guns.

Gunowners in a safe community: 66% own guns.

75% of those who own a gun say the world has become a more dangerous place.

50% of adults in the United States say they grew up in a gun-owning household.

72% of Americans say they have fired a gun at some point in their lives.

2018: <u>130,000,000 (million) people own 400,000,000 guns.</u>

<u>**The 130,000,000 people in United States with a gun is a ready-made group to develop the largest citizens militia in history**</u>. A certain force

to eliminate crime in America. At present our efforts are mainly to respond to it and not decrease it. The arming of teachers can be a part of this.

Wake up America!
The FBI processes 2,500,000-gun purchases per month. No one knows the true number of guns owned because many gun owners do not or will not report them. The actual number must be **magnanimous**. (The most descriptive word in the English language.)

In 20 years, there have been 299,697,888 or 300,000,000, background checks for gun ownership.

Wake up America: Our schoolchildren are dying. In 2018 up to May 25, 21 weeks into 2018 there have been at least 21 school shootings or more than one shooting a week.

School Shootings By Saeed Ahmed and Christina Walker, CNN (Updated 11:05 AM ET, Fri May 25, 2018,

www.cnn.com/2018/03/02/us/**school-shootings**-2018. (accessed on January 29, 2019).

School Shootings:
- May 25: Noblesville, Indiana
- May 18: Santa Fe, Texas
- May 11: Palmdale, California
- April 20: Ocala, Florida
- April 12: Raytown, Missouri
- April 9: Gloversville, New York
- March 20: Lexington Park, Maryland
- March 13: Seaside, California
- March 8: Mobile, Alabama
- March 7: Birmingham, Alabama
- March 7: Jackson, Mississippi
- March 2: Mount Pleasant, Michigan
- February 27: Norfolk, Virginia
- February 27: Itta Bena, Mississippi

- February 24: Savannah, Georgia
- Feb. 14: Parkland, Florida
- February 9: Nashville, Tennessee
- February 5: Oxon Hill, Maryland
- Feb. 1: Los Angeles, California.
- January 31: Philadelphia, Pennsylvania
- Jan. 23: Benton, Kentucky
- Jan. 22: Italy, Texas
- Jan. 20: Winston-Salem, N.C.

Gun Control (8, pp.189-198)

The issue in this book concerns the freedom of the individual citizen to own and use private firearms such as pistols and rifles. This has been an issue for hundreds of years even before our country became a country. The main issue of the individual is that a life of freedom also gives him a responsibility to protect his private property. In this case, the ability to own and use private arms is the issue. There are those who strongly approve and those who strongly disapprove. The problem is that one needs the tools to protect oneself, and family against tyranny, including crimes. In all human societies, there has always been crime. **Crime in this country has increased tremendously through the last 50-100 years. The police and FBI have proven to lack the ability to control crime, they just react to it.**

Older people who for years would walk in their neighborhood at night when it was cool, but now because of crime they are unable to do this. **They are prisoners in their own homes by the known criminals**. The rising crime rates include: robbery, homicide, rape, destruction of property, etc.

In the Bible Jesus told his disciples that if they did not have a sword, to "go sell your clothes and buy one". They said they have two. He knew that they had to protect themselves from robbers of other villages that would invade their place and rob all their valuable property, including even their wives.

The potential for war and terrorism has never been so great. Nuclear war seems to be in the background, but local crimes **including terrorism,** is a major and expected situation these days. The right and responsibility of defending oneself and their family has been present for hundreds of years. **Plato related**, **"the right and duty of keeping and knowing the use of arms of the country and times".** **Aristotle said**, "The nobility of an oligarchy (a government of a few people) could afford the most expensive form of defense". **Rousseau, Machiavelli, and Adam Smith** saw the decline of the Roman Empire when it transferred its base army from a citizen to a mercenary (one who works for money in an army) one.

In a citizen army, the individual has duty to the state. <u>**The idea of a militia**</u> (a citizen-soldier) army is prepared to fight to save his home, family, property, and country. **King Henry III** (1216-1272) decrees that the militia should possess arms according to their respective possessions in land and property. (8, p. 190)

During Saxon times (450 A.D.) in England there was a national militia service. There were various levels of the militia, but generally they served only as defense and in case of emergency. This, in general, relates to the **concept of our National Guard.** The Saxons (English) on the continent in Germany were ruled by the Franks until the end of the eighth century. They were conquered by Charlemagne and forced to convert to Christianity. (Treaty of Verdun, 843) (8, p. 190)

Before 602 A.D. the right to keep and bear arms was considered a basic right of Englishman. This was confirmed by the Assize of Arms, King Henry II, 1181.

In 1869, William and Mary, as King and Queen, issued **the English Bill of Rights to confirm the essential freedom of Englishmen to keep and bear arms.** The defense of the nation for the most part was an **obligation and a right**. The military force at that time was the **militia.** (8, p. 190)

In the 17th and 18th centuries the militia was called **a military force,** especially the body of soldiers in the service of the sovereign of the state. It was a **citizen army** distinguished from a professional or mercenary army.

The Hague Convention of 1899 recognized the principle in international law and here **codified** it for the first time.

During the 18th-century **England was dependent upon armed citizens that could rise and make use of firearms and other weapons already in there keep.** The American colonies accepted the right of the Englishman to keep and bear arms. The colonists had constant problems, which they could solve only by **recourse to arms.**

The same problem exists today in America where crime is not controlled by the police or the FBI **who react to crime** only. They have in no way been able to prevent the widespread rise of crime in America. **The militia principal came to America with the first colonists.** This cannot be disputed. Miles Standish and the Pilgrims in Massachusetts, and John Smith in Virginia organized the first real defense force to defend themselves from the native savages. Our "savages" are the criminals.

The Plymouth Colony, 1633, passed an ordinance which **required all men to own certain items of military equipment. Every man was a soldier who owned his own weapons.** The official designation was the **Colonist Organized Militia.** George Washington's brother, Lawrence, was a member. **The North Carolina Militia Act of 1746** required all **freemen, citizens,** and servants to be in the **militia service.** In Virginia in 1632 each man was ordered to **bring his gun to church,** so he could practice with it afterwards. By the end of the 17th century **the militia system had been firmly established in the colonies.** (8, p. 191)

During the American Revolution, due to the lack of regular recruits (they never reached their quota), the use of the militia was forced into use from 1776-1781 to fill existing gaps. In 1775, British General Thomas Gage attempted to remove military supplies from the colonist militia, but he failed. His second attempt failed and brought his troops to armed confrontation with **American militia.** The shot heard around the world was viewed in terms of the colonials defending, by force of arms, a right derived from duty, the right to keep and bear such arms as they had use to defend self and property. They rose up in defense of freedom. The militia remained during and after the Revolution as an integral part of defense.

The Militia Act of May 8, 1792, created the enlistment of every able-bodied male between the ages of 18 and 44 in the militia of his state. Service in the militia was considered evidence of patriotism above and beyond the normal requirement of militia responsibility. When a state of the union has control of a well-regulated and lawfully organized militia it can resist the encroachment of tyrants, dictators, or criminals. (8, p. 192)

This could also include crime and radical Islam. The National Guard could, with proper direction, leadership, and increased recruitment, be a force needed to defend crime and radical Islam. Thomas Paine related that the American cause during the revolution had faith in the militiamen who could leave his place to defend his own location. Women were also enrolled in the militia. There was no distinction between age and sex. (8, p. 192)

The United States Constitution did not specifically sanction the right to bear arms, but sufficient authority to require each able-bodied man between 18 and 45 the obligation to keep and bear arms for defense of the state. The Militia Act of May 8, 1792, to furnish for his individual use a good musket with appropriate equipment and ammunition. This 1792 Militia Act still exists at least in theory. (8, p. 192)

The Second Amendment: A well-regulated militia being necessary to the security of a free state, the right of the people to keep and bear arms shall not be infringed. The attempt to limit the right of keeping and other gun related supplies was listed in the Declaration of the Causes of Necessity of Taking up Arms dated July 6, 1775, as one of the reasons for the American Revolution. The right to bear arms forced the American Revolution. I hope this is not repeated.

A ruling of the Supreme Court held that the right of people to keep and bear arms was not guaranteed in the Constitution, but that it also was not dependent upon that instrument for its existence. The Court did hold that it was true that all citizens, regardless of age or sex, constitute the reserved military force or reserve militia of the United States. The states cannot, even having the Constitutional provision in question out of view, **prohibit the people from keeping and bearing arms,** so as to deprive the United States in their rightful resource for the **army and the militia.**

The citizen reserves to himself the right to protect himself and his property from unwarranted invasion in instances where such guarantee cannot be provided by the state for any one of a variety of reasons. In the United States firearms have been associated with self-defense. Recently this has included self-defense in the citizen's resistance to riots and civil disruption. **This today includes all the personal crimes against the citizen.**

In English common law (*Blackstone's Commentaries on the Law of England* on which America's common-law has been based) **all citizens have the obligation to prevent a crime being committed. A citizen was required** to take whatever steps necessary to prevent successful perpetration of a crime. The right was based on **self-defense** when trying to prevent a crime. The general rule offered was one of reasonable **apprehension of harm.** This right was also extended in **resistance to riots or similar disturbances.** If three or more citizens were the threat. This was whether such a threat was against one's own property or life. (8, p. 193)

The Right of Self-Defense:
1. The right to defend oneself, his family, his employees, and his property.
2. The right to stand one's ground or be compelled to retreat when under attack.
3. One may shoot to kill presumably when under attack. (8, p. 193)

A court held that a man's obligation to protect his family was deeply rooted in both

American and English common law.
1. Individual right to use weapons in defense of himself or the state: Arizona, Washington, Alabama, Connecticut, Michigan, Texas.

2. Right of all men to bear arms in defense of themselves and the state: Florida, Idaho, Indiana, Kentucky, Oregon, Pennsylvania, South Dakota, Vermont, Wyoming.

3. Right to bear arms for their security and defense: New Mexico, Ohio, Utah.

4. Right to bear arms in defense of his home, person, property: Colorado, Mississippi, Missouri, Montana, Oklahoma.

5. People have the right of common defense: Arkansas, Kansas, Maine, Massachusetts.

6. Right of the citizen to self-defense: Alaska, Hawaii, Louisiana, North Carolina, South Carolina, New York. (8, p. 194)

In some states, there has been a law allowing weapons for self- defense, but also a law making carrying a weapon. This was later ratified. Elements that justify the use of force in the defense of a person:

1. That force is threatened against a person
2. That any person threatened is not the aggressor
3. That the danger of harm is imminent
4. That the force threatened is unlawful
5. That the person threatened must believe
   a) That a danger exists
   b) That the use of force is necessary to avert the danger
   c) That the kind and amount of force which he uses is necessary.
4. That the above beliefs are reasonable. A further principle:
   a) The threatened force will cause death or great bodily harm or
   b) The force threatened is a forcible felony.

The right of the individual to be secure in his home and in his person, is universally recognized. Such divergent philosophies as **Christianity, Buddhism, and Islam recognize that right.**

The United Nations, in 1948, adopted The Universal Declaration of Human Rights and included the right of self-defense.

History notes it is possible in a future war that citizens would need their arms to defend the state. It is a common belief and quoted by several great leaders of this country that the best way to avoid a war is to be prepared for war. History reveals that America has had enemies that would "bury us" if they were given the opportunity. These groups have been noted to have murdered over 50 million plus people. When America arms it is for defense reasons.

Civilizations have changed. War is local and is violence on citizens by people who have already invaded America. They would bury us if they could. Radical Islam has no country. Its objective is to overtake the world with their Islamic law. The thing that has saved our country from war inside our country is that which has been called from the old days, we are a nation of "riflemen mentality". (8, p. 195)

We take up our arms and go in the world to fight for freedom. Since a large percentage of **Americans have arms, they just trade them for military ones**.

There are numerous countries that have well-organized trained "people militia" including: China, the Soviet Union, Albania, etc. They are "citizen-soldiers". In these countries, there is a much lower crime rate. It is becoming a new way in keeping with human dignity and civil liberties. It appears to be the only way to reduce crime in America. This would use the base organization of the American National Guard. There would have to be one militia in every block in America, which would require millions. This is a resource that could control riots and reduce property damage and local injuries. Those in riots (insurrectionists) have all sorts of weapons. Gasoline and other flammable liquids have been used. This happened in Washington, D.C., in the place of guns. (8, p. 195)

We must add to our view of self-defense to address the rise of riots and other insurrections. The **militia** must be trained and have the right to, if necessary, shoot a rioter, a rapist, or would-be murderer. It is the obligation of all American citizens to defend our country in the defense of internal enemies. We must realize that the criminal is self-serving and is without principles or ethics. He is a criminal voluntarily and of his own free will.

He knows his calculated risk which was much reduced in America by previous leaders.

From the ancient laws of mankind, the citizen had not only the right, but the obligation to prevent the action of a crime. The courts in America have become so liberal that sometimes the courts punish the citizen rather than the criminal. After the riots of 1967- 68 in United States many public officials and organizations called for the formation of a voluntary citizen group to back up the police. The National Rifle Association for years has said that the best police force on earth, alone, cannot stop the kind of violence that has swept many American cities. That was thirty-eight years ago, and the crime rate is still rising!

Wake Up America!! <u>We have enemies inside and outside America and we are not defeating either one</u>. At that time Cook County Sheriff, Joseph I. Woods, sought to form a 1000-member riot control squad composed of private citizens who were to have the full power of deputies during major emergencies. This never happened. Recently in late 2016, Chicago asked for 1000 new policeman. (8, p. 196)

Arlington County Virginia and Montgomery County Maryland have asked for civilian volunteers to help the police. The use of firearms to resist criminal attempts, either by groups or by single individuals, must be made by trained professionals and citizens. This is not to be the old-style "vigilante techniques", but a legally organized group.

The second amendment indicates that the right of the people to keep and bear arms shall not be infringed. Some ask if this is a collective or an individual, right? It is clear that the act wholly disarms aliens for all purposes. The courts have not always agreed on the distinction between unmaterialized foreign residents and citizens. High crime rate states have generally pushed for some form of weapon registration. Many states do not have this law.

There has been "bitter" controversy as to who controls the militia units; local or federal. It is clear that the right to keep and bear arms is an individual right at both state and federal levels. There is no such thing as "collective" rights, which has no counterpart for individual citizens. If a right exist collectively it exists individually. It may be regulated to exclude certain classes of individuals for cause, but it is otherwise universal. The earliest Militia act was the Militia Act of 1792, which the courts continue to study.

A system would require "five unique" system problems: data collection, data conversion, and data storage and retrieval, data dissemination, and data communication. This would require hundreds of people years to accomplish to add all Americans with guns at which time the data would have changed again. Many of the gun crimes are with stolen guns and there are many other weapons or tools used for crimes. From 1954 - 1964 an estimated 16,000 firearms were stolen from the U. S. military from both active and reserve installations. (8, p. 197)

In two years, a questionnaire was sent to all 50 states concerning guns. Three states never replied including: Alabama, Massachusetts, and Rhode Island. It is doubtful whether all the guns in America could ever be successfully registered. Gun opponents have stated, "The United States is a very special type of insane asylum in that all the inmates are permitted to have guns." They are ignorant of the many citizen militia in foreign countries. **Wake Up America** and be prepared to defend yourself and your family with a gun just is Jesus told his disciples to get a sword to protect themselves. (Luke, the doctor 22:36) (8, p. 197)

Firearms education is the primary key to the reduction of war, violence, and the killing of man. Correctly organized this would create a relationship between the police and citizens. There are at least (1972) 10 million knowledgeable gun owners that could correct the ignorance regarding to guns. It is noted that the states that have restricted gun laws have no reduction in crime. (8, p. 197)

It would be possible to suggest that the very glorification of violence spawned by the media themselves is by far and away more responsible for acts of violence and are guns.

We continue to note the pro-firearms stance by our forefathers and leaders in the foundation of our country of wise men that believed the American citizen had the right to defend himself, his family, and his property.

XIII. Christianity

Christianity had **a part in fashioning medieval warfare in both theory and practice**. (3, p. xxiv) The central idea of a just Christian war for the sake of punishing evildoers were of little real significance for practices. Knighthood with its strong individualist moral code of chivalry shaped a common Christian outlook. The Christian faith had a widespread belief in the chivalrous virtue. Christians helped prevent the bloody and total kind of activity common among the ancients. The medieval Christian soldier could think only of his Christian faith as the supreme end which all activities were destined to. This was alien to the idea of religion which could be effective in increasing morals, determination, and loyalty. All a means for the ultimate good of victory.

The English Colonies
The English Colonies founded in (1587-1707) was to become the United States of America. The first English colony was in Virginia in 1607. The second was Newfoundland in 1610, claimed for England in 1497, by John Cabot (1450-98). The third was in Massachusetts, New England in 1624. 60,000 English emigrated in the first half of the 17th century and 200,000 in the second half. Many of the British colonies had religious motives. New England Puritans were the most famous. Later the Quakers founded settlements in Pennsylvania, and the Catholics in Maryland. The motives were mostly economic: for raw materials, metals, timber, and foodstuffs. They purchased manufactured goods from England which increased their trade. (8, p. 134)

The English colonies was funded by private rather than government capital. Under the leadership of John Smith (1580-1631) the colonies became successful. John Rolfe's (1585-1622) tobacco production in 1612 provided the colonies with a valuable cash crop.

The English colonies established its own elected assembly in 1619. Pilgrim fathers arrived on November 21, 1620, at Cape Cod and began the settlement of New England. One hundred and two were on board the Mayflower. They founded the Plymouth Colony on Massachusetts Bay. The Puritans were regarded as England's state church, but it was close to the Roman Catholic Church in practice. They believed in **religious freedom**, **self-government**, and **local democracy** in New England.

A **"Great Migration" of 20,000** settlers arrived in New England during the 1630s. Boston was a flourishing port. They wanted to create a Bible Commonwealth (1614) with citizenship and the right to vote for the governor. Dissenters were expelled and founded their own colonies where greater religious tolerance was protected: Rhode Island, New Hampshire, and Connecticut.

The New England Confederation was formed for mutual defense. The last serious challenge to English colonization was King Philip's War of 1675. Five hundred settlers were killed, and many towns burned. The Indians were again defeated with heavy losses. They were now too numerous to be moved. **These wars were fought by local militias**. Next came the American Revolution and the creation of the United States. (8, p. 135)

France lost its North American colonies to Britain in the French and Indian war (1754 - 1763) An extension of the Seven-Year War in Europe. Louisiana still retains many French cultural traits.

The French states spread Catholicism to the native people. Many Jesuit missionaries were killed by the Indians. Immigration from France in the 17th and 18th centuries were around 60 to 70,000 people. The French plantations began importing African slaves for labor. English-speaking naval dominance, and landless poor immigrants pushed France out and England was dominant. (8, pp. 134, 135, 136)

What Does the Bible and Jesus Say about War?

There are 242 verses in the Bible that refer to war describing battles of the Old Testament or spiritual warfare.

Christ only mentioned war two times:

1. *"And ye shall hear of wars and rumors of wars. See that ye be not troubled, for all these things must come to pass."* (Matt. 24:6, Mark 13:7, Luke 21: 9)

2. The second time Jesus mentioned war is whether a king with 10,000 men could fight a king with 20,000. If not, he should go and ask for conditions of peace. (Luke 14:31, 32) The statement ends here, but one must assume that if one king thought he could go against the other king then the battle should begin.

Jesus knew we had to protect ourselves when He said, *"He that hath no sword...buy one".* (Like 22:36)

Religion, Churches
The whole question of church and state has become a bigger question.

In 1922 there were 167 Protestant seminaries in the United States:

- Baptist 29
- Methodist 27
- Presbyterians 27
- Lutheran 22
- Episcopal 13
- Congregational 12
- Undenominational 8
- Others 29

In these 95 years there has been a "falling away" from Christianity. (8, p. 263)

<u>**Churches are closing and becoming restaurants, museums, or business property**</u>. Our personal church, First Baptist Brandon, Florida where our pastor, Rev. Tim Keith, is truly God's spokesman from the Scriptures and lifts us into the clouds every Sunday.

Losing Faith:
America remains unusual among rich democracies as being highly religious. Yet, our country is becoming much less devout. Little notice has been given

to how much less devout the country has become. The term "**Nones**" has been coined to refer to atheists, agnostics, and those who say they have no religion. "**Nones**" already outnumber Catholics and mainline Protestants. In 2019, it is expected that they will also outnumber evangelicals. Soon there will be more "**Nones**" than any single group of Christians.

People of all generations are leaving churches. The oldest generations are the most religious and the youngest the most non-believing. The Catholic Church has suffered the most. Sexual abuse scandals seem to bear much of the blame. Other countries have noticed that America is secularizing. (5, p.41) Some politicians are already comfortable telling a pollster that they are atheist or agnostic. Christians are losing our country in so many ways.

The world's population is on the move because of technical and economic globalization by wars, religions conflicts, terrorism, crime, divorces, economy, poverty, fear, lack of security, etc. History continues to be full of migrations. Building a new life in a foreign country requires initiative with action and courage. For hundreds of years Europe has been the main world source of migration to other countries. Time, with its ethnic, cultural, economy has changed Europe into an importer of migrants.

To study the human race, one must study the effect of migrations on culture, economy, and government. Migrations create the history of the world. I have found no country that has been free of migrations. Migrations in many cases changed their culture and government leadership. The philosophy of the country may also be changed by its migrants. Migrations can have both positive and negative effects on countries. Some communities became stronger and others became weaker with their migrations. (8, p. 122)

Wake up America. For survival our country must return to the love of Christianity and Christ.

Books of Religion - King James Bible Version

Frequently in Books of Religion Famous Leaders are Listed. (None Can Compare with Christianity's known leaders. No other religion has a book that even compares with these listed leaders.) 170 Biblical leaders are listed. (Their names are continuing for thousands of years.)

Figures in the Hebrew Bible (Old Testament)

- **Aaron** - Brother of Moses and Miriam, and the first High Priest.
- **Abel** - Second son of Adam and Eve, slain by Cain.
- **Abraham** - Founder of monotheism; Patriarch; also called Abram.
- **Adam** – First human according to Genesis.
- **Amos** – Herdsman; prophesized against social injustice and oppression of the poor.
- **Bathsheba** - Queen, wife of King David, and mother of King Solomon.
- **Cain** – First son of Adam and Eve; killed his brother Abel.
- **Cyrus** – Persian ruler; sent the Jews home from exile.
- **Boaz** - Husband of Ruth and ancestor of King David.
- **Daniel** – Cast into the lion's den for violating decree of Darius; saved.
- **David** - Israel's greatest king; shepherd, warrior, musician, psalmist.
- **Deborah** – Prophet and judge; ruled over Israel.
- **Elijah** – Great prophet, was victorious over the priests of the Phoenician god Baal.
- **Elisha** – Prophet; successor to Elijah.
- **Esther** – Jewish wife of the king of Persia; saved Jews from annihilation.
- **Eve** – First woman according to Genesis.
- **Ezra** – Great Jewish leader; rededicated worship and Torah law after exile.
- **Goliath** – Giant Philistine warrior; slain by David.
- **Hannah** – Childless; promised child to God; mother to the prophet Samuel.
- **Hosea** – Enacted prophecy; asked God's forgiveness for Israel's unfaithfulness.
- **Isaac** – Son of Abraham and Sarah; saved form sacrificial altar.
- **Isaiah** – Highly educated prophet; avoided war with Assyria; Israel destroyed; Jerusalem survived.
- **Jacob** – Son of Isaac; father of the Twelve Tribes; renamed "Israel" by Angel.
- **Jeremiah** – Confronted leaders and urged surrender to Babylon.

- **Jezebel** – Phoenician queen of Ahab; had Israelite prophets killed.
- **Job** – "Blameless" man; allowed by God to lose family, health, and possessions in a test of this faith.
- **Jonah** – Swallowed by a great fish; prophesied destruction of the city of Nineveh, averted when the people repented.
- **Jonathan** – Son of King Saul; friend of David.
- **Joseph** – Favorite of Jacob; interpreted Pharaoh's dreams; brought Hebrews to Egypt.
- **Joshua** – Successor of Moses led the Hebrews into Canaan.
- **Josiah** – Reformist king; repaired Solomon's Temple; restored worship; reintroduced Passover.
- **Leah** – Matriarch; older sister of Rachel; wife of Jacob.
- **Micah** – Prophet; predicted the end of war and beginning of peace.
- **Miriam** – Prophet and great leader of the Hebrews; sister of Moses and Aaron.
- **Moses** – Most important Hebrew prophet; leader of the Israelites; received the Torah.
- **Nathan** – Prophet; confronted King David over his seduction o Bathsheba.
- **Nebuchadnezzar** – Babylonian king; destroyed Jerusalem.
- **Nehemiah** – Led Jews back to Jerusalem from Babylonian exile.
- **Noah** – Man of great faith who, according to Genesis, saved his family and two of every living thing on Earth from a great flood.
- **Rachel** - Matriarch; younger sister of Leah; wife of Jacob; Joseph's mother.
- **Rebecca** - Matriarch; wife of Isaac; mother of Jacob.
- **Ruth** – Moabite convert; ancestor of David.
- **Sampson** – Judge and military leader of Israel; possessed super-human strength.
- **Samuel** – Prophet; anointed Saul king of Israel and later anointed David to succeed him.
- **Sarah** – First matriarch of Israel; wife of Abraham; mother of Isaac.
- **Saul** – First king of Israel; father of Jonathan.

- **Solomon** – King of Israel at its zenith; known for great wisdom.
- **Zechariah** - Prophet; encouraged rebuilding of Solomon's Temple destroyed by Babylonians.

Figures in the Bible (New Testament) King James Bible Version
- **Andrew** – One of the Twelve Apostles; brother of Peter and former fisherman; one of the earlier disciples.
- **Barabbas** – Disciple of Jesus; closely connected with Paul.
- **Bartholomew** – A lesser-known member of the Twelve Apostles; cheerful and prayed often.
- **Cornelius** – Roman convert; defended by peter, allowing Gentiles to become Christians.
- **Elizabeth** – Mother of John the Baptist; relation to the Virgin Mary.
- **Gabriel** – Archangel; appeared to the Virgin Mary to announce that she was to give birth to the Messiah.
- **Herod** – May refer to Herod the Great, wo ordered the death of children after Jesus's birth, or to his son, Herod, who had John the Baptist beheaded.
- **James** – May refer to either of two Apostles: James the son of Zebedee, brother of John the Apostle, or the lesser-known James, son of Alphaeus.
- **Jesus** – Central figure of the Gospels; believed to be the Messiah and son of God; crucified by the Romans.
- **John** (Apostle) - Beloved disciple of Jesus; one of the Twelve Apostles; possible author of fourth gospel; brother of James.
- **John the Baptist** – Known as John the Baptist; important prophet and forerunner to Jesus; relation of the virgin Mary.
- **Joseph** – Husband of the Virgin Mary; descendent of King David.
- **Judas Iscariot** – Betrayer of Jesus; prominent member of the Apostles; committed suicide.
- **Judas Thaddeus** – One of the Twelve Apostles; also called Jude to distinguish him from Judas Iscariot.
- **Lazarus** – Brother of Mary and Martha of Bethany; raised from the dead by Jesus at their request; possibly the same Lazarus who appears in Jesus's parable of the rich man.

- **Luke** – Traditional author of the Gospel of Luke; possibly a follower of Paul.
- **Mark** – Traditional author of the Gospel of Mark; possibly a disciple of Peter.
- **Mary** - The mother of Jesus – Traditionally believed to be a virgin who conceived without sin; wife of Joseph.
- **Mary Magdalene** – Important female disciple of Jesus; witness to his death and resurrection.
- **Matthew** – One of the Twelve Apostles; possible author of the Gospel of Matthew; former tax collector.
- **Matthias** – Often included on lists of the Twelve Apostles as the apostle who replaced Judas Iscariot after his betrayal.
- **Paul (Saul)** – Writer of nearly a quarter of the New Testament; a former persecutor of Christians, converted after a vision; played a significant role in spreading Christianity.
- **Peter** – Considered the foremost of the Twelve Apostles author of epistles; also called Simon and Simon Peter.
- **Phillip** – One of the Twelve; considered pragmatic and sensible.
- **Pontius Pilate** – A Roman prefect; played a large role in the trial and crucifixion of Jesus.
- **Simon** – One of the Twelve Apostles; known as "the zealot" to distinguish him from Simon Peter.
- **Stephen** – Fervently preached that Jesus was the Messiah; stoned to death by angry mob, including Saul; important figure in Saul's conversion.
- **Thomas** – One of the Twelve Apostles; known as "Doubting Thomas" because he did not believe Jesus was risen until he could touch him.
- **Timothy** – A disciple closely connected with Paul; recipient of epistles.
- **Zacharias** – Father of John the Baptist; husband of Elizabeth; struck dumb when he doubted his barren wife could become pregnant. **(8, pp.72-77)**

215 million Christians experience persecutions, which is one in 12 Christians. (8, p. 143)

"8 main engines of persecution:"

1. Islamic Extremism
2. Religious Nationalism
3. Ethnic Antagonism
4. Secular Intolerance
5. Communist and Post-Communist Oppression
6. Denominational Protectionism
7. Organized Corruption and crime
8. Dictatorial Paranoia

The Persecution of Christians Score Range

Extreme	81-100
Very High	61-80
High	53-60

Countries and Score Comments (8, pp. 143-146)

Atheism	**North Korea**	**The Worst Place on Earth for Christians** – Paranoia
Islam	Somalia	Martyrdom is Commonplace
Islam	Afghanistan	When it costs Everything
Islam	Pakistan	Unjust Treatment, Violent Attacks
Islam	Sudan	Persecution and Sectarian Strife
Islam	Syria	Persecution and Civil War
Islam	Iraq	Near Extinction
Islam	Iran	A "Threat" From the West
Islam	Yemen	War and Islamic Extremists
Islam	Eritrea	Shipping -Container Prisons
Islam	Libya	Anarchy and Persecution
Islam	Nigeria	Brutal Violence in the North
Islam	Maldives	A False Paradise

Islam	Saudi Arabia	Defined by Islam. Christians must live their faith in deepest secrecy.
Hinduism	India	A Hindu Nation, and Christianity
Islam	Uzbekistan	Constant Surveillance
Buddhism	Vietnam	Restrictions and Discrimination
Christianity	Kenya	A Persecuted Majority – the main religion is Christianity
Islam	Turkmenistan	Lack of Freedom
Islam	Qatar	Private Worship Only
Islam	Egypt	War and Islamic Extremists
Christianity	Ethiopia	A Persecuted Majority
Islam	Palestinians	Caught in the Middle
Buddhism	Laos	The Cost of Deviation
Islam	Brunei	The Islamic Sultanate
Islam	Bangladesh	A Growing Minority - Christianity
Islam	Jordan	A Turning Tide – Tribal Antagonism
Buddhism	Myanmar	Violent Attacks, Legal Opposition
Islam	Tunisia	Rising Extremism
Buddhism	Bhutan	Underground Fellowship
Islam	Malaysia	Fading Tolerance
Islam	Mali	Undermining Freedom
Christianity	Tanzania	Militant Threats
Catholic	Central Africa Republic	Displacement and Violence
Islam	Tajikistan	Pressure to Turn Back
Islam	Algeria	Home to Extremists
Islam	**Turkey**	**Nationalist Pressure**
Islam	Kuwait	A False Sense of Freedom
Atheism	**China**	**Restrictions Through the Country**

Islam	Djibouti	Persecution Spilling Over from Neighboring Countries
Christianity	Mexico	Persecution in a Christian Nation
Islam	Comoros	A History of Persecution
Islam	Kazakhstan	Every Form of Persecution

Total Number of Countries - 50

Country	Religion	Population	Christians
North Korea	Islam	25,405,000	300,000
Somalia	Islam	11,392,000	Few hundred
Afghanistan	Islam	34,169,000	Thousands
Pakistan	Islam	196,744,000	3,938,000
Sudan	Islam	42,166,000	1,996,000
Syria	Islam	18,907,000	794,000
Iraq	Islam	38,654,000	230,000
Iran	**Islam**	**80,946,000**	**800,000**
Yemen	Islam	28,120,000	Few thousand
Eritrea	Islam-Christianity	5,482,000	2,741,000
Libya	Islam	6,409,000	20,000
Nigeria	Christianity	191,836,000	95,918,000
Maldives	Islam	376,000	Few thousand
Saudi Arabia	Islam	32,743,000	**1,406,000**
India	Hinduism	1,342,513,000	**63,970,000**
Uzbekistan	Islam	30,691,000	350,000
Vietnam	Buddhism	95,415,000	8,368,000
Kenya	Christianity	48,467,000	39,749,000
Turkmenistan	Islam	5,503,000	69,900

Qatar	Islam	2,338,000	210,000
Egypt	Islam	95,215,000	9,521,500
Ethiopia	Christianity	104,345,000	**65,737,400**
Palestinians	Islam	4,928,000	70,800
Laos	Buddhism	7,038,000	225,000
Brunei	Islam	434,000	54,800
Bangladesh	Islam	164,828,000	**866,000**
Jordan	Islam	7,877,000	169,000
Myanmar	Buddhism	54,836,000	4,369,000
Tunisia	Islam	11,495,000	23,500
Bhutan	Buddhism	793,000	20,000
Malaysia	Islam	31,164,000	2,865,000
Mali	Islam	18,690,000	448,600
Tanzania	Christianity	56,878,000	31,739,000
Central Africa Republic	Christianity	5,099,000	3,772,000
Tajikistan	Islam	8,858,000	62,200
Algeria	Islam	41,064,000	37,700
Turkey	Islam	80,418,000	187,000
Kuwait	Islam	4,100,000	349,000
China	**Atheism**	**1,370,000,000**	**85,000,000**
Djibouti	Islam	911,000	11,100
Mexico	Christianity	130,223,000	**124,869,000**
Comoros	Islam	798,294	3,300
United Arab Emirates	Islam	9,398,000	**1,220,000**
Sri Lanka	Christianity	20,300,000	1,400,000
Indonesia	Christianity	263,510,000	31,925,000
Mauritania	Islam	4,266,000	5,000

Bahrain	Islam	1,419,000	186,000
Oman	Islam	4,741,000	204,000
Columbia	**Christianity**	**49,068,000**	**46,657,000**

Islam	36
Christian	10
Buddhism	4
Atheism	1

52 Countries (2 Islamic Countries counted with another religion.)

Total 50 Countries

"Today, our fellow citizens, our way of life, our very freedom, came under attack". (President George W. Bush) **This was more than were killed in a surprise attack at Pearl Harbor. (2,343 killed, Pearl Harbor)** (2, p. 1153) The United States had intercepted intelligence of an attack, but the leaders in Washington and Pearl Harbor were in disbelief and totally unprepared. President Roosevelt made a famous statement, "This date will live in infamy". In 2001, New York was awakened, but the leaders of America remain asleep.

The face of war has allowed a man to look a stranger in the face and strike to kill him. The machine-gun in the 19th century replaced the pistol, pike, and sword. **The amount of killing on the battlefield has increased from century to century**. Firearms have made skill in fighting irrelevant. The technology between civilians and military life has been brought closer together. (8, pp. 182-187)

The right for conscientious objection and capital punishment has dropped from the education system. **The concept of fraternalism has been pushed by self-reliance and self-defense.** Modern warfare has given the average soldier a sense of unimportance as it made the lives of the opponents unimportant. The Hague Convention in 1899 put the rise of "thing-killing" as differentiated from man killing. Previous artillery and Calvary made it personal killing. Battles remain to the strong and the young.

There has been an appearance of drugs preparing our soldiers for battle. **Alcohol and marijuana** were used in Vietnam. Marijuana was used on European ships before battle.

The Realities of War and the Horrors of Combat Reformations Bring on Many Wars

<u>There is no such thing as getting used to combat</u>. A certain number of casualties occurs because of exhaustion or from psychiatric reasons. The first hours of combat disable some of a fighting force.

I gave this section a good deal of thought before I included it in this book. I am including it because it reveals some of the **realities of war** and descriptive scenes of the **horrors of combat**. For those of us who have been in combat and experienced seeing those we know killed and torn apart it will be a reality in a different way and to the others it will be informative.

The Roman Catholic Cantons started with cruelty towards all who were attached to the Gospel. This included fines, imprisonment, torture, scourge, confiscation of property, banishment, cutting out minister's tongues, beheading them, and burning at the stake. They took away all the Bibles and all the evangelical books. This was countryman against countrymen. **Hatred prevailed over patriotism**. (8, p. 183)

The Catholic men charged with their long and pointed halberds. (A battle axe and spike on a handle six feet long.) They screamed, "You heretics! Sacrilegious! We have you at last." The Zurichers replied, "You Man-sellers, idolaters, impious papists! Is it really you?" Both parties suffered, and many were wounded and killed. The Zurichers were in disorder, but with sword and halberds they drove the soldiers of the Five Cantons backwards. When the Zurichers advanced and became entangled in the marsh the Catholics said they fell into their trap. (8, p. 184)

In vain the bravest of the Zurichers fought with fearlessness. Spies fell among the Zurichers crying, "Turn, run, brave men you have been betrayed!" An older Zuricher raised the Gospel banner with a firm hand. The bannerette said, "Let us lower the banner, my lord, and save it, for our people are running shamefully." The old warrior said, "Warriors, stand firm." The old man stood like an oak beaten by a frightful hurricane. He received unflinchingly the blows that fell upon him, and alone he resisted the terrible storm. They said to him, "My lord, lower the banner or else we shall lose it, there is no more glory to be reaped here!" The bannerette that was already mortally wounded said, "Alas, must the city of Zurich be so punished?" (8, p. 185)

The old man dragged him but did not have the strength to cross a ditch. He was still holding the glorious standard whose folds dropped on the other bank. The colors of the flag caused the enemy to run up like a bull to the gladiator's flag. The old man leaped to the bottom of the ditch still holding the staff with his dying hands. The bannerette was still supporting him. When the bannerette died the old man tore it away from his hands. The last of the Zurichers reached the ditch. They fell over one another upon the expiring bannerette, which hastened his death. The old man was gunshot, but he still defended himself and the banner. (8, p. 185)

The Catholics surrounded him with their swords. The enemy grabbed the flag and tore it. The old man with one blow from his sword, cut his throat and cried, "To the rescue, brave Zurichers! Save the honor and the banner of our Lord." He was about to fall. Adam Naeff rushed up with his sword and cut off the head of the enemy who tore and rolled up the banner. His blood soaked the flag of Zurich. Another Christian warrior arrived to support Naeff with his halberd. They had the banner but were now severely wounded. They sprang forward with the banner. (8, p. 185)

They rushed with sword in hand among enemies and friends leaving a trail of their own blood. The enemy chased after them saying, "Heretics! Villains! Surrender and give us the banner." The Zuricher replied, "You will have our lives first." The enemy had to stop and take off their boots. They ran with the flag and climbed up a mountain. One died from his wound climbing the mountain. A colonel-general who fought as a private died close to the church. His two sons died drunk in their father's blood. The old man had gotten up and retrieved the banner, but he found his enemy had surrounded him and the bloody colorful flag. His eyes grew dim, he could not see, all was dark. A hand of lead knocked him to the ground. He threw the flag to the other side of a hedge and said, "Is there any brave Zuricher near me. Let him preserve the banner and the honor of our Lord. I can do no more! He looked to heaven, May God be my helper!" (8, p. 186)

Dahtyler, a Zuricher, jumped over the hedge, "With the aid of God I will carry it off." He climbed the Albis and placed the ancient standard of Zurich in safety. The noblest blood of the republic had been spilt. The enemy had worn. A man and his brother were in a glorious tomb, side by side. Their house was desolate. All the pride of the population of Zurich lay on the field of battle; seven members of the council, nineteen of the two hundred sixty-five citizens, four hundred and seventeen from the rural area including a father; all of his children and brothers lay where they fell in battle. There had probably never been a battle where so many men of the Word of God lost their life in battle. Ministers marched with their flocks. Joner, a minister, died within sight of his church. Many pastors met the Lord of whom they had preached. (8, p. 186)

Zwingli, with his helmet on his head, sword hanging by his side, and battle-axe in his hand stopped to console a dying man. A stone thrown by the enemy struck him on his head. He got up and was hit by two other blows to the legs and he was down again. Twice he got up, but the next time he received a thrust from a lance. He staggered and fell to his knees. Will this darkness cover our church? Gazing on his trickling blood he exclaims, **"What matter this misfortune? They may kill the body, but they cannot kill the soul"**. These were his last words. (8, p. 186)

He fell backwards under a pear tree. He was on his back, his eyes to heaven with his hands clasped. Two soldiers searching the field did not recognize him and asked if he wanted a priest. He was weak, but shook his head no. They asked again, and he again shook his head no. They began to curse him. "You must be one of the heretics of the city. Another came by with a torch and recognized him. "Zwingli! The vile heretic, Zwingli! That rascal, the traitor!" He took his sword and struck him in throat and said, "Die, obstinate heretic!" Zwingli gave up the Ghost. Zwingli lay dead at age forty-eight. A crowd reached the pear tree. The Catholics tried the dead body and decreed that he should be quartered for treason and burned for heresy. The executioner of Lucerne carried out the sentence. They mixed his ashes with those of a pig. The lawless crowd threw his ashes to the four winds of heaven. (8, p. 187)

He had been the only minister that had nursed victims of the plague. The others were too afraid to go near them. Zwingli got the plague but was a rare recovery. His body was no more than a handful of dust in the hand of a soldier. He was a minister, a general in the army, and a head of government. People even today ask can he be all three of these the sight of God. (8, p. 187)

It may be that battle has already abolished itself? This certainly has not happened against ISIS, but the battles of the future may be fought in never-never land. (Such as the atomic bomb if it is not restricted by all of us!)

It took atomic power to win World War II and it may come to that again.

WWII was popular, but there were still 40,000 American soldiers who deserted. Many ministers volunteered for war, as they were needed for the men. However, many stayed behind to get openings created in the big churches. I heard a minister who went to a big church say, "He could do more good by staying home."

Some college professors openly rooted for a Viet Cong victory. Some young men burned American flags and draft cards. A future president (Clinton) deserted to Canada. During Vietnam 576 Americans deserted to Canada, 337 to Sweden, and 88 to Mexico, for a total of 1001. There were 403 "soldiers" who deserted to foreign countries as of 1 July 1966.

General Võ Nguyên Giáp said, "100,000 people die every minute. Life and death don't matter". This kind of war was more political than military, but they say, "**Political power grows out of the barrel of a gun**. Peace is to be used to gain strength while the enemy relaxes and grows soft." "The life of this world is but sport and pastime." (Quran 47:30)

Since the 1950's there has been fear of war in America. **There have been 75 wars since WWII**. The United Nations has had no effect on the incidence or outcome of any war.

We let the 17th parallel in Vietnam fall and <u>lost the only war in American history</u>.
"War is undertaken for the sake of peace. If we want peace we must win".
(**Plato**)

"In war there is no substitute for victory." (**General Douglas McArthur**)

XIV. Suicide and Drug Overdoses

America is the only country in which suicide has increased by 18% since year 2000. Globally it is down by 29%. (**5, p. 13**)

Life expectancy has decreased. There were 70,000 more deaths in 2017 than in 2016. This is the most than in the last 100 years. Middle-age people have had the largest impact. Suicide deaths are the highest than in the last 50 years. (1975) **There were 47,000 suicides**. The United States has the longest period of a generally declining life expectancy since the 1910's. **Gun deaths, mostly suicides**, increased in the last three years from 35,500 to 40,000. The percentage of suicides to drug overdoses has been going down slightly. (**Nation and World**, *"Suicides, Drugs Push Down Life Expectancy"*, Tampa Bay Times, November 30, 2018, p.4A) Alcohol consumption suicide rates have soared upward. (5, p. 52)

XV. Defensive Walls (8, pp. 205-213)

Biblical Walls
- **Jericho** city wall (Joshua 2:15) (7800 B.C.) Earliest known walls.

- **Solomon**: Walls of Jerusalem, (1 Kings 9:15) Hazor, Megiddo - 970 B.C., Gezer.
- **Rehoboam** built walls and fortresses for the defense of Judah in Bethlehem, 450 - 400 B.C., Etam, Tekoa, Beth-zur, (2 Chronicles 11:5-10) Soco, Adullam, Gath, Mareshah, Ziph, Adorain, Lachish, Azekah, Zorah, Aijalon, Hebron.
- **Asa** also built fortified cities of Judah and surrounded them with "walls and towers, gates, and bars". The land is ours as we have sought the LORD our God. They built and prospered.
- **Jehoshaphat** built in Judah fortresses and stone cities. (2 Chronicles 17:12)
- **Nehemiah** in 430 B.C. returning from captivity in Babylonia repaired the walls of Jerusalem that were broken down. Its gates had been destroyed by fire. (Nehemiah 1:8; 2:13) He said to the people, **"Let us rise up and build"**. (Nehemiah 2:18) With their hands and good work they built the wall. He was opposed by Sanballar and Tobiah (ancient Democrats). (Nehemiah 2:19) The people prospered.
- The wall at **Damascus** was where the gates were watched day and night. Saul escaped by being let down at night from the wall. (Acts 9:25) (63-70 A.D.)

From the very beginning of their history as a nation the Israelites were acquainted with fortified cities.

The New Jerusalem
The Heavenly Jerusalem (Revelation 21:10-27) written between 68-69 A.D. or 81 – 96 A.D.)

A New Heaven and a New Earth:
Even here is a great wall – Revelation 21:12, 14, 15, 17, 18, 19.
"And he carried me away in the spirit to a great and high mountain, and shewed me that great city, the holy Jerusalem, descending out of heaven from God, Having the glory of God: and her light was like unto a stone most precious, even like a jasper stone, clear as crystal; And **had a wall great and high**, and had twelve gates, and at the gates twelve angels, and

names written thereon, which are the names of the twelve tribes of the children of Israel: On the east three gates; on the north three gates; on the south three gates; and on the west three gates. And **the wall of the city had twelve foundations**, and in them the names of the Twelve Apostles of the Lamb. And he that talked with me had a golden reed to measure the city, and the gates thereof, and the wall thereof. And the city lieth foursquare, and the length is as large as the breadth: and he measured the city with the reed, twelve thousand furlongs. The length and the breadth and the height of it are equal. And he measured the wall thereof, an hundred and forty and four cubits, according to the measure of a man, that is, of the angel. **And the building of the wall of it was of jasper**: and the city was pure gold, like unto clear glass. And the foundations of the wall of the city were garnished with all manner of precious stones. The first foundation was jasper; the second, sapphire; the third, a chalcedony; the fourth, an emerald; The fifth, sardonyx; the sixth, sardius; the seventh, chrysolite; the eighth, beryl; the ninth, a topaz; the tenth, a chrysoprasus; the eleventh, a jacinth; the twelfth, an amethyst. And the twelve gates were twelve pearls; every several gate was of one pearl: and the street of the city was pure gold, as it were transparent glass. And I saw no temple therein: for the Lord God Almighty and the Lamb are the temple of it. And the city had no need of the sun, neither of the moon, to shine in it: for the glory of God did lighten it, and the Lamb is the light thereof. And the nations of them which are saved shall walk in the light of it: and the kings of the earth do bring their glory and honour into it. And the gates of it shall not be shut at all by day: for there shall be no night there. And they shall bring the glory and honour of the nations into it. And there shall in no wise enter into it anything that defileth, neither whatsoever worketh abomination, or maketh a lie: but they which are written in **the Lamb's book of life."**

In God's description of His construction of a better place for us to live in eternity where there is no evil, **God mentions His wall in seven verses. The wall is important. In President Trump's many efforts to make America great again he also needs a wall**! There is nothing magnanimous enough to fully set forth the glory of heaven. **We must contemplate in our minds such a wall**, and such gates, how amazing, how glorious, would the prospect be.

History and Walls
The 12th century saw the construction of large new schemes of defensive walls.

- Paris (Notre Dame) set the pattern. The walls were of stone. King Philip Augustus built city walls, first on the right bank of the Seine (1190) And then on the left bank (1210) These walls surrounded 625 acres.
- Charles VI enclosed the right bank of Paris (1080 acres) comprising the commercial and the rich quarters within **a new wall making the city the most populous in Europe.**

Competitions in Constructing Walls:
- **Prague:** The king wanted to make his capital the seat of the Holy Roman Empire. In 1348, Emperor Charles IV founded a new city on the right bank of the Vltava River that wrapped around the old town. **Walls were built around houses in the towns.** He built streets that were 82 feet wide and 1,650 houses all made of stone. Then he enclosed everything by an **11,500-foot-long wall**. (71, p. 31)
- **Paris:** The tower of the Louvre (1190) included 20 circuitous towers 102 feet high and 49 feet wide. Some including construction of moats.

Walls provided the primary defense of a city or fortress along with towers and gate complexes. **Solid parallel walls were built with rooms between the walls**. **Siege walls were built by the invading enemies since biblical days.** "Neither shall Pharaoh with his mighty army and great company make for him in the war, by casting up mounts, and building forts, to cut off many persons." (Ezek. 17:17) **A Roman siege wall of 68 A.D. during the Jewish Revolt is still visible around the mountain fortress of Masada.**

History of the Development of Walls:
- The walls of **Jericho**, 7800 B.C. are the earliest known walls.
- There were massive defensive walls at **Palestine** (3000 B.C.). Arab (859-824 B.C.)
- Walls and towers were recorded.

(2200 - 586 B.C.) There were walls at Megiddo, Tell Beit Mirsum, Hazor, Tel Dan, Akko, Yavnnehn-Yarn, Tel Kabri, Gezer, **Lachish**, Tell en-Nasbeh. Ashdod (1000-600 B.C.) had walls.

- **Jerusalem** (early seventh century) had massive walls.
  Persian period (586-332 B.C.) had massive walls at Tell abu Hawan. Tel Megadin had a double wall.
- <u>**Greek and Roman walls were massive**</u> **(332 B.C. - 324 A.D.). <u>Hasmonean rulers</u> (152-37 B.C.) built massive walls around Jerusalem. Herod (37 B.C. - 870 A.D.) restored and <u>enlarged the walls and towers</u>.**

Techniques used for defending walls:
<u>Siege warfare walls</u> also noted in Deuteronomy 20:20, 2 Samuel 20:15, Psalms 89:40, Jeremiah 6:6, Ezekiel 4:1-3, 26:7-10; Joel 2:7-9; Luke 19:43.

Samaria was besieged for three years. (2 Kings 17:5) For 4000 years there are no recorded walls in the Bible. **The walls of Megiddo and Gezer were erected in 3000 B.C. From 3000 B.C. until the <u>Roman beginning in 63. BC. cities were almost always surrounded by walls</u>.**

Walls in the Bible:
The city of Jerusalem had the glory of God.
Jericho
Babylon
Damascus
Tyre

Walls were so important in the ancient world that they were referred to as a most potent figurative expression.

Other Walls:
- **The Berlin Wall** (1961 - 1989) was probably the most famous wall of modern times.

The United States government now plans to build a $5.7 billion wall along the Mexican border. **<u>India is planning a similar wall for its 2,550-mile borders with Bangladesh</u>.**

Walls are also important to get rid of pigs.

In Denmark they are building a 43-mile steel wall between Denmark and Germany to prevent pigs from carrying into the country African Swine Fever. The wall is to prevent devastation of their 5 billion-dollar pork industry. (It is harmless to humans.) (***Tampa Bay Times***, Page A2, Tuesday, January 29, 2019)

- **Hadrian** (76 - 138 A.D.) built Hadrian's Wall (121 A.D.) to hold back the barbarians from Britain. Aurelian walls of Rome were built by Hadrian.
- **Constantine** (11 May 330) built landward walls for the city.
- **Ctesiphon**, **capital city of the** **Persian Empire had vast rings of walls encircling the city** that stretched the immensity of the irrigation system moat after endless moat.
- **Amida**, a heavenly fortified stronghold with massive basalt walls just above the reaches of the Tigris River.
- An army of Greeks laid siege to **Troy**. They found it impossible to break through. After a siege of ten long and terrible years spies finally managed to break through. (**There have been spies among immigrants throughout all ages.**)
- In **Khorasan**, **a red brick immense wall extended 150 miles and was the greatest barrier ever constructed in the Near East. (484 B.C.)**
- **There was a raw fortress on the red wall beyond the Alborz Mountain in northern Iran.** (8, pp. 205-213)

XVI. Other Groups

1. The Jews

The Jews are unique in that they have been in a state of near permanent migration for 2000 years, known as the Diaspora. They are in every continent and are the most widespread people in the world. They have been pushed by persecution and pulled by new opportunities. Their survival is remarkable. They are motivated by their religion. They believe that they have a special covenant with God, and in the coming of the Messiah, who will restore the kingdom of Israel.

The Persian King Cyrus the Great (550-530 B.C.) conquered Babylon and gave the Jews permission to return home and rebuild the Temple in Jerusalem.

In the 1930's, Jews were at their most numerous, about 18 million. In 2013, there were 13.6 million. The Jews are 0.2% of the world population. **1948** (May 14) – Israel's Declaration of Independence

2. The Mormons (1846-1869) The first group arrived in 1856.
The Mormons in search of a Promised Land (1846-1869) migrated as a community and was one of the driving forces for over 20 years to the west by Joseph Smith (1805-1844) After Joseph Smith's death, Brigham Young (1801–1877) developed a plan for the Mormons to head West, which became known as the "Great Migration". In 1846, they crossed the Mississippi River and 3,500 Mormons spent the winter at "Winter Quarters" in Nebraska. Another 10,000 Mormons were scattered along the trail. In 1847, Young led the first party of the hundred forty-eight pioneers out of Winter Quarters for the Rockies on the Oregon Trail to Fort Bridges. He left the Oregon Trail and arrived in the valley of the Great Salt Lake in Utah, in late July 1847. (8, pp 137, 138)

3. Slavery
The largest forced migration in history was the estimated 14 million African slaves that were to work in the American plantations. They made up **12% of the population of the United States**. In all the Americas, it was estimated to be over **120 million people** of African descent.

Slavery was one of the major causes of the Civil War (1861-1865). The defeat of the Southern Confederacy resulted in the abolition of slavery, but it was another hundred years before African-Americans had equal civil rights with white Americans. The African-American population in Mississippi and South Carolina was 50%. In the 20th century there was a drift of African-Americans to the cities. In the South this included Atlanta, New Orleans, Memphis, and Houston. The drift was even greater in the North with: New York, Washington, DC, Philadelphia, Detroit, and Chicago. African-Americans are the most on urbanized ethnic group in the United States. (8, p. 136)

Juvenile Delinquency

Juvenile delinquency is usually related to the ages 16 – 20. A high proportion of adult criminals have a background of early delinquency. *"Culture of poverty"* is a term from poverty-level neighborhoods. Gangs are also frequently related. Since 1899, the juvenile court was separated from the adult court. There are many juvenile correction institutions and other agencies. All of these have not solved the problem that keeps occurring in juveniles. Most of our agencies work to fix the problem after it occurs. (1, p. 1083)

Be Prepared for History as you are Making it!

We must always be prepared for war.

"Proclaim ye this among the Gentiles; Prepare war, wake up the mighty men, let all the men of war draw near; let them come up: Beat your plowshares into swords, and your pruninghooks into spears: let the weak say, I *am* strong." (Joel 3:9, 10)

"The LORD is a man of war." (Exod. 15:3)

"A time of war, and a time of peace." (Ecclesiasts 3:8)

Wars mark the big turning points of history. War is the people's examination. War is the most spectacular social phenomena.

War shatters psychological and religious isolation. It is said that war creates a new moral universe. During war "Christians" become "sinners" and "sinners" become "Christians".

Hippocrates said in 460 B.C., "He who wishes to be a surgeon should go to war." I went to war to learn war surgery. An old quotation, "A doctor sees men not at their best, as does the minister, not at their worst, as does the lawyer; the doctor sees men as they are."

In a study of war here are three points to note: They are **loyalty to country**, **military and civilian discipline**, and **the influence of religion on war**.

Both the Bible and the Quran speaks of pacifism as being bad. "If the ruler rises against you, do not yield, pacifying allows more offences against you". (Ecclesiastes 10:4) President Trump seems to be our only leader that knows this. "When you encounter a force of disbelievers, do not turn your backs on them, if you do, you draw the wrath of Allah on yourself." Quran Surah 8:16

Otto van Bismarck (a strong Protestant) said, "We fear God and nothing else in the world. It is the fear of God that makes us love peace and keep it. Evil that fights against us will learn the meaning of "warlike love".

Every war has strong opposition. The most notable is The American Revolution - a classic example. Over half the population did not support it, if that half had had their way, America would not be America today. War has permanent effects on the minds of men.

XVII. My Thoughts of Thunder and Word Storms Today

Here are some thoughts of today by this 89-year-old retired admiral and neurosurgeon:
- Cyrano De Bergerac was a French novelist, playwright, epistolarian and duelist. A bold and innovative author, his work was part of the libertine literature of the first half of the seventeenth century. Today he is best known as the inspiration for Edmond Rostand's most noted drama Cyrano de Bergerac which, although it includes elements of his life, also contains invention and myth. On his last day, "I wave bye to the world with my plume." (Those of you who do not know the Plume is a white feather.)
- The Lord said what I have done to the least of us, I have done it to Him. (Matthew 25:40)
- "For all have sinned and come short of the glory of God." (Romans 3:23) Do not judge others.

- Cathy and I have One Love, which is not a thing, but a spirit. **Even when we are apart, we are together** on earth or in heaven.
- "But the fruit of the Spirit is love, joy, peace, longsuffering, gentleness, goodness, faith, meekness, temperance: against such there is no law. (Gal. 5: 22-23)
- The Word of God's plan and purpose for mankind is clearly revealed.
- "In whom the god of this world hath blinded the minds of them which believe not, lest the light of the glorious gospel of Christ, who is the image of God, should shine unto them." (2 Cor. 4:4)
- "Hath in these last days spoken unto us by *his* Son, whom he hath appointed heir of all things, by whom also he made the worlds; Who being the brightness of *his* glory, and the express image of his person, and upholding all things by the **word of his power**, when he had by himself purged our sins, sat down on the right hand of the Majesty on high." (Heb. 1: 2, 3)
- **The Word of God is the means by which God makes himself known, declares His will, and brings about His purposes**.
- God, through His Word, "Thus the heavens and the earth were finished, and all the host of them." (Gen. 2:1)
- "And the LORD God formed man *of* the dust of the ground and breathed into his nostrils the breath of life; and man became a living soul." (Gen. 2:7) He made man a living soul.
- "And the rib, which the LORD God had taken from man, made he a woman, and brought her unto the man." (Gen. 2:22) Man and his wife shall be one flesh.
- "The husband shall rule over the woman." (Gen. 3:16)
- "In the beginning was the Word, and the Word was with God, and the Word was God." (Jn 12:1) **The Word of God occurs throughout the Bible**. "Grace and truth came into the world by Jesus Christ." (Jn 1:17)
- Jesus said to John, *"Behold the Lamb of God, which taketh away the sin of the world."* (Jn 1:29)

THE END:

Glory, power, honor, beauty, greatness, authority are all seen in God's character.

A. **"The LORD *is* high above all nations, *and* his glory above the heavens."** (Psa. 113:4)

B. **God's moral beauty and perfection as a visible presence.**
   1. "And the LORD went before them by day in a pillar of a cloud, to lead them the way; and by night in a pillar of fire, to give them light; to go by day and night." (Exod. 13:21)
   "And Moses said unto the people, Fear ye not, stand still, and see the salvation of the LORD, which he will shew to you today: for the Egyptians whom ye have seen today, ye shall see them again no more forever. But lift thou up thy rod, and stretch out thine hand over the sea, and divide it: and the children of Israel shall go on dry *ground* through the midst of the sea. And Moses stretched forth his hand over the sea, and the sea returned to his strength when the morning appeared; and the Egyptians fled against it; and the LORD overthrew the Egyptians in the midst of the sea. And the waters returned, and covered the chariots, and the horsemen, *and* all the host of Pharaoh that came into the sea after them; there remained not so much as one of them." (Exod. 14: 13, 16, 27, 28)
   2. "And Moses and Aaron went into the tabernacle of the congregation, and came out, and blessed the people: and the glory of the LORD appeared unto all the people. And there came a fire out from before the LORD and consumed upon the altar the burnt offering and the fat: *which* when all the people saw, they shouted, and fell on their faces." (Lev. 9:23, 24)
   3. The Temple: "So that the priests could not stand to minister because of the cloud: for the glory of the LORD had filled the house of the LORD. Then spake Solomon, The LORD said that he would dwell in the thick darkness. I have surely built thee an house to dwell in, a settled place for thee to abide in for ever." (1 Kings 8:11-13)

4. "And there came a voice out of the cloud, saying, This is my beloved Son: hear him." (Luke 9:35)

"This beginning of miracles did Jesus in Cana of Galilee and manifested forth his glory; and his disciples believed on him." (Jn 2:11)

"And now, O Father, glorify thou me with thine own self with the glory which I had with thee before the world was. I have manifested thy name unto the men which thou gavest me out of the world: thine they were, and thou gavest them me; and they have kept thy word. And the glory which thou gavest me I have given them; that they may be one, even as we are one." (Jn 17:5, 6, 22)

"But we all, with open face beholding as in a glass the glory of the Lord, are changed into the same image from glory to glory, *even* as by the Spirit of the Lord." (2 Cor. 3:18)

"By whom also we have access by faith into this grace wherein we stand and rejoice in hope of the glory of God." (Rom. 5:2)

"When Christ, *who is* our life, shall appear, then shall ye also appear with him in glory." (Col. 3:4)

"And the nations of them which are saved shall walk in the light of it: and the kings of the earth do bring their glory and honour into it." (Rev. 21:24)

C. **Love the LORD**

"I love the LORD, because he hath heard my voice *and* my supplications." (Psa. 116:1)

Every creature on earth will give Him glory.

"Saying with a loud voice, Worthy is the Lamb that was slain to receive power, and riches, and wisdom, and strength, and honour, and glory, and blessing." (Rev. 5:12, 13)

CONTENTS

Book Two

Rear Admiral Joseph H. Miller

A servant to Christ, was a sinner in death, and born again to eternal life; and blessed as a husband, father, neurological surgeon, author, patriot, military leader, deacon, teacher of God's word, and thankfulness as in our prayer of grace: "Thank you, God, for undeserved blessings too numerous to count!

I. CURRICULUM VITAE – (A Professional Life Revealed)

A curriculum vitae is made for the eyes of man.

NAME: Joseph H. Miller, M.D., F.A.C.S.
                        Rear Admiral (MC) USNR-Ret.

BIRTHDATE: 09 April 1930

BIRTHPLACE: Thrift, Texas, USA

MARITAL STATUS: Married- Cathy Gail Miller

CHILDREN:

                        Leta-Fern
                        Joseph (deceased),
                        Paul, Dwight (deceased)

Netta Sue
Angelique
John Copeland (Step-Son)

EDUCATION:

HIGH SCHOOL: Ludowici, Georgia, 1947

UNDERGRADUATE: **Mars Hill College** 1947-49, A.A.
May King in 1949, Alumni of the Year in 1967. Listed as One of the Outstanding Alumni in the 150 Years of the School, April 23, 2007
East Texas College 1950
Mercer University 1951, A.B.

MEDICAL SCHOOL: Medical College of Georgia
August 1951-June 1955, M.D.

INTERNSHIP:

Surgical, Baptist Memorial Hospital, University of Tennessee School of Medicine, Memphis, TN July 1955- June 1956

RESIDENCY: Neurosurgery, Baptist Memorial Hospital, University of Tennessee School of Medicine, June-1956- June 1959
National Institute of Neurological Diseases and Blindness, June 1959 - 1960

MILITARY SERVICE:

Rear Admiral, (MC) USNR – Retired United States Naval Reserve

September 1952 – October 1986

Deputy Surgeon General for Reserve Affairs (OP093R), Pentagon, 1983-1986

Commander Naval Reserve Force, Force Medical Officer (006) 1983-1986

U.S. Public Health Service, National Institute Neurological Diseases and Blindness National Institute of Health, 1959-1960

Chief, Department of Neurosurgery, National Naval Medical Center, 1960 – 1961

6 Navy Selection Boards Washington, D.C.: 1976, 78, 81, 82, 85, 90. 7-12 January 1984 (First Active Duty Commodore Selection Board in history in peace time), 29 January- 9 February 1984, (President of First Commodore Reserve Selection Board in history in peace time)

Duty at Commander in Chief U.S. Central Command, MacDill Air Force Base, Tampa, Florida, 28 December 1982, 7-10 February 1983, 24-26 February 1984

Named as Top Navy Reservist, Navy Reserve Readiness Command Nine, Public Affairs Office, 27 October 1983

Neurosurgical Consultant:
U.S. Naval Hospital, Millington, Tennessee
U.S. Public Health Service, Memphis, Tennessee
Veteran's Administration Hospital, Memphis, Tennessee
U.S. Naval Hospital, Da Nang, Republic of Vietnam, June – September 1969
Special Consultant to the Surgeon General

United States Coast Guard
U.S. Merchant Marine Officer, Captain
Member American Professional Captains Association, U.S. Coast Guard Auxiliary
U.S. Coast Guard Auxiliary 2002-Present

LARGE AND MINATURE MEDALS:
Legion of Merit
Navy Commendation Medal with Combat V
National Defense Service Medal

Vietnam Service Medal, SBS
Armed Forces Reserve Medal
Republic of Vietnam Gallantry Cross Unit Citation, GF+BP
Republic of Vietnam Civil Action First Class, GF+BP
Navy Expert Pistol

MILITARY RIBBONS:
Combat Action Ribbon

Navy Unit Commendation
Meritorious Unit Commendation
Navy and Marine Corps Oversees Service Ribbon

BOARD CERTIFICATION:
American Board of Neurological Surgery 1966

MEDICAL LICENSURE:

Tennessee MD 004013	1961-(Retired status 2008)
Georgia 007535	1955- 2000
Missouri MDR5432	1974- 2000
Arkansas R2244	1975- 2000
Mississippi 12020	1989- 2000

SOCIETY MEMBERSHIPS:

Society of Neurological Surgeons

American Association of Neurological Surgeons (Harvey Cushing Society),
    Military Liaison Committee, Joint Socio-Economic Committee, Joint
    Section on Neurotrauma and Critical Care
Congress of Neurological Surgeons:
    Surgery, 1973
    Chairman: Committee for Registry of Sabbaticals for Neurological
    Surgeons, 1970-1973
American College of Surgeons, 5 October 1967
American Heart Association, Stroke Council, 1985-2000

Member Affiliate Liaison Program Committee, 1992

Society of Medical Consultants to the Armed Forces-Member of Advisory Board to the Chairman, Reserve Affairs Committee, 1975-1983, Member of the Constitution and By- Laws Committee 1984

Southern Neurosurgical Society

Tennessee Neurosurgical Society, President 1970
Speaker 15 September 1991

Memphis Neurological Society, President 1972-1975
Memphis and Shelby County Medical Society: Chairman, Medicine and Religion Committee, 1966- 1973: House of Delegates, 1971-1978

American Medical Association

American Association of Advancement of Science

Society of Sigma XI (National Honorary Scientific Society) 1959

Aerospace Medical Association

Civil Aviation Medical Association

Beta Beta Beta Biological Honor Society

Association of Military Surgeons of the United States: Speaker 1978, 1983

Naval Order of the United States (Founded July 4, 1890) New York Commandery May 1, 1978

Association of Military Neurological Surgeons

Flying Physicians Association

Memphis, Medical Journal Club, Number One, 1962-1988

Baptist Medical–Dental Fellowship

The Gerontological Society of America

American Geriatrics Society, January 1987

UNIVERSITY APPOINTMENTS:

Instructor, Neurosurgery, 1962

Assistant Professor, Neurosurgery, 1970

Associate Professor, Neurosurgery, July 1, 1977-2000 (Emeritus)

Training Director, Neurosurgery, Department of Neurosurgery, University of Tennessee at Methodist Hospital, July 1, 1983-December 31, 2000.

University of South Florida Medical School, Voluntary Faculty 2002 to Present.

HOSPITAL APPOINTMENTS:

Methodist Hospitals of Memphis
    Director and Founder Memphis Neurosciences Center   1985- 2000
    Chairman- Department of Neurosciences   1985-2000
    Director- Neurosurgical Training   1983-2000
    Chairman, Medical Education Committee   1975-1977
    Vice President- Medical Staff   975-1976
William F. Bowld Hospital
    Courtesy
City of Memphis Hospital
    Consultant
St. Francis Hospital
    Consultant
Baptist Memorial Hospital
    Consultant

SPECIAL ACTIVITIES:

International Interchange of Experts Program under the auspices of the U.S. State

Department and Administered by the Department of Health, Education, & Welfare, (Lecturing and demonstrating neurosurgical techniques in various Neurosurgical Centers in India) January-February 1967

Sabbatical Leave-Special Neurosurgical Consultant to the Surgeon General in Vietnam, Japan, Philippines & Guam June - September 1969

Awarded Navy Commendation Medal with Combat V

Study of Patients Reported Under the Head and Spinal Injury Program, NINDB, Washington D.C., 8 March 1971

Member National Committee for Employer Support of the Guard and Reserve, Washington, D.C., 8 December 1972 and New Orleans, Louisiana, 4-5 February 1974

U.S. Naval Medical Research Unit #2, Taipei, Republic of China, 27 October 1975

Evaluated New Navy Hospital and Marine Field Medical Operations, Okinawa, Japan, 10-24 September 1977

Medical Reserve Policy Board: 14 July 1977 and 26-28 November 1978

Temporary Active Duty to Survey and Evaluate Neurosurgical capabilities: Portsmouth, VA (3 days), San Diego, CA, (3 days), Oakland, CA (3 days), Washington, D.C. (3 days), 10-21 April 1983

Mission Service Corps, The White House, May 1978 Invited by the President to an organization meeting of the Mission Service Corps for increasing U.S. involvement in countries where U.S. activities are minimal.

Developed Academic Neurosurgical Interchange between The Memphis Neurosciences Center and thirty-nine leading International Neurosurgical Centers throughout the world.

Developed a new word in 1984: *"Gerastheniatrology"* (The care of the acutely ill old person as opposed to Gerontology.)

Brain Reconstruction:
Hausman model completed, 1961
Model of Retina completed, 1962
Model of Amygdala completed, 1963
Model of Brachial Plexus completed, 1964
Model of Lumbar, Sacral, and Coccygeal Plexus completed, 1965
Model of Thalamus, completed, 1976

DEVELOPMENT OF NEW METHOD OF RAPID LEARNING USED AS A TEACHING TECHNIQUE:

Clinical protocols for patient evaluation have been established. This has provided a standardization of the clinical examination, which is reproducible for the major neurological conditions. The following unpublished protocols have been presented in multiple invited professorships and to all University of Tennessee neurosurgical residents since 1969 with periodic revisions.

Miller, J.H.: *Course in the Clinical Evaluation of the Peripheral Nerves, Upper Extremity* (1 hr.), *Lower Extremity* (1 hr.), *Brachial and Lumbosacral Plexus* (1hr)

Miller, J.H.: *Classification of Head Injuries to be used in the Initial Evaluation Clinical* (1 hr.), *Anatomical* (1 hr.), and *Complications* (1 hr.)

Miller, J.H.: *The Immediate Support of the Unconscious Patient*, (1 hr.)

Miller, J.H.: *The Clinical Evaluation of Headaches*:
1. *Vascular Headaches*, Diagnosis by Identification of Clinical Syndromes, Medical Treatment of the Acute Phase, Elimination of the Precipitating Factors and Prevention by Medical Prophylactic Protocols. (1 hr.)
2. *Headache and Face Pain* (1 hr.)
3. *Organic Headaches* (1 hr.)

Miller, J.H.: *The Clinical Evaluation of Low Back Pain*:
1. Classification of Low Back Pain (1 hr.)
2. Clinical Evaluation of Low Back Pain (1 hr.)
3. Non-Organic Findings in Low Back Pain (1hr.)

Miller, J.H.: *The Clinical and Anatomical Evaluation of Scoliosis* (1 hr.)

Miller, J.H.: *The Five Questions for the Clinical Evaluations of Ankylosing Spondylitis*, (30 min.)

Miller J.H.: *The Cervical Disk Syndromes Clinical Evaluation and Treatment* (1hr.)

Miller, J.H.: *The Neurovascular Syndromes of the Shoulder and Their Clinical Evaluation with Comments on Treatment* (1 hr.)

Miller, J.H.: *Introduction to the Clinical Examination of the Comatose Patient* (1 hr.)

Miller J.H.; *Classification of Metabolic Encephalopathy*, (1 hr.)

Miller, J.H.: *Osmolarity and the Nervous System* (30 min.)

Miller, J.H.: *Metabolic Brain Requirements and Their Significance in the Clinical Environment,* (30 min.)

Miller, J.H.: *The Carotid Artery Syndrome, Indications for Surgical Treatment with a Classification of the Twelve Risks Factors* (1 hr.)

Miller, J.H.: *A Classification of Intracranial Tumors* (30 min.)

Miller, J.H.: *A Classification of Metastatic Brain Tumors with Comments on Surgical Versus Medical Treatment* (1 hr.)

Miller J.H.: *The Clinical Evaluation of the Cranial Nerves* (3hrs.)

Miller, J.H.: *Third Nerve Abnormalities, A Clinical Anatomical, and Pathological Evaluation* (1hr.)

Miller, J.H.: *The Suprasegmental Auditory Systems* (30min.)

Miller, J.H.: *The Suprasegmental Optic System* (1 hr.)

Miller, J.H.: *The President's Commission on Brain Death Guidelines, and Interpretative, Implementation and Verification Protocol*, (30 min)

Miller, J.H.: *Reflex Sympathetic Dystrophy, Clinical Evaluation and Scoring for Verification of Diagnosis* (1hr.)

Miller, J.H.: *A Simple Clinical Classification of the Muscular Dystrophies for the Neurosurgeon*, (30min.)

OTHER POSITIONS OF LEADERSHIP:

Union University Trustee, 1970-1976
    Chairman–Board of Associates, 1970–1975
    Academic Affairs Committee, 1970–1975
    Commencement Speaker, May 1972 "The Challenges of Life"

Mars Hill College
    Associate Trustee, 1971-1980
    Alumnus of the Year, 1967

Samford University
    Board of Advisors 1998-2004

Memphis Rotary Club, 1970–1995
Regions Bank Director, 1984-2000
President Music Mountain Mineral Water, Inc. Hot Springs, Arkansas, 1969-1970

TEACHING EXPERIENCE:

Neuro-didactics, Methodist Hospital, weekly, on Monday and Thursday. Series of lectures given to the U.T. Medical Students assigned to Methodist Hospital, the transitional interns and surgical residents at Methodist, and the neurosurgical residents at Methodist Hospital, 1983-2000.

Neurosurgical Resident Teaching Veterans Hospital, Weekly 7:30-9:30 Tuesday. 1962-2000

Chairman, Neurosurgical Journal Club, Methodist Hospital–6:30 AM Wednesday

Conduct weekly Neurosurgical Resident Teaching Rounds, Memphis Neurosciences Center–8:00 AM–Wednesday

PUBLICATION: BOOK CHAPTERS:

Handbook of Head Trauma, Acute Care to Recovery, Editors: C.J. Long and L. K.

Ross. Chapter 1, *"Management and Evaluation of head Trauma"*, pp. 3-17. Plenum Press, New York and London, 1992

Monograph: **Stroke, Cerebrovascular Occlusions and Intracerebral Hemorrhages**, Editor, Methodist Healthcare Press, 2000

BOOKS SINCE RETIREMENT:

1. *Mysteries of the Southern Baptist Beliefs Revealed or Biblical Baptist*
2. *You Live! You Die! Who Decides?*
3. *Faked Disability A Shame of America*
4. *Explore the Brain for the Soul and Overcome the World*
5. *Calvin, The Psychopath*
6. *The One Love*
7. *Eighty Years Behind the Masts* (My autobiography)
8. *After 400 Years of the King James Bible*
9. *The Few*
10. *Scriptures for Life*
11. *Obedience*
12. *Radical Islam Hopes to Take Over Our Country (The Sword of Islam)*
13. *Eternal Truth*
14. *100-Years first Baptist church Brandon, Florida, It's Mission and vision for the Future* (19 December 1915 to 19 December 2015)
15. *War*
16. *Civilian Militia* (2019)

II. Publications, Journals, Video, Committees, Offices Held., Lectures. Visiting Professorships Posters, Practices

"Regional Enteritis, A Review of the Literature", M. Med. J., 31: 60-63, 1956

"The Neural Control of the Pituitary Gland", M. Med. J., 32: 289-299, 1957

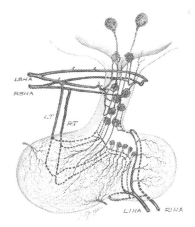

The hypophyseal portal system supplies blood to the anterior gland.

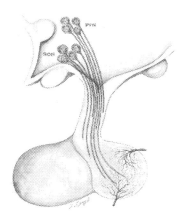

The SON and PVN supplies hormones from the hypothalamus to the posterior gland.

In some of our studies we showed that the anterior pituitary gland did not receive a direct anterior flow of blood but was supplied by the hypophyseal portal system. I made a drawing that reveals this and had a professional artist to make it into the beautiful drawing that you see here.

My first paper on this was in 1957. (***Neural Control of the Pituitary Gland with Particular Reference to Conditions of Stress***, Journal of the Memphis and Shelby County Medical Society. 32:289-301 (September 1957)

This is common knowledge now, but it was not 62 years ago.

The "Stroke", M. Med J., 33: 187-199, 1958

"Carotid Insufficiency–Diagnosis and Surgical Treatment", (with Murphy, Francis), Journal of Neurosurgery, 16: 1-23, 1959

"Brain Tumors in the Newborn", The Southern Medical Journal, (with DeSaussure, R.L. & Strickland, C.R.), 53: 918-921, 1960. Presented Southern Medical Association, November 1959

"Arteriosclerotic Disease of the Carotid Artery", American Surg., 27: 116-128, 1961 (Winning paper-Scientific Award Contest, Southeastern Surgical Congress)

"Intravasation of Opaque Media During Myelography", Journal of Neurosurgery, 18: 610-613, 1961

"Pneumococcal Vertebral Osteomyelitis in an Adult", The Southern Medical Journal, (with Gelfand, M.), Vol. 80 #4, 534-35, April 1987

"The Disposition and Cerebrospinal Fluid Penetration of Morphine, Its Ten Major Glucuronide Metabolites in Adults Undergoing Lumbar Myelogram", Pharmacotherapy (with Laizure, S., Stamens, R., Donahue, D., Laster, R., and Brown, D.) Vol. 13 35, Sept./Oct. 1993

"Meningeal Melanocytoma, An Uncommon Diagnostic Pitfall in Surgical Neuropathy", (with O'Brien, Moran, Hinsley). Arch. Pathol Lab Med. Vol 119, June 1995

"The Importance of Risk factors as Related to the Surgical vs. Medical Treatment of Carotid Artery Disease", Stroke Prevention Series. Tennessee Medicine, pp. 101-102, March 1997

"Further Discussion: Surgical vs. Medical Treatment of Carotid Artery Disease in Asymptomatic Patients", Tennessee Medicine, pp. 364-366, September 1997

PUBLICATIONS: VIDEOS:

Miller, J.H.: ***"Positioning in Neurosurgery"***, Video Series, Department of Education, Methodist Hospital, 1986

Miller, J.H.: ***"Medical Bulletin in Neuroscience"***, Video Series, Department of Education, Methodist Hospital, 1989

Miller, J.H.: ***"Memphis Neurosciences Center"*** and short course in Neurosciences. MPL, Video/Film, Post Production, Memphis, TN 1986

COMMITTEES AND OFFICES HELD:

American Association of Neurological Surgeons
    Military Liaison Committee, 1975–Present, Chairman, 1986
    Joint Socio-Economic Committee, 1978
    Section on Neurotrauma and Critical Care

American Heart Association Stroke Council, 1985-2000
    Members Affiliate Liaison Program Committee, 1992

Congress of Neurological Surgeons
    International Committee, Chairman Committee on Continuing Education in Neurological Surgery, 1973
    Chairman, Committee for Registry of Sabbaticals for Neurological Surgeons, 1970-1974

Government and Public Affairs of the Board of Managers, Methodist Hospital 1973-1980

Building and Planning Committee, Board of Trustees, Methodist Hospital 1973-1990

Society of Medical Consultants to the Armed Forces
    Chairman, Reserve Affairs Committee, 1975-1983
    Constitution and By-Laws Committee, 1984-1985

Society of Neurological Surgeons
    International Committee 1994

Tennessee Neurosurgical Society, President, 1970

Memphis Neurological Society, President, 1972-1975

Memphis and Shelby County Medical Society

Chairman, Medicine and Religion Committee, 1966-1973

House of Delegates, 1971-1978

INVITED LECTURES:
Trigeminal Neuralgia & The Historical Evolution of its Treatment with the Report of an Unusual Case. Resident award, Essay Contest, Memphis & Shelby County Medical Society 1956

Observations on the Uptake of Fluorescein Labeled Protein by The Nervous Tissue in Vitro & Vivo. American Association of Neuropathologists, June 1960

Carotid Endarterectomy. Travel Club of Neurosurgical Society of America, June 1968

The Reticular Formation, National Institute of Neurological Diseases and

Blindness, Annual Course on Brain Reconstruction, 1960

Human Endurance in Outer Space, NIH Seminar, March 1961

Trauma to the Central Nervous System. Trauma Seminar, National Naval Medical Center, Bethesda, MD, March 1961

Neurological Problems of Sustained Life in Outer Space. Honorable Mention, United States Naval Institute, 1961

Cicatrizing Enteritis Involving Duodenum: Report of a Case, (with Farrar, Turley & Strain, S. Fred, Sr. Memphis Surgical Society, 1956

Clinical Value of Muscle Biopsy, BMH Medical Seminar, 1958

Intracranial Aneurysms, The Association of Operating Room Nurses, 1974

Pathophysiology of Stroke. American Heart Association Memphis Chapter November 4,1977

Central Nervous System Involvement with Neoplastic Disease, Continuing Education Course-Cancer Update-Methodist Hospital and UTCHS, October 1-2, 1976

Emergency Surgery to Penetrating Head Wounds Sustained in War

This Monograph was prepared after circulation to 30 Navy neurosurgeons who served in Vietnam, published by U.S. Navy for Navy wide distribution.

Introduction to Coma. Association of Military Surgeons of the United States, 1978; Foreign Mission Conference, Medical Symposium, 1977; International Congress of Military Physician, Caserta, Italy, 1980

Clinical and Anatomical Classification of Head Injuries to be Used in the Initial Evaluation. Association of Military Surgeons of the United States, Foreign Mission Conference-Medical Symposium, Glorieta NM., 1978

Classification of Headaches, Foreign Mission Conference-Medical Symposium Glorieta, NM, 1979; Ridgecrest, NC, 1979

Head Injury Protocol. Navy Medical Seminar with UTCHS, Baptist Hospital & Methodist Hospital, 1979

(Head Injury Lecture) Uniformed Services University Conference Garmisch-Partenkirchen, Germany, 2-6 May 1985

Clinical Evaluation of Comatose Patients. Midwest Spring Conference, Moline, IL, 1980

Physician Reservist in Medical Universities and Schools (PRIMUS), Council of Deans, American Association of Medical Councils, Washington, D.C. 7 November 1983

The Value of Patriotism, Civitan International Clergy Night, Dyersburg, TN, 6 February 1986

Classification of Head Injuries LCRAN. International Conference on Recent Advances in Neuro-traumatology, Sevilla, Spain, September 1987

Metastatic Brain Tumors, The Japan Neurosurgical Society, Tokyo, October 13, 1987

Evaluation of Head Injuries, March 22,1987

20 Annual Family Practice Review Course, University of Tennessee

Evaluation of Unconscious Patients, April 9,1987

American Railroad Association, Annual Medical Conference, Memphis, TN

Evaluation of Head Injuries, University of Tennessee and St. Francis, Trauma Update, January 14, 1988

Late Effects of Head Trauma, Mid-South Head Injury Assoc., St. Francis Medical Center, March 3, 1985

(1) *Evaluation of Unconscious Patients*. (2.) *Transient Ischemic Attacks*, University of Arkansas and University of Tennessee, Annual Critical Care Conference, Hot Springs, AR, April 7-8,1988

Neurosciences in Memphis, 21ˢᵗ Century Healthcare: *Designs for the Future–The Biomedical Research Zone*. International Healthcare Exposition, Memphis, Cook Convention Center, 23-25 May 1989

Introduction to Coma and Immediate Support of the Unconscious Patient, Annual Navy Physician's Assistant Course, Millington, TN September 3, 1988

Philosophy of War with Comments on Pearl Harbor, Pearl Harbor Survivors Association, Memphis, Tennessee, December 1989

Metastatic Brain Tumors with Emphasis on Long Term Survival, Breakfast Seminar, American Association of Neurological Surgeons, Nashville, TN, May 3, 1990

Development of a Neuroscience Center, May 11, 1990
University of Tennessee Neuroscience Symposium Chairman, Dr. Steve Kitai

The Decade of the Brain, Rotary Speaker, January 15, 1991

Surgery of Multiple Metastatic Brain Tumors, 14ᵗʰ International Symposium on Controversies in Neurosurgery, Frankfurt, Germany, June 19, 1991

Management of Metastatic Brain Tumors, European Congress of Neurosurgery, Moscow, USSR, June 26, 1991

Classification of Head Injuries, Tennessee Neurosurgical Society, Nashville, TN September 15, 1991

Spinal Epidural Hematoma, Australian-Asian Congress of Neurosurgery, Seoul, Korea, October 25, 1991

Evaluation of Head Injuries, 121ˢᵗ Army Evacuation Hospital, Seoul, Korea, October 24, 1991

(1.) *Classification and Treatment of Headaches.* (2.) *Immediate Support of the Unconscious Patient* University of Tennessee, and Methodist Hospital Annual Course on Advances in Medicine, Bermuda, November 11-12, 1991

Carotid Artery Dissection, Hong Kong Neurosurgical Society, Hong Kong, February 11,1992

Low Back Pain, University of Tennessee, Annual Review Course, March 18, 1992

Criteria of Brain Death and Comments on Irreversible Coma, Memphis Neurosciences Center and Methodist Hospital Seminar July 16,1992

Low Back Pain and *Evaluation of Minor Head Injuries*; Memphis Neurosciences Center and Methodist Hospital Seminar, July 17, 1992

Irreversible Coma Without Brain Death and Management of Hopeless Cases-1993 Medical Education Program Schedule, Kneibert Clinic, Poplar Bluff, Missouri, January 29, 1993

Carotid Artery Dissection, Turkish Neurosurgical Society, Belek, Turkey, May 6, 1993

Clinical Evaluation of the Peripheral Nerves, Three-Hour Course:
1.   Upper extremity
2.   Shoulder girdle and lower extremity
3.   Brachial, Lumbar, Sacral Plexuses
Turkish Neurosurgical Society, Belek, Turkey, May 7,1993

Carotid Artery Dissection with Emphasis on Trauma and Diagnosis by MRA, MRI, and Arteriography (with Clarence Watridge, M.D.), 2ⁿᵈ International Conference on Stroke, Geneva, Switzerland, May 14,1993

Brain Death and Vegetative State, Methodist Hospital House Staff, January 19,1994

The Evaluation of the Comatose Patient and *The Evaluation of the Patient with Acute Low Back Pain*, the University of Arkansas and University of Tennessee Critical Care Conference, Hot Springs, Arkansas, March 31, 1995

The Magnitude of China's Humanity (One Institute Caring for 800 Million People) Southern Medical Association, Memphis Cook Convention Center, 13 May 1995

Modern Management of Headache, University of Tennessee Twenty-Ninth Annual Review Course for the Family Physician, Memphis, TN, March 17-23, 1996

Is New in Spinal Surgery Really Better? A Two Year and a Twelve Year Post-Operative Review of Forty-Six Cases of Unilateral Facetectomy at L5, S1 for Lateral Foraminal Stenosis. European Association of Neurosurgical Societies. Zaragoza, Spain. February 20-22, 1997 and The Department of Neurosurgery, University of Tennessee School of Medicine, Memphis, Tennessee. September 12, 1997

The Clinical Evaluation of the Comatose Patient. Annual Neurological Lecture. Methodist Hospital. July 30, 1997

Stroke, New Concepts of Diagnosis and Treatment. (Summary of the recommendations of the American Heart Association Stroke Council, The Memphis Neurosciences Center and The Department of Neuroscience Methodist Hospital Annual Conference, Kneibert Clinic, Poplar Bluff, Missouri, August 15, 1997, and The Department of Neurosurgery, University of Tennessee Methodist Hospital, September 18, 1997

Surgery for Large Metastatic Brain Tumors and Comments on Long Term Survival, Bayfront Medical Center, St. Petersburg, Florida, April 14, 2003

VISITING PROFESSORSHIPS:

St. Louis University, June 15, 1987. *Course on Clinical Evaluation of Peripheral Nerve Function*

Kyorin University, Tokyo, Japan, October 16, 1987

Beijing Neurosurgical Institute, Beijing, China, October 22, 1987

Belize Medical Center, *Intracranial Pressure in Head Injured Patient*, December 2, 1988

Frei University, Berlin, Germany, September 24, 1989

Agean University, Izmir, Turkey, *Metastatic Brain Tumors*, September 28, 1989

University of Heidelberg, Heidelberg, Germany, September 28, 1990

National Institute of Neurosurgery, *Metastatic Brain Tumors with Emphasis on Long Term Survival*, Budapest, Hungary, October 1990

University of Prague, CSFR, July 4, 1991

University of Tokyo
1. *Melanocytoma of the Brain*
2. *Carotid Artery Dissection*

Tokyo, Japan, February 7, 1992

University of Hong Kong and Kwan Wah Hospital, February 11, 1992

Guangzhou Medical College and Neuroscience Institute, Lectures:
1. *Melanocytoma*
2. *Classification* of Head Injuries

Guangzhou, China, February 13-14, 1992

University of Sydney and Westmead Hospital, Lecture:

Carotid Artery Dissection as a Cause of Stroke, Sydney, Australia, May 20, 1992

Tan Tock Seng Hospital and Medical College, Singapore, November 18, 1992

Marmara University, Istanbul, Turkey, *Metastatic Brain Tumors*, March 1, 1994

Agean University, Izmir, Turkey, *Spontaneous Spinal Epidural Hematoma*, March 1994

University of Athens, Athens, Greece, International Academic Interchange, March 15, 1994

Aristotle's University, Thessaloniki, Greece, *Metastatic Brain Tumors, Source, Long Term Survival and Comments on Multiple Lesions*, March 17-18, 1994

Erfurt University and Clinic for Neurosurgery, Erfurt, Germany, May 4-6, 1995

SEMINAR PROGRAM COORDINATOR (CHAIRMAN):

Congress of Neurological Surgeons and the University of Tennessee Center for the Health Sciences College of Medicine Continuing Education Course *Management of Peripheral Nerve Injuries*, with Kline, David, M.D., January 31, 1975

Methodist Hospital, the University of Tennessee Center for the Health Sciences College of Medicine, Memphis Regional Cancer Center, American Cancer Society, Memphis and Shelby County Unit, Continuing Education Course, *Cancer Update*, October 1-2, 1976

Methodist Hospital, and the University of Tennessee Center for the Health Sciences College of Medicine, Continuing Education Course, *Emergency Medical Care Seminar*, January 12-13, 1978

Navy Medical Seminar, University of Tennessee Center for the Health Sciences. Methodist Hospital and Baptist Hospital–Naval Regional Medical Center, Memphis, Tennessee 1979

Methodist Hospital Continuing Education, *Neurological Disorders*, January 17-18, 1980

Memphis Neurosciences Center and Methodist Hospital-*Seminar on Pan Ethics*, July 16, 1992 and *Acute Neurological Disorders*, July 17, 1992

POSTERS:

Diagnosis and Surgical Results in Seventy Patients with Thoracic Disk Ruptures (with Drs. Clarence Watridge and Shelley Timmons)
American Association of Neurological Surgeons
Orlando, Florida April 22-27, 1995
and

10th European Congress of Neurological Surgery
Berlin, Germany, May 7-12, 1995

PRACTICE (PROFESSIONAL EXPERIENCE:

Private Practice at Methodist Hospital of Memphis, July, 1961-2000
Vice President, Neurosurgical Group of Memphis, July 1961- 31 March 1995
Semmes-Murphey Clinic 1995-2000

NON-PROFESSIONAL PAPERS PRESENTED:

On the Occasion of Mrs. Bonnie Schneider's Retirement After Forty-Two years at The Bureau of Medicine and Surgery, Washington, D.C. 3 April 1998 *"One of Navy Medicines Most Visible and Valuable Supporters of this Century"*

The Philosophy of War–History, Causes, Results. (Presented more than 95 times to all types of civic, academic and medical organizations.) Memphis Rotary Club, October 1969

A Surgeon Looks at the Problems in Vietnam (Presented to civic, medical, and Naval groups)

My First Benign Brain Tumor. (Presented to House Staff, UTCHS, Memphis, TN, 1958)

How Did One Become a Neurosurgeon? **Nerve Net**, The Center for Neuroscience Quarterly Newsletter. The University of Tennessee, Memphis Vol. 6 #2 pp. 1-5. July 1998

RELIGION:

Bible Teacher or Sunday School Superintendent
Member First Baptist Church Brandon, Florida 2002-Present
Deacon, First Baptist Church Brandon
Teacher, Berea Sunday School Class (Senior Adults)
Speaker, Dedication of the Miller Building, Southern Baptist Missionary Learning Center, Richmond VA, 9 October 1984

Church Positions:
Committees: Finance, Budget, Stewardship, Host, Athletic, Missions
Superintendent Adult Sunday School Department
First Baptist Church, Washington, D.C. 1959-1961
Teacher Adult Bible Class *Sunday School teacher 58 years)
Ordained as Deacon, First Baptist Church, Augusta, GA, December 1953
(Youngest deacon in the history of the church)
A Baptist Deacon for 66 years.
Deacon, First Baptist Church, Brandon, FL 2004-Present.
Advisory Committee, 2006-Present.

<u>PRIVATE PILOT</u> (5,258 HOURS) (150 hours in a Citation Jet)
Graduate Aviation Training Enterprises Instrument School
    (Member Silver Seal Club)–Chicago, Illinois
Graduate, United Airlines Courses: Airborne Weather Radar Meteorology

Graduate–Naval Course, Aviation Physiology Naval Air Station Beaufort,
S.C., 1970

Flight Safety Course, Citation Jet Training, Wichita, Kansas, August 28-
30, 1995 (Revised November 2000)

III. The Miller Code of Ethics

(How to live dealing with good and evil.)

Outline:

Introduction: We Must Have Knowledge
We believe:

> Our nations motto
> As in the *"Star Spangled Banner"*
> Heaven and Earth
> The King
> Our Prayer
> Our Favorite Scriptures

Our Christian Ethics
Our Favorite Teaching
Our Favorite Anticipation
Our Favorite Hymn
Our Personal Oath of Allegiance
Our Work Motto
Our Answer To, "So what?"

What Do We Know?

A Great Promise
Our Victory Promise
What Can **We** Do?
Who Will Lead Us?
God Listens

Our Favorite "Grace" Scripture
Our Prayer Before Battle and Travel
The Big Question, "Who Am I?"
To God Be the Glory

Introduction:
A Christian's Code of Ethics is based on God's Word in contrast to their Curriculum Vitae, which is made for man.

<u>**We must have knowledge**</u> to inform our hearts. God describes Himself in His word when He opened the mysteries of God and gave us direction as to the word of truth. Christian lives must be based on faith and <u>**knowledge**</u>. Faith then becomes works. When we understand; we know how to walk. How can we do if we do not know? Millers are men of action and our action is the action of truth. (Millers have fought in all the wars of our country.) Obedience leads to holiness; holiness leads to heaven. Holiness is from being quiet and listening to God, looking at our true selves, and loving our brother.

We Believe:
We believe along with our nation's motto "In God we trust".

Psalm 7:1
"O Lord my God, **in thee do I put my trust**: save me from all them that persecute me, and deliver me:"

Psalm 18:2
"The Lord is my rock, and my fortress, and my deliverer; my God, my strength, **in whom I will trust**; my buckler, and the horn of my salvation, and my high tower."

Psalm 31:1
"In thee, O Lord, do I put my trust; let me never be ashamed: deliver me in thy righteousness."

Psalm 91:2
"I will say of the Lord, He is my refuge and my fortress: my God; **in him will I trust**."

Psalm 143:8
"Cause me to hear thy lovingkindness in the morning; for **in thee do I trust**: cause me to know the way wherein I should walk; for I lift up my soul unto thee."

We Believe as in The Star-Spangled Banner:
"Land of the free and home of the brave; where there is no terror of defeat or gloom of the grave."

We Believe Jesus:
"Heaven and earth will pass away; but my words shall not pass away."
Luke 21:33

We Believe in The King:
1 Timothy 1:17
"Now unto the King eternal, immortal, invisible, the only wise God, be honor and glory for ever and ever. Amen."

Our Prayer:
Matthew 6:9-13

"After this manner therefore pray ye: Our Father which art in heaven, Hallowed be thy name. Thy kingdom come. Thy will be done in earth, as it is in heaven. Give us this day our daily bread. And forgive us our debts, as we forgive our debtors." And lead us not into temptation, but deliver us from evil: For thine is the kingdom, and the power, and the glory, forever. Amen.

Our Favorite Scripture:
John 3:16, 17
"For God so loved the world, that he gave his only begotten Son, that whosoever believeth in him should not perish, but have everlasting life. For God sent not his Son into the world to condemn the world; but that the world through him might be saved."

Our Christian Ethics:
Romans 12

1. I beseech you therefore, brethren, by the mercies of God, that ye present your **bodies** a living sacrifice, holy, acceptable unto God, which is your reasonable service.

2. And be not conformed to this world: but be ye transformed by the renewing of your **mind**, that ye may prove what is that good, and acceptable, and perfect, will of God.

3. For I say, through the grace given unto me, to every man that is among you, not to think of himself more highly than he ought to think; but to **think soberly**, according as God hath dealt to every man the measure of faith.

4. For as we have many members in one body, and all members have not the same office:

5. So we, being many, are one body in Christ, and **every one members one of another**.

6. Having then **gifts** differing according to the grace that is given to us, whether **prophecy**, let us prophesy according to the proportion of faith;

7. Or **ministry**, let us wait on our ministering: or he that teacheth, on teaching;

8. Or he that **exhorteth**, on exhortation: he that giveth, let him do it with simplicity; he that ruleth, with diligence; he that **sheweth mercy**, with cheerfulness.

9. **Let love be** without dissimulation. Abhor that which is evil; cleave to that which is **good**.

10. Be kindly affectioned one to another with brotherly love; in honour **preferring one another**;

11. Not slothful in **business**; fervent in spirit; serving the Lord;

12. Rejoicing in **hope**; patient in tribulation; continuing instant in prayer;

13. Distributing to the necessity of saints; given to **hospitality**.

14. **Bless** them which persecute you: bless, and curse not.

15. Rejoice with them that do **rejoice**, and weep with them that **weep**.

16. Be of the **same mind** one toward another. Mind not high things, but condescend to men of low estate. **Be not wise in your own conceits**.

17. Recompense to **no man evil for evil**. Provide things honest in the sight of all men.

18. If it be possible, as much as lieth in you, **live peaceably** with all men.

19. Dearly beloved, **avenge not yourselves**, but rather give place unto wrath: for it is written, **Vengeance is mine**; **I will repay, saith the Lord.**

20. Therefore if **thine enemy** hunger, feed him; if he thirst, give him drink: for in so doing thou shalt heap coals of fire on his head.

21. Be not overcome of evil but **overcome evil with good**.

Our Favorite Teaching:
("Teaching on the Mount")
Matthew Chapter 5

1. And seeing the multitudes, he went up into a mountain: and when he was set, his disciples came unto him:

2. And he opened his mouth, and taught them, saying,

3. *Blessed are the poor in spirit: for theirs is the kingdom of heaven.*

4. *Blessed are they that mourn: for they shall be comforted.*

5. *Blessed are the meek: for they shall inherit the earth.*

6. *Blessed are they which do hunger and thirst after righteousness: for they shall be filled.*

7. *Blessed are the merciful: for they shall obtain mercy.*

8. *Blessed are the pure in heart: for they shall see God.*

9. *Blessed are the peacemakers: for they shall be called the children of God.*

10. *Blessed are they, which are persecuted for righteousness' sake: for theirs is the kingdom of heaven.*

11. *Blessed are ye, when men shall revile you, and persecute you, and shall say all manner of evil against you falsely, for my sake.*

12. *Rejoice, and be exceeding glad: for great is your reward in heaven: for so persecuted they the prophets which were before you.*

13. *Ye are the salt of the earth: but if the salt have lost his savour, wherewith shall it be salted? it is thenceforth good for nothing, but to be cast out, and to be trodden under foot of men.*

14. *Ye are the light of the world. A city that is set on an hill cannot be hid.*

15. *Neither do men light a candle, and put it under a bushel, but on a candlestick; and it giveth light unto all that are in the house.*

16. *Let your light so shine before men, that they may see your good works, and glorify your Father which is in heaven.*

17. *Think not that I am come to destroy the law, or the prophets: I am not come to destroy, but to fulfil.*

18. *For verily I say unto you, Till heaven and earth pass, one jot or one tittle shall in no wise pass from the law, till all be fulfilled.*

19. *Whosoever therefore shall break one of these least commandments, and shall teach men so, he shall be called the least in the kingdom of heaven: but whosoever shall do and teach them, the same shall be called great in the kingdom of heaven.*

20. *For I say unto you, That except your righteousness shall exceed the righteousness of the scribes and Pharisees, ye shall in no case enter into the kingdom of heaven.*

21. *Ye have heard that it was said by them of old time, Thou shalt not kill; and whosoever shall kill shall be in danger of the judgment:*

22. *But I say unto you, That whosoever is angry with his brother without a cause shall be in danger of the judgment: and whosoever shall say to his brother, Raca, shall be in danger of the council: but whosoever shall say, Thou fool, shall be in danger of hell fire.*

23. *Therefore if thou bring thy gift to the altar, and there rememberest that thy brother hath ought against thee;*

24. *Leave there thy gift before the altar, and go thy way; first be reconciled to thy brother, and then come and offer thy gift.*

25. *Agree with thine adversary quickly, whiles thou art in the way with him; lest at any time the adversary deliver thee to the judge, and the judge deliver thee to the officer, and thou be cast into prison.*

26. *Verily I say unto thee, Thou shalt by no means come out thence, till thou hast paid the uttermost farthing.*

27. *Ye have heard that it was said by them of old time, Thou shalt not commit adultery:*

28. *But I say unto you, That whosoever looketh on a woman to lust after her hath committed adultery with her already in his heart.*

29. *And if thy right eye offend thee, pluck it out, and cast it from thee: for it is profitable for thee that one of thy members should perish, and not that thy whole body should be cast into hell.*

30. *And if thy right hand offend thee, cut it off, and cast it from thee: for it is profitable for thee that one of thy members should perish, and not that thy whole body should be cast into hell.*

31. *It hath been said, Whosoever shall put away his wife, let him give her a writing of divorcement:*

32. *But I say unto you, That whosoever shall put away his wife, saving for the cause of fornication, causeth her to commit*

adultery: and whosoever shall marry her that is divorced committeth adultery.

33. *Again, ye have heard that it hath been said by them of old time, Thou shalt not forswear thyself, but shalt perform unto the Lord thine oaths:*

34. *But I say unto you, Swear not at all; neither by heaven; for it is God's throne:*

35. *Nor by the earth; for it is his footstool: neither by Jerusalem; for it is the city of the great King.*

36. *Neither shalt thou swear by thy head, because thou canst not make one hair white or black.*

37. *But let your communication be, Yea, yea; Nay, nay: for whatsoever is more than these cometh of evil.*

38. *Ye have heard that it hath been said, An eye for an eye, and a tooth for a tooth:*

39. *But I say unto you, That ye resist not evil: but whosoever shall smite thee on thy right cheek, turn to him the other also.*

40. *And if any man will sue thee at the law, and take away thy coat, let him have thy cloak also.*

41. *And whosoever shall compel thee to go a mile, go with him twain.*

42. *Give to him that asketh thee, and from him that would borrow of thee turn not thou away.*

43. *Ye have heard that it hath been said, Thou shalt love thy neighbour, and hate thine enemy.*

44. *But I say unto you, Love your enemies, bless them that curse you, do good to them that hate you, and pray for them which despitefully use you, and persecute you;*

45. *That ye may be the children of your Father which is in heaven: for he maketh his sun to rise on the evil and on the good, and sendeth rain on the just and on the unjust.*

46. *For if ye love them which love you, what reward have ye? do not even the publicans the same?*

47. *And if ye salute your brethren only, what do ye more than others? do not even the publicans so?*

48. *Be ye therefore perfect, even as your Father which is in heaven is perfect.*

Matthew Chapter 6

1. *Take heed that ye do not your alms before men, to be seen of them: otherwise ye have no reward of your Father which is in heaven.*
2. *Therefore when thou doest thine alms, do not sound a trumpet before thee, as the hypocrites do in the synagogues and in the streets, that they may have glory of men. Verily I say unto you, They have their reward.*
3. *But when thou doest alms, let not thy left hand know what thy right hand doeth:*
4. *That thine alms may be in secret: and thy Father which seeth in secret himself shall reward thee openly.*
5. *And when thou prayest, thou shalt not be as the hypocrites are: for they love to pray standing in the synagogues and in the corners of the streets, that they may be seen of men. Verily I say unto you, They have their reward.*
6. *But thou, when thou prayest, enter into thy closet, and when thou hast shut thy door, pray to thy Father which is in secret; and thy Father which seeth in secret shall reward thee openly.*
7. *But when ye pray, use not vain repetitions, as the heathen do: for they think that they shall be heard for their much speaking.*
8. *Be not ye therefore like unto them: for your Father knoweth what things ye have need of, before ye ask him.*
9. *After this manner therefore pray ye: Our Father which art in heaven, Hallowed be thy name.*
10. *Thy kingdom come. Thy will be done in earth, as it is in heaven.*
11. *Give us this day our daily bread.*
12. *And forgive us our debts, as we forgive our debtors.*
13. *And lead us not into temptation, but deliver us from evil: For thine is the kingdom, and the power, and the glory, for ever. Amen.*
14. *For if ye forgive men their trespasses, your heavenly Father will also forgive you:*

15. *But if ye forgive not men their trespasses, neither will your Father forgive your trespasses.*

16. *Moreover when ye fast, be not, as the hypocrites, of a sad countenance: for they disfigure their faces, that they may appear unto men to fast. Verily I say unto you, They have their reward.*

17. *But thou, when thou fastest, anoint thine head, and wash thy face;*

18. *That thou appear not unto men to fast, but unto thy Father which is in secret: and thy Father, which seeth in secret, shall reward thee openly.*

19. *Lay not up for yourselves treasures upon earth, where moth and rust doth corrupt, and where thieves break through and steal:*

20. *But lay up for yourselves treasures in heaven, where neither moth nor rust doth corrupt, and where thieves do not break through nor steal:*

21. *For where your treasure is, there will your heart be also.*

22. *The light of the body is the eye: if therefore thine eye be single, thy whole body shall be full of light.*

23. *But if thine eye be evil, thy whole body shall be full of darkness. If therefore the light that is in thee be darkness, how great is that darkness!*

24. *No man can serve two masters: for either he will hate the one, and love the other; or else he will hold to the one, and despise the other. Ye cannot serve God and mammon.*

25. *Therefore I say unto you, Take no thought for your life, what ye shall eat, or what ye shall drink; nor yet for your body, what ye shall put on. Is not the life more than meat, and the body than raiment?*

26. *Behold the fowls of the air: for they sow not, neither do they reap, nor gather into barns; yet your heavenly Father feedeth them. Are ye not much better than they?*

27. *Which of you by taking thought can add one cubit unto his stature?*

28. *And why take ye thought for raiment? Consider the lilies of the field, how they grow; they toil not, neither do they spin:*

29. *And yet I say unto you, That even Solomon in all his glory was not arrayed like one of these.*

30. *Wherefore, if God so clothe the grass of the field, which to day is, and to morrow is cast into the oven, shall he not much more clothe you, O ye of little faith?*

31. *Therefore take no thought, saying, What shall we eat? or, What shall we drink? or, Wherewithal shall we be clothed?*

32. *(For after all these things do the Gentiles seek:) for your heavenly Father knoweth that ye have need of all these things.*

33. *But seek ye first the kingdom of God, and his righteousness; and all these things shall be added unto you.*

34. *Take therefore no thought for the morrow: for the morrow shall take thought for the things of itself. Sufficient unto the day is the evil thereof.*

Matthew Chapter 7

1. *Judge not, that ye be not judged.*

2. *For with what judgment ye judge, ye shall be judged: and with what measure ye mete, it shall be measured to you again.*

3. *And why beholdest thou the mote that is in thy brother's eye, but considerest not the beam that is in thine own eye?*

4. *Or how wilt thou say to thy brother, Let me pull out the mote out of thine eye; and, behold, a beam is in thine own eye?*

5. *Thou hypocrite, first cast out the beam out of thine own eye; and then shalt thou see clearly to cast out the mote out of thy brother's eye.*

6. *Give not that which is holy unto the dogs, neither cast ye your pearls before swine, lest they trample them under their feet, and turn again and rend you.*

7. *Ask, and it shall be given you; seek, and ye shall find; knock, and it shall be opened unto you:*

8. *For every one that asketh receiveth; and he that seeketh findeth; and to him that knocketh it shall be opened.*

9. *Or what man is there of you, whom if his son ask bread, will he give him a stone?*

10. *Or if he ask a fish, will he give him a serpent?*

11. *If ye then, being evil, know how to give good gifts unto your children, how much more shall your Father which is in heaven give good things to them that ask him?*

12. *Therefore all things whatsoever ye would that men should do to you, do ye even so to them: for this is the law and the prophets.*

13. *Enter ye in at the strait gate: for wide is the gate, and broad is the way, that leadeth to destruction, and many there be which go in thereat:*

14. *Because strait is the gate, and narrow is the way, which leadeth unto life, and few there be that find it.*

15. *Beware of false prophets, which come to you in sheep's clothing, but inwardly they are ravening wolves.*

16. *Ye shall know them by their fruits. Do men gather grapes of thorns, or figs of thistles?*

17. *Even so every good tree bringeth forth good fruit; but a corrupt tree bringeth forth evil fruit.*

18. *A good tree cannot bring forth evil fruit, neither can a corrupt tree bring forth good fruit.*

19. *Every tree that bringeth not forth good fruit is hewn down, and cast into the fire.*

20. *Wherefore by their fruits ye shall know them.*

21. *Not every one that saith unto me, Lord, Lord, shall enter into the kingdom of heaven; but he that doeth the will of my Father which is in heaven.*

22. *Many will say to me in that day, Lord, Lord, have we not prophesied in thy name? and in thy name have cast out devils? and in thy name done many wonderful works?*

23. *And then will I profess unto them, I never knew you: depart from me, ye that work iniquity.*

24. *Therefore whosoever heareth these sayings of mine, and doeth them, I will liken him unto a wise man, which built his house upon a rock:*

25. *And the rain descended, and the floods came, and the winds blew, and beat upon that house; and it fell not: for it was founded upon a rock.*

26. *And every one that heareth these sayings of mine, and doeth them not, shall be likened unto a foolish man, which built his house upon the sand:*

27. *And the rain descended, and the floods came, and the winds blew, and beat upon that house; and it fell: and great was the fall of it.*

28. *And it came to pass, when Jesus had ended these sayings, the people were astonished at his doctrine:*

29. *For he taught them as one having authority, and not as the scribes.*

(I have memorized the Teachings on the Mount.)

Our Favorite Anticipation:
"The Blessed Hope"
Titus 2:13
"Looking for that **blessed hope**, and the glorious appearing of the great God and our Saviour Jesus Christ;"

Our Favorite Hymn:
We thank Dr. Luke 15:32 for giving John Newton the words of *"**Amazing Grace**."*
"It was meet that we should make merry and be glad: for this thy brother was dead, and is alive again; and was lost, and is found." **Luke 15:32**
The most amazing grace: "God will remember our sins no more." **Hebrews 8:12**

Our Personal Oath of Allegiance:
"…as for me and my house, **we will serve the Lord**." **Joshua 24:15**
Our work motto:

Galatians 6:4
"But let every man prove his own work, and then shall he have rejoicing in himself alone, and not in another."

Colossians 3:17

"And whatsoever ye do in word or deed, do all in the name of the Lord Jesus, giving thanks to God and the Father by him."

Our Answer to, "So What?"
Ephesians 5:13-17

13. But all things that are reproved are made manifest by the light: for whatsoever doth make manifest is light.
14. Wherefore he saith, Awake thou that sleepest, and arise from the dead, and Christ shall give thee light.
15. See then that ye walk circumspectly, not as fools, but as wise,
16. Redeeming the time, because the days are evil.
17. Wherefore be ye not unwise but understanding what the will of the Lord is.

What Do We Know?
2 Timothy 1:12

12. For the which cause I also suffer these things: nevertheless I am not ashamed: for **I know whom I have believed,** and am persuaded that he is able to keep that which I have committed unto him against that day.
A Great Promise:

I Corinthians 2:9

9. But as it is written, Eye hath not seen, nor ear heard, neither have entered into the heart of man, the things which God hath prepared for them that love him.
Our Victory Promise

Romans 8:31

31. What shall we then say to these things? <u>**If God be for us, who can be against us**</u>?

What Can We Do?
Philippians 4:13

13. I can do <u>**all things**</u> through Christ which strengtheneth me.

Who Will Lead Us?
Dr. **Luke 12:12**
For **the Holy Ghost shall teach** you in the same hour what ye ought to say.

God Listens:
Jeremiah 29:12-13
12. Then shall ye call upon me, and ye shall go and pray unto me, and I will hearken unto you.
13. And ye shall seek me, and find me, when ye shall search for me with all your heart.
Our Favorite Grace Scripture:

Romans 11:6
6. And if by grace, then is it no more of works: otherwise grace is no more grace. But if it be of works, then is it no more grace: otherwise work is no more work.
Our prayer before battle and travel:

Psalm 121
1. I Will lift up mine eyes unto the hills, from whence cometh my help.
2. My help cometh from the Lord, which made heaven and earth.
3. He will not suffer thy foot to be moved: he that keepeth thee will not slumber.
4. Behold, he that keepeth Israel shall neither slumber nor sleep.
5. The Lord is thy keeper: the Lord is thy shade upon thy right hand.
6. The sun shall not smite thee by day, nor the moon by night.
7. The Lord shall preserve thee from all evil: he shall preserve thy soul.
8. The Lord shall preserve thy going out and thy coming in from this time forth, and even for evermore.

IV. The Big Question, "Who Am I?"

Do not be afraid to ask. Moses, David and Solomon asked it.

Exodus 3:11

11. And Moses said unto God, **Who am I,** that I should go unto Pharaoh, and that I should bring forth the children of Israel out of Egypt?

I Samuel 18:18

18. And David said unto Saul, **Who am I** and what is my life, or my father's family in Israel, that I should be son in law to the king?

II Samuel 7:18

18. Then went king David in, and sat before the Lord, and he said, **Who am I,** O Lord God? and what is my house, that thou hast brought me hitherto?

I Chronicles 17:16

16. And David the king came and sat before the Lord, and said, **Who am I,** O Lord God, and what is mine house, that thou hast brought me hitherto?

I Chronicles 29:14

14. But **Who am I,** and what is my people, that we should be able to offer so willingly after this sort? for all things come of thee, and of thine own have we given thee.

II Chronicles 2:6

6. But who is able to build him an house, seeing the heaven and heaven of heavens cannot contain him? **who am I** then, that I should build him an house, save only to burn sacrifice before him?

The Answer to the Question, "Who Am I?"

"A little lower than the angels crowned with glory and honor." **Psalm 8:5:** "kings and priests unto God" Revelation 1:6.

To God Be the Glory!
Romans 11:36

36. For of him, and through him, and to him, are all things: to whom <u>be glory</u> for ever. Amen.

Ephesians 3:21

21. Unto him **be glory** in the church by Christ Jesus throughout all ages, world without end. Amen.

I Timothy 1:17

17. Now unto the King eternal, immortal, invisible, the only wise God, <u>**be honour and glory**</u> forever and ever. Amen.

2 Timothy 4:18

18. And the Lord shall deliver me from every evil work, and will preserve me unto his heavenly kingdom: to **whom be glory** for ever and ever. Amen.

I Peter 4:11

11. If any man speak, let him speak as the oracles of God; if any man minister, let him do it as of the ability which God giveth: that God in all things may be glorified through Jesus Christ, **to whom be praise and dominion** for ever and ever. Amen.

II Peter 3: 18

18. But grow in grace, and in the knowledge of our Lord and Saviour Jesus Christ. To **Him be glory** both now and for ever. Amen.

Revelation 1:6

6. And hath made us kings and priests unto God and his Father; <u>**to Him be glory**</u> and dominion forever and ever. Amen.

V. How Does One Define Himself?

(Look Through A Window at Yourself.)

Joseph Hardy Miller, Jr.
Rear Admiral Joseph H. Miller
Physician-Neurosurgeon
Teacher of Medicine
Teacher of God's Word

A "Born-Again" Christian, A Man of Prayer
A Follower and Soldier of Jesus Christ
Bank Director, College Trustee, Author, Pilot, Deacon

All the Other Things I Have Been Called

"Admiral" Joe, "Dr. Joe", Husband, Father, Son, Dad, Granddaddy, Brother, Mentor to My Students, and Friend.

"My life has been one of working, and learning; read this and you can learn without working". For the young doctor he or she can be stimulated to plan his or her next 30 years. For the young minister there are many life's sermon illustrations. For the lawyer or judge, life's purpose, and right from wrong is always revealed. For the military patriot, "God will always be with them." For all of us we can learn how to prolong our days. For some of us we can learn a definition of a "Broad Mentality". And for a few of us we can learn stimulation, technique, and results of learning.

My Dad taught me, "Son, you can always learn something, even if it is what not to do!"

1948:
"The Great Beyond":
The purpose of this book will be to define the title, as the author would have the reader understand it. In order to understand the content of the ideas presented, it is necessary that the theme be viewed from the mind of a youth or in the mind of an older person who can in some way reverse the thinking of their mind back to the days of their youth and think and dream without the aid or pitfalls of their own experiences. The subtitle of this book when read alone will have different understanding to different people depending particularly on the age of the reader, but also on their surroundings and training thus far. To an elderly Indian *"The Great Beyond"* would of course mean, *"The Happy Hunting Ground"* with the *"Long Journey"* yet to come. The religious philosopher would perhaps interpret *"The Great Beyond"* as being **Heaven.** The Christian who knows, dreams, and lives for the promise of God will make this interpretation, which is indeed an excellent one. Within these covers *"The*

Great Beyond" will refer to the time certain young men and young women have before them in this life. If history continues to repeat itself there is a "Beyond" for all young people, but *"The Great Beyond"* is only for a few. Certain questions are discussed:

- "Why just a few"?
- "Am I predestined for a *'Great Beyond'*"?
- "What do I need to know to have a *'Great Beyond'*"?
- "When does this *'Great Beyond'* begin?"
- "When will it be too late for me to have a *'Great Beyond'*"?

The intellectual minds of modern medicine nor the vast expanse of the field of science cannot slow down, stop, or reverse one second of the "Beyond". Life can only be handled by medical doctors while it is present. The mystery of life is the same secret that it was in the beginning of time. With this in mind it seems fitting to present one's ideas about *"The Great Beyond"* if it can be obtained by those who know of it in time and who desire the possibilities it presents. This is a challenge to the author's generation to think on these things for the time is at hand. We are destined for one thing and one thing only. Moral obligations and tremendous responsibilities will soon be ours. If we are prepared it will be a *Great Beyond*, but if not, history will again record a generation that failed not only itself, but also those who taught us and those we will teach.

Consider these ideas with the hope that we all may see *"The Great Beyond"*. May God have mercy on those of us who do not. Joe H. Miller, Jr. (In 1948, while at Mars Hill College.)

January 2019, seventy-one years later:
"The Great Beyond," as we now suppose is from that moment in 1948 unto the end of my days of life on earth. In 1948 I could not write it but could only live it from moment to moment.

What is a *"Great Beyond"?* It is a life of happiness and service.

Seventy-one years later instead of looking toward *"The Great Beyond"*, I am now looking back at it. I have seen my Great Beyond. Read on and see a *Great Beyond* unfold for one person! I challenge you, every young person, to plan and do your own *"Great Beyond"* Develop a "window" of yourself for the future. "Man is not born but made." **(Erasmus)**

Develop a *Broad Mentality*

I have defined it as a knowledge of:

1. The Bible, (One is illiterate without a knowledge of the greatest book of all time.)
2. God
3. Man
4. Salvation of man from death.
5. The Church
6. The Lord's Day (Who does not know the meaning of Sunday?)
7. God's Kingdom
8. The Last Things (The end of the world.)
9. Social Order
10. War
11. Religious Liberty
12. The Family
13. Education
    a. Learn from study and experiences
    b. Their professional qualifications (Doctors, lawyers, ministers, teachers, etc.)

If one does not have some knowledge of these 13 Things, they cannot claim to have a *Broad Mentality*.

Learn what will prolong your days from the Promises of God:
1. "Keep my commandments." (Exodus 20:12, Deuteronomy 5:33, 6:2; Proverbs 3:1. 2, 4:6, 8, 10; Isaiah 53:10)
2. "Learn my sayings." (Proverbs 4:10)
3. "Get understanding and wisdom." (Proverbs 3:13, 16) "full of days" (Genesis 35:29) Job 42:17

Learn what will bring:
1. Happiness or "a merry heart". (Proverbs 3:13, 15:15; 1 Peter 3:10)

2. Honor (Proverbs 4:8)
3. Glory (Proverbs 4:9)

Summary:

Psalm 37; 18, 55:23 (deceitful man), 90:10-12, 11, 14; 102:31 (days like smoke, a shadow), 103:15-18; Lamentations 5:21; Romans 13:12-14; 14: 5-8, (Live or die we are the Lords.), 2 Corinthians 6:2, 3, 4; Hebrews 10:25, 26) James 5:3; 2 Peter 3:8; Revelation 22;1, 2 (healing of nations)

The Bottom Line:

In the first book of the Bible God says, "I am with thee and will keep thee in all places where you go…" (Genesis 28:15)

"God's faithful ones are preserved forever." (Psalms 37:28)

"God will deliver me and preserve me for His Heavenly Kingdom." (2 Timothy 4:18)

What can a man create that lasts forever? - A book, A song or a Tombstone monument!

To know man as God's creation is to know God. God says He will direct our paths and light them. (Psalms 119:105, 16: 11; Proverbs 3:6) God's shadow is light. If you walk with God, you will always be in the light.

Adam and Eve: The Ancestors of All People. (Genesis 5:1)

Our ancestry starts with **Adam and Eve. Adam means "a man" or "all people"**. Eve is the Hebrew word for "living", but it refers only to the first woman. The best source of genealogy is from Dr. Luke. It starts with Luke 3:38 and goes backwards to Luke 3:23. God's Creation: Adam is described as the Son of God. (Luke 3:38) There is no way that he could have been recreated with the concept man called, "the Original sin." The genealogy proceeds through Seth, Enos, Cain, Maleleel, Jared, Enoch, Mathusala, Lamech, Noah, Sem, Arphaxad, Cainan, Sala, Heber, Phalec, Ragau, Saruch, Nachor, Thara, Abraham, Isaac, Jacob, Juda, Phares, Esrom, Aram, Aminadab, Naasson, Salmon, Boaz, Obed, Jesse, David, Nathan, Mattatha, Menan, Melea, Eliakim, Jonan, Joseph, Juda, Simeon, Levi,

Matthat, Jorim, Eliezer, Jose, Er, Elmodam, Cosam, Addi, Melchi, Neri, Salathiel, Zorobabel, Rhesa, Joanna, Juda, Joseph, Semei, Mattathias, Maath, Nagge, Esli, Naum, Amos, Mattathias, Joseph, Janna, Melchi, Levi, Matthat, Heli, and Joseph, the virgin Mary's husband.

It continues through the Patriarchs. (The Patriarchs date is uncertain, but probably between 2000–1500 B.C. and goes from Abraham to the twelve sons of Jacob (Israel), the last being Joseph.) It continues with Methuselah, Isaac, Jacob, Judah, and Salmon who married Rahab (the harlot, Joshua 2:1). Their son Boaz was the rich man who married Ruth. Boaz and Ruth begat Obed, who begat Jesse, the father of King David. (This was the 32nd generation from Adam and Eve.)

The kings of Judah and Israel.
The Twenty Kings of Judah (and Benjamin) [I have underlined the good kings. All the others were bad kings and did evil in the sight of the LORD.] Rehoboam, Abijah, **<u>Asa</u>**, **<u>Jehoshaphat</u>**, Jehoram, Ahaziah, Athaliah, **<u>Joash</u>**, **<u>Amaziah</u>**, **<u>Uzziah</u>**, **<u>Jotham</u>**, Ahaz, **<u>Hezekiah</u>**, Manasseh, Amon, **<u>Josiah</u>**, Jehoahaz, Jehoiakim, Jehoiachin, and Zedekiah. (There were only eight good kings out of the twenty.)

The Nineteen Kings of Israel (Ten Northern Tribes)
There were no good kings in the nineteen kings of Israel. (931 B.C.-712 B.C.) They include: Jeroboam I, Nadab, Baasha, Elah, Zimri, Omri, Ahab, Ahaziah, Joram, Jehu, Jehoahaz, Jehoash, Jeroboam II, Zechariah, Shallum, Menahem, Pekahiah, Pekah, and Hoshea. Of the total of thirty-nine kings of both groups only eight were good and these were all among the kings of Judah. The Israel and Judah lineage ended in 722 B.C. and 586 B.C. respectably.

The Millers of Tennessee:
The Millers of Tennessee mainly under the leadership of Mr. and Mrs. Gustavus Hindman Miller published a book at a great cost of $38,000 in 1922. The book was titled, ***The Millers of Millersburg***. Millersburg refers to Millersburg, Tennessee.

The book traces the Millers to King Egbert of Wessex. (800-836 A.D.) Thomas R. Miller from Tennessee died in the Alamo.

Thrift Texas: My Birth

Newton, Texas became Waggoner, Texas and Waggoner, Texas became Thrift, Texas.

The house where I was born was torn down and the Thrift Baptist Church was built in its place. The church building was picked up and moved to Burkburnett, Texas. This is the only remnant of Thrift, Texas. My birth certificate is the only historical record that proves that I am also a remnant of Thrift, Texas. "So here it is, take it or leave it."

Religious songs written by men born in 1930: *Name of all Majesty*, by Michael Boughen; *Lord, Here Am I*, by John Ness Beck (Words by Fanny J. Crosby 1820-1915) and four songs by Wesley LM Forbus; *Break Out, O Church of God, Creator of the Universe, O God of Prophets, Known of Old, Go with God, The King of Glory Comes* by Willard F. Jabusch, <u>*Holy Holy*</u> by Jimmy Owens and *Go Now in Peace* by Natalie Sleeth.

Other Happenings in 1930 Were:
- The first radio broadcast of the "Lone Ranger".
- The Supreme Court rules that buying liquor does not violate the constitution.
- The first scheduled transcontinental air service began.
- Constantinople is renamed Istanbul (From Christian to Greek to Islam).
- Germany bans the film, "All Quiet on the Western Front".
- Emigration from the United States exceeds immigration to the United States.
  (Religious freedom was not cut out like it was supposed to be.)
- Frozen foods are first sold commercially.
- The U.S. Open winner is Bobby Jones (and short pants arrived.)
- Twinkies cakes and Snickers candy are invented.
- Gasoline is 10 cents a gallon.
- The U.S. postage stamp for a letter is 2 cents.

- Famous people born in 1930, were astronauts "Buzz" Aldrin and Neil Armstrong, and actors; Clint Eastwood, Sean Connery, and Steve McQueen.
- Music in 1930: "*I can Dream Can't I*", (Tommy Dorsey), "*Happy Days Are Here Again*", (Benny Meroff), "*Strike Up the Band*", (Red Nichols)

When I was five years old, I have a fairly clear memory of a doctor who immediately relieved me a severe earache. (He must have opened the eardrum to allow pus to escape.) I said to myself, "I am going to be a doctor."

My mother gave me a book by Harvey Cushing, the father of neurosurgery, when I was age 15. I read it and from that time on my objective was to be a "brain surgeon."

The third experience that I had in Cleburne is one that I remember clearly including all the details. I have no memories clearer to me than this. It was the time that **I gave my heart to the Lord**. It was Sunday afternoon after church. I was home alone in 1942. I felt suddenly a horrible feeling. I ran out to the garage into our workroom. I was trapped by something invisible. It suddenly occurred to me that it was God convicting me. The horrible feeling was that I was lost and a sinner and going to Hell. I prayed and asked to be saved. I immediately felt a joy that seemed to light up the whole world. Dad baptized me at Southside Baptist Church in Cleburne, Texas. (I have pictures of me being previously baptized in an irrigation canal in Kamay, Texas, but I have no memory of it whatsoever.) I have never doubted my salvation for one second as I have heard that some people have. I know that God paid the price for my sins and I will fly to Heaven to my mansion and see all my family and friends. I have bragged about having questions when I get to Heaven, but an old Christian friend reminded me that I would know it all in Heaven; there will be no questions.

Henderson Mother owned a boarding house and she needed sugar for baking. She would buy 100 lbs. of sugar on the "black market". I would load it into the pick-up for her. During Thanksgiving and Christmas

Henderson Mother always took baskets of food to the poor. She would fill 2-3 baskets and I would drive her to the little shacks. One day I was there when she was filling the baskets. On the table next to the baskets were some oranges. I thought the oranges looked pretty so I, on the spur of the moment, took one and put it on the top of the basket. When we drove to the little shacks Henderson Mother went in and told them what she had. I took the basket in and put it on the table. When I sat it down one of the little boys grabbed the orange from the basket and hugged it to his chest. I have never forgotten that till this day.

I did a lot of reading when I was young. I read all the funny books. Buck Jones, etc. anything I could get. I was 14 or 15 years old when mother bought me a book for five dollars, that is now priceless, at a store basement sale. It was by Harvey Cushing, the father of neurosurgery, and was written after he had done his 2,000[th] brain tumor operation. After reading that book, (Cushing wrote it like a novel) I decided I wanted to become a "brain surgeon". I never altered my decision from that time on. I was criticized by my school for making up my mind so early in my life. Looking back these 65 years later considering our financial standing **at that time it was impossible for me to become a "brain surgeon"**, but as noted all things are possible with God. I am certain that God was with me because of the devotion to Him of my Father and Mother. They sacrificed all through my training years.

I learned many beautiful lessons at Mars Hill. One that I particularly have benefited from was this. My second-year English teacher to me was so ugly I could not even look straight at her. By the end of that year, she was one of the most beautiful ladies I have ever known even to this day. Beauty is not only in the "eyes of the beholder", but also in the object of vision.

My new wife and I re-dedicated our lives to the Lord. Night was turned to day and only light has been shining since. All of the great things in my life have happened since 13 October 1979, the date of my second marriage.

In my third year I attended East Texas Baptist College in Marshall, Texas. The president, Dr. Bruce, when he heard I was a student called me to his office. I will never forget it. The thing I remember about the conversation is, "You are going to be a doctor. Look out for three things: Look out for drugs, alcohol and women, and not necessarily in that order. Dismissed."

VI. Brain Modeling

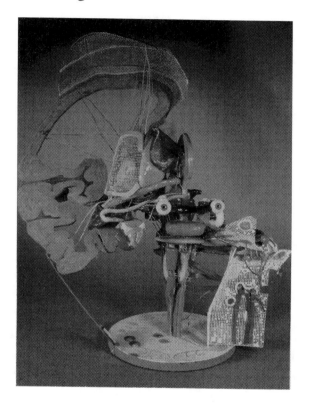

Demonstration of a Method of Brain Modeling
Joseph H. Miller, M.D.
1961

Brain reconstruction or Brain Modeling began with Adolf Meyer and Louis Hausman as they reported in Arch. Neural and Psychiat. in 1922 and 1928. The interest began at John Hopkins and with Meyer and Hausaman. They moved, and Brain Modeling moved to Cornell University in New York. They retired and Dr. Francis McNaughton who had visited Meyer

151

and Hausman took up the interest at the Montreal Neurological Institute in 1937. Murray L. Barr gave a brief report on modeling of the brain in 1946. (University of Western Ontario, Med. Jour). Choh-Luh Li and Kenneth M. Earle reported the anatomy and reconstruction of the brain in 1956. (***Texas Reports on Biology and Medicine***, Volume 14. Number 2, pp. 208-225, summer, 1956. This was reprinted by the U.S. Department of Health, Education, and Welfare, Public Health Service)

The interest in Brain reconstruction then moved to the National Institute of Neurological Diseases and Blindness where I became involved.

I continued my interest in nervous system reconstruction when a six-month course was offered at NINDB, October 1959-March 1960. I was one of 15 instructors. I had presented a paper on the "Reticular Formation" and they gave me the part on "Association (or reticular) plate of the brain stem". There were about 45, all post-graduates that took the Course. I was the only one who finished with a complete brain model. Each week the wastebasket would have the remains of a failed model. If one made a mistake early the results was a "monster" and had to be discarded. I only know of four other Hausman Models that were completed. I only saw one of them made by Dr. John Kurtzke, a neurologist in Washington, D.C.

VII. Learning: A System of Threes (Discover the Magic Number Three)

The Number 3
The number 3 is a key number embedded in the mind of all English-speaking peoples. This is proved by the world's literature being filled with author's dividing in groups of 3. The Number "3" is important in many areas of the Bible including the Trinity. I have collected a vast literature on the times that the number 3 has been used to divide groups unto teaching or making a point. There are many "Rules of Three".

Here is an example of 9 things being divided into groups of 3:
(Reference unknown)
3 Things to Admire

Dignity, Intellectual Power, Graciousness

3 Things to Give

Needy, Comfort, Appreciation

3 Things to Govern

Temper, Tongues, Conduct

3 Things to Cultivate

Courage, Affection, Gentleness

3 Things to Commend

Thrift, Industry, Promptness

3 Things to Despise

Cruelty, Arrogance, Ingratitude

Other "3's" in History

Three Emperor's League (1872)

Austria-Hungary, Germany, Russia

Three Holy Children

Abed-nego, Shadrach, and Meshach who Nebuchadnezzar threw into the fiery furnace.

Three Chinese Kingdoms of History

Wei, Shu, Wu

(***Romance of the Three Kingdoms***, a novel by San Kuo Chih Yen 1)

Three Kings

Wise Men of the East (Magi or Three Kings)

(Came from the East to adore Jesus Matthew 2:1)

Three Pagodas Pass

The chief route between S.E. Burma and Thailand

Three Rivers (Trois Rivierës) 1737

A famous small town in Canada named by the 3 channels of the St. Maurice River as it enters the St. Lawrence River. A starting point for explorers and missionaries.

Three Taverns (Tres Tabernae)

Ancient town of Latium, Italy on the Appian Way where St. Paul met friends on the way to Rome who gave him "courage and he thanked God." (Acts 28:15)

(Dr. Luke wrote this: One wonders if that is why the Three Taverns are mentioned.)

The United States Marine Corp is based on the Number 3:

3 Marines make a Fire Team

3 Fire Teams make a Squad

3 Squads make a Platoon

3 Platoons make a Company

3 Companies make a Battalion

3 Battalions make a Regiment

Now the greatest discovery of all in groups of 3:

The Ten Plagues God sent by Moses over Egypt to force the Pharaoh to let the Israelites leave Egypt can be divided into 3 Groups of three each and 1 victory when Pharaoh "let them go". (*Moses and His vision,* by David Daiches, 1912, p. 63) The plagues are presented in Exodus as three groups of three with a final victory for Moses.

1. Water to blood (All rivers, lakes, and water in vessels of wood and stone)
2. Frogs (Covered all Egypt and died in the houses and fields and stank. They gathered them up and threw them in the river.)
3. Lice, Gnats (They were in all Egypt on man and beast)
4. Flies - There were swarms in all Egypt that covered Pharaoh, his servants, and all his people. The land Goshen where the Israelites were, was free of flies.)
5. Livestock plagues - (Killed all horses, camels, oxen and sheep.) The Israelites cattle were not harmed.
6. Boils - (Upon man and beast in all Egypt.)
7. Hail, thunder, fire - (All men and beast left – the towns and fields died.) The Israelites were spared.
8. Swarms of Locusts - They covered all the earth so that it was dark, all herbs left were eaten.
9. Darkness - There was a thick darkness over all Egypt for three days.
10. The Passover - The first born of all the Egyptians, including Pharaoh's son, died. He let the Hebrews go!

Now a little science from an old scientist and a little knowledge from a young theologian, me. Sometimes I mix scriptures. numbers and science:

(Keep in mind my theory depends on all knowledge being relative.) In the Scriptures we read, "There be three *things which* are too wonderful for me, yea, four which I know not: The way of an eagle in the air; (One) the way of a serpent upon a rock;(Two), the way of a ship in the midst of the sea;(Three) and the way of a man with a maid." (Four) (Proverbs 30: 18, 19) In science creation depends upon DNA 1, selecting 2, in advance selects 3, and this results in 4. For a creative purpose it has the same features of intelligence." (Gulirizza) To develop a system of learning, information must be available. Localized together at the right time. Capable of functioning together. And for an intended purpose such as to develop a system of learning and knowledge. It requires an agent to establish these conditions such as a teacher.

VIII. The Miller Knowledge Relativity Theory (KRT)

(Adding the name Miller to this is not for the sake of ego, but it is there so that no one else would ever get the blame for it.)

To begin my discussion of the KRT (Knowledge Relativity Theory) I refer to an old historical term "aether", which was related as a medium that filled all unoccupied space through which all waves are propagated. Water waves go through water, sound waves go through air, and I propose that knowledge waves go through the unoccupied space in the brain. Our conscious effort to learn causes the transmission of similar "electromagnetic" waves thorough the brain looking for a place to store it. When it invariably finds something relative it adds and stores it. The practical concept of this can be viewed in the following example. Frequently in a conference we hear something valuable and new to us that we describe as a "pearl of knowledge", which we must remember. A year later we are in a conference and remember a "pearl", but we can't remember what the "pearl" was. The cerebral software that I describe acts as a stored skeleton of knowledge where one can attach the "pearl" in a part of the stored knowledge relative to it. In this way it will be remembered since it is now stored in software previously added to the memory in the brain computer related to that subject.

The Theory of Relativity replaces the older concept that space and time are separate entities. Space and time have been joined into another dimension. Hendrik Lorentz showed the space and time coordinates of one moving system could be **correlated** with any other system. (1887) This established the basis for Einstein's theory of relativity. Einstein showed that it was the equivalence of the two systems with the other laws of nature. (1905). There are three space-like coordinates and one timetable coordinate. They simultaneously exist only as a relation between two events and a particular observer. Because the cerebral software may be different or even absent in one observer simultaneous events for one observer will not be simultaneous for the other observer. (It has clearly been shown in "The Musical Brain" if certain circuits of the brain are not activated between the age of 8 and 12, they may be eliminated. (Journal of World Neurosurgery, May 2010, pp. 442-457) The relativistic effect of the structure of space-time is opened up by the presence of a learned knowledge stored in a "cerebral software"!

IX. Neurosurgery

(Surgery of the Brain, Spinal Cord, Peripheral Nerves, and Spine that covers the Spinal Cord and Nerves)

There is no question; real neurosurgery is life and death, and death and life. Days, days, days, patients, patients, patients, surgery, surgery, surgery with no horizon and too busy for a sunset.

Rear Admiral Joseph H. Miller Was Medical Licensed in the Following States:

STATE	Date	License Number
TENNESSEE	1 JANUARY 1961	MD 004013
MISSOURI		R5432
MISSISSIPPI	6 MARCH 1989	12020
ARKANSAS		R-2244
GEORGIA	15 JULY 1955	007535

Certifications:
American Board of Neurological Surgeons, 1966
American College of Surgeons, 1967

10,000 Operations

"Tricks of the Trade"

Be prepared for the patient who comes in with this complaint. "Doctor, I have had headaches for fifty years. I was told that they would go away when I went through menopause. I am past menopause and I still have headaches. I want something done, now!" I said, "Lady, I am referring you to a man in Mexico who is the only person I know that can cure your headaches." She said, "I will go anywhere, do anything!!" Here is a picture of his treatment.

"Thanks, doctor, my headaches are not that bad!"

MY OFFICIAL RETIREMENT FROM NEUROSURGERY
31 DECEMBER 2000
(AGE 70 PLUS 8 MONTHS)
I RECEIVED 201 LETTERS OR CARDS.
(MOSTLY LETTERS)
FROM THE CONTINENTIAL UNITED STATES

INTERNATIONAL 157 FROM 31 COUNTRIES

Since 2005 I have been a voluntary faculty member of the University
of South Florida Department of Neurosurgery, Tampa, Florida.

X. Summary of Navy Orders (For 62 Years)

**The Millers have fought in all the wars of our country! My first set of
orders were dated: 12 August 1952.**

There were three years during my residency training that I was unable to
drill or go on Active Duty for Training (ACDUTRA) and thus I received
no Navy Credits for those years.

There were 34 years with:
Active Duty
Temporary Active Duty
Special Active Duty
Active Duty for Training (acdutra)

There were 28 years with:

Permissive Orders
(Permissive Orders are voluntary, non-pay, and carry no military credit. They allowed me to volunteer my services to most of the Navy hospitals and clinics around the world.)

For a total of 62 years
I paid my own way to many military hospitals in the United States. (I have been to Washington over 120 times, Hawaii 20 times, Japan 40 times, Republic of China -Taipei, Taiwan, Guam, Philippines, Puerto Rico, etc.)

There were more Admirals (23 Admirals) in Memphis for my retirement than any other time in history! August 1986

XI. Seventy-one International Centers and Twenty- four Countries Associated with the Academic Interchange Program with the Memphis Neurosciences Center:

(All travel money for the Interchange Program for the Center; I either raised it or paid for it myself. A number of those who could not afford it I paid for their visit to the Center.)

Argentina (Buenos Aires)
Dr. Alberto Dubrovsky

Australia (Westmead, Sydney)
Dr. N.W.C. Dorsch

Belize (Dangriga)
Dr. Kevin R. Murphy

Chile (Santiao)
Dr. Pablo Danoso

China (Guangzhou)
Dr. Zhaoming Cai
Dr. Deshu Zheng
Dr. Li Jingrong
Dr. Zhu Jian Kuan
Dr. Sang-Lin Ding
Dr. Lei Zhang
Dr. Tong Zheng

China (Beijing)
Dr. Chung-ching Wang
Dr. Zhang-xue Wu
Professor Zhi Hu Zhang

Czech Republic
Professor Ivo Fusek, M. D. (Stresovice)
Oldrich Subrt, M.D., Ph.D (Prague)
Vladimir Benes, Jr., M.D, Ph.D (USTI)

England (Bristol)
Professor Brian H. Cummins, Ch.M. F.R.C.S.

Germany
Dr. Ruediger Lorenz (Frankfurt)
Dr. med. Daniel Rosenthal (Frankfurt)
Dr. Allen V. Norman (Landstuhl)
Prof. Dr. Dr. H.C. Maro Brock (Berlin)
Prof. Dr. med. Dr. h.c. Jondi Cervas-Navarro (Berlin)
Prof. Dr. Helmut Pothe (Erfurt)
Prof. Dr. Horst P. Schmitt (Heidelberg)
Prof. Werner Hacke (Heidelberg)

Greece
Prof. George Foroglou (Thessalonica)
Dr. John Tsirimbas (Athens)
Professor C. Th. Pagageorgiou (Athens)
Dr. Panos Varelos (Athens)

Guam
Dr. E.J. Cruz (Tamuning)

Hong Kong
Dr. Hsiang-Lai Wen (Hong Kong)
Dr. John Ching Kwong Kwok (Kowloon)
Dr. Kwan –Hon Chan, F.R.C.S.E. (Hong Kong)
Dr. Peter H.T. Wu (Hong Kong)
Dr. Wai S. Poon (Hong Kong)

Hungary
Professor Emil Pasztor (Budapest)
Dr. Thomas Pentelenyi (Budapest)

Professor Istran Nijary (Budapest)

India
Dr. M. Sambasivan, B. Sc., M.B.B.S. (Kerala)
Dr. H.M. Dastur, M.S., F.R.C.S. (Bombay)

Japan
The Kameda Medical Center (Kamogawa City)
Dr. Toshitada Kameda
Dr. Takaaki Kameda
Dr. Shinsuki Kameda
Dr. Shogo Kameda
Dr. Tsundyoshi Eguchi (Neurosurgeon)
Dr. Kazuo Takeuchi (Neurosurgeon–Tokyo)
Dr. Isamu Saito, (Neurosurgeon–Tokyo)
Dr. Kintomo Takakura (Neurosurgeon–Tokyo)
Dr. H. Narabayashi (Neurologist–Tokyo)
Dr. Shiro Waga (Tsu, Mie)

Korea
C. Jin Whang, M.D., F.A.C.S. (Seoul)
Jung Kyo Lee (Seoul)

The Netherlands
H. August Van Alphen, M.d., Ph.D. (Amsterdam)
(He wrote a chapter on Euthanasia in my book, *"You Live! You Die! Who Decides?"*)

Peru
Dr. Alfredo Duran (Lima)

Puerto Rico (San Juan)
Dr. Nathan Rifkinson

Spain
Dr. Jose Carlos Perez De Salcedo Bustos (Madrid)
Maria L. De Ceballos, Ph.D. (Madrid)

Switzerland
Hans F. Reinhardt (Basel)

Thailand
Dr. Charas Suwanwela (Bangkok)

Turkey
Dr. Aykut Erbengi (Ankara)
Professor Erdem Tuncbay (Izmir)
Professor Ture Tuncbay (Iszmir)
Professor Dr. M. Necmettin Pamir (Istanbul)

USSR (Commonwealth of Independent States)
Dr. Valeriy P.Bersnev (Leningrad)
Professor Edward I. Kandel (Moscow)
Professor Alexander N. Konovalor (Moscow)

Yugoslavia
Prof. Boris Klun (Ljubljana)
Prof. Vinko V. Dolenc (Ljubljana)

XII. Retirement

A. RADM Joseph H. Miller – Activities for 2001and 2002

When we first moved to Florida, we joined the St. Petersburg Yacht Club. We bought a 34-foot twin diesel Sea Ray Yacht (The "Admiral Joe") and cruised to all the Yacht Clubs in the Florida Council of Clubs. During this time, I memorized the Sermon on the Mount. ("Teachings on the Mount.")

Cathy named the boat the "Admiral Joe" and had an artist paint our Miller Coat of Arms on the back of the boat.

B. World Cruise Voyage of the Seven Wonders, 65 Days

New York to Hong Kong, 9 January - 15 March 2006

We embarked in New York and from there we cruised to Ft. Lauderdale, Florida, Willemstad, Curacao, Panama Canal, Acapulco, Mexico, Los Angeles, California, Honolulu, Hawaii, Pago Pago, American Samoa, Crossing the International Dateline, Lautoka, Fiji, Noumea, New Caledonia, Auckland, New Zealand, Tauranga, New Zealand, Wellington, New Zealand, Sydney, Australia, Melbourne, Australia, Adelaide, Australia, Perth, Australia, Exmouth, Australia, Taipei, Taiwan, Kobe,

Japan, Kagoshima, Japan, Shanghai, China, Hong Kong (Hong Kong Disneyland!)

C. IMPORTANT BOOKS

BOOKS I HAVE READ FROM COVER TO COVER
(Not a complete list)

It has been said many times,
"One can tell about a man by the books he reads."
One can tell about a man by the books in his library.
One can tell about a man if he has no books in his house.
Man can learn about himself by reading good books by great men.

1. ***The Bible*** (King James Version)
   Author: God, The Book That Speaks!
2. ***The Return of the Native***
   By Thomas Hardy
   (This was an assignment during my first year of college in 1947)
3. ***Spoon River Anthology***
   Edgar Lee Masters (1915)
4. ***The Riddle of the Sands***
   Erskine Childers (1903)
5. ***America's God and Country***
   William J. Federer, 2000
6. ***The World's Great Speeches***, 1942-1999.
   Lewis Copeland, Lawrence W. Lamn and Stephen J. McKenna.
7. ***In Search of a Soul***
   Horatio W. Dresser (1897)
8. ***Royal Truths***
   Henry Ward Beecher (1886)
9. ***The Brotherhood***
   Reverend Thomas G. Bcharrell, A.M. (1868)
   (The Bible is Our Text Book)

Desiderius Erasmus (1466-1536):
(The name of Erasmus will never perish, the greatest scholar and writer of his age.)
1. ***The Manual of the Christian Knight* (1905)**
2. ***The Complaint of Peace* (1516)**
3. ***The Praise of Folly***
4. ***Praise of Folly***
5. ***Erasmus 2004***
6. ***Erasmus***
7. ***Christian Humanism and the Reformation***
8. ***Select Colloquies***

Eusebius (260-339 A.D.)
The History of the church from Christ to Constantine
Eusebius Ecclesiastical History

Josephus 37-10 A.D.
Antiquities of the Jews;
A History of the Jewish Wars.
Complete Works of Josephus
Josephus, the Essential Writings
The Ancient Historians
Heresies, Heresy and Orthodoxy in the History of the Church.

D. History of Christianity

The Faith (A History of Christianity) Brian Moyhahan 1941-2002. This is a must read.

Anthologia Sacra or Select Theological Extracts on Doctrinal, Practical and Experimental

Christian Theology, Russell R. Byrum
(Professor of Systemic Theology in Anderson Bible School and Seminary, Anderson, Indiana.) 1925. This is a must for the scholar.

The Church in America, William Adams Brown, Ph.D., D.D. (Chairman of the Committee on War and the Religious Outlook

Short History of the Christian Church,
C.P.S. Clarke, M.A. 1929
Islam means to turn one to God in prayer. Mohammed said, "The sword is the key to Heaven and Hell."

The Goodly Fellowship of the Prophets
Christopher R. Seitz

Orthodoxy
G.K. Chesterton, 1908
Descartes' said, 'I think; therefore, I am'.

Pocket History of the Church
D. Jeffery Bingham, 2002
This little book is a must.

Discourse on Free Will, Erasmus–Luther,
Translated by Ernst f. Winter, 1524 (copyright 1961)

Two Living Traditions, Essays on Religion, and the Bible. Samuel
Sandmel, 1972.

Documents of the Christian Church
Selected and edited by Henry Bettenson and the Third edition by Chris Mounder. 1949-1999

Memoirs of a Superfluous Man by Albert Jay Nock, 1964. I heard this book referred to in a lecture by a great neurosurgeon (Dr. Frank Mayfield). He told of the man who went to Iceland to study owls and after two years found there were no owls in Iceland.

Hope of a Nation. Our Christian Heritage by Nelson Beecher Keyes and Edward Felix Gallager, 1952

Charles Spurgeon (1839-1892)
The Forgotten Spurgeon by Pain Murray 1966

Spurgeon's Sermon Illustrations Edited and condensed by David Otis Fuller, D.D., MCMLXII

The Problem with Evangelical Theology:
Testing the Exegetical Foundations of Calvinism, Dispensationalist,
and Wesleyism
Ben Witherington III 2005

The 100 Most Important Events in Christian History
Kenneth Curtis, J. Stephen Lang, Randy Peterson, 1991

Rizal's Poems, Jose Rizal, (1861-1896) 1992 He is the hero of the Philippines nationalist, author poet, physician (Ophthalmologist). I was a guest of two medical schools in Manila and read the poem the first time in 1969. Dr. Rizal was a Philippine martyr and was executed in 1896. This caused the Philippines to rise up and obtain their freedom. The book lists 39 of his poems. His last poem written the night before his execution is 14 pages. It is a love letter to the Philippines.

The Wisdom of the Great Chiefs
The Classic Speeches of Chief Red Jacket, Chief Joseph, and Chief Seattle.

Chief Joseph (50 pages –abbreviated)
Buffalo Bill said, "Chief Joseph was the greatest American ever produced."

Chief Joseph, 1879
"The earth is the mother of all people, and all people should have equal rights upon it.

The Wisdom of the Forest by Geoffrey Parrinder,1975.
"Do not wander away as a beggar in a holy place."

Men cannot see the soul, for if he were to be seen he would be incomplete. In breathing his name is breath, in speaking his name is voice, in seeing his name is the eye; in hearing his name is the ear; in thinking his name is the mind. But these are simply names of action. The Soul is a trace of everything for it knows the whole universe. Can you explain the breath of life and Space? My answer to that is Read, the Bible!"

The Christian Philosophy of St. Thomas Aquinas by Etienne Gilson and L.K. Shook
The Results of My Study of Bible Translations:

Acceptable:
1. Authorized King James Version 1911-**1769** (our version)
2. English Standard Version
3. New Revised Standard Version

National Geographic Essential Visual History of the Bible, this is a must read for any Bible scholar or student.

Ten Fingers for God: The Life and Work of Dr. Paul Brand by Dorothy Clarke Wilson

Fearfully and Wonderfully Made
Paul Brand and Philip Yancey. This is a quote from Psalms 139:14
"I praise thee, for I am
Fearfully and wonderfully made"

The Parson of The Islands
A biography of Reverend Joshua Thomas (1776-1853) by Adam Wallace, 1978.

A Survey of Bible Doctrine
Charles C. Ryrie, 1972)

Books of the Non-Christian Religions that I have read:
They are all a learning experience. I have over 50 non-Christian Religious books in my library. I have scanned them all, but I have read all of only a few:

The Tibetan Book of Living and Dying Sogyal Rinpache, 1994. (118,500 copies have been sold in 12 printings.)

Bushido, The Soul of Japan Inazo Nitobe, AM. PhD., 1969

Hagakure The Book of The Samurai
Yamamoto Tsunetomo 1700 (Translated by William Scott Wilson, 1979) "The way of the Samurai is found in death."

E. Books I Have Read on Islam:

The Trial of Benazir (Bhutto) Rafig Zakaria, 1989.

Ninety-nine Names Of Allah (Shems)

Islam - Ismail R. Al Faruqi, Ph.D., 1974

The Crisis of Islam - Bernard Lewis (Holy War and Unholy Terror, 2004

The Crescent Through the Eyes of the Cross - Nabell T. Jabbour, 2008

Black Gold and Holy War by Ishak Ibraham

F. The "So-Called" Reformation:

(Nothing was reformed, but Protestantism was born!)

Trouble with The Tulip - Frank S. page, Ph.D. 2000, 2006

The Plague, 1571 a year of famine and death. Luther 1611, The Protestants were cowards in plague epidemics.

The Pursuit of God - A.W. Tozier, A Beloved, Timeless classic.

The Hiding Place - Corrie Ten Boon with John and Elizabeth Sherrill, 1971.

The Pre-Wrath Rapture of The Church - Marvin Rosenthal, 1990.

The Criminalization of Christianity - Janet L. Floger, 2005. This is a must read.

Twelve Ordinary Men _How the Master Shaped His Disciples for Greatness._ - John MacArthur, 2002.

Are We Living in The End Times? - Tim LaHaye and Jerry B. Jenkins, 1999.

The DIDACHE or Teaching of the Twelve Apostles

Damien the Leper - John Farrow, 1954

Opium, A History - Martin Booth, 1996

War Books: - (I have at least 155 books on war in my library.

War
By Gaston Bouthoul. This is the first book written on the Philosophy of War. It was first published in French in 1953 but was not translated into English until 1962. Bouthoul first used the term *"Polemogy"* for the study of war. This is a Must!

Days of Anguish, Days of Hope
Billy Keith gives the story of Lieutenant Robert Taylor, a chaplain in the Bataan Death March. He was a prisoner of the Japanese for five years. He was declared dead. His wife remarried, and he returned home. She met him in New York and took him to a small restaurant to give him the news. She said, "I have remarried and have a new life." He said, "But, but, you are my wife." She said, "I have a new life now." He walked out into the streets of New York and took a bus to Texas. He became Major General Robert Preston Taylor, Chief of Chaplains of the Air Force. This book is a must, must, must read!

On War by **Carl von Clausewitz**

The Fall of Empires - Cornoc O'Brien

In 60% of the empires that failed it was due to immigration that changed the culture of the country. Very revealing at this time.

__The Fifteen Decisive Battles of the World__ - Sir Edward S. Creasy

Books I Cannot Do Without:
__Bible__ (**King James Version**)
__Thompson Chain Reference Bible New International Version__
__An Encyclopedia of World History__
__The Merriam – Webster Dictionary__
__Oxford Dictionary of the Christian Church__ - Editors: F.L. Cross and E.A. Livingstone, 1997

__Matthew Henry's Commentary__
Hendrickson Publishers 2002 (Published since 1706)
George W. Truett "This is the best."
Charles H. Spurgeon "This is first among the mighty commentaries."
Joseph H. Miller "If I could only have one, this would be it, by far."

__An Encyclopedia of Religion__ - Edited by Vergilius Fern, 1940.

__The Catholic Encyclopedia__ - Editor, Robert C. Broderick, 1986

__The Encyclopedia of the Jewish Religion__

G. My Favorite Songs

Faith:

Victory in Jesus
Tell It to Jesus
Take Time to Be Holy
To God Be the Glory
Jesus, Lover of my Soul
Jesus Loves Me
Sweet By and By

Jesus Saves, Jesus Saves
The Old Rugged Cross
Because He Lives
How Great Thou Art!
Amazing Grace
Holy, Holy, Holy

Patriotic:

The Star-Spangled Banner   *A Mighty Fortress Is Our God*
Battle Hymn of the Republic   *The Red White and Blue*
My Country, 'tis of Thee   *My Bonnie*

Spiritual:

The Old Time Religion
Swing Low Sweet Chariot
Now the Day Is Over

Music of the World:

Bach: on Faith Johann Sebastian Bach (1685-1750) In 1940 music experts declared Bach the greatest musician of all time.

Handel: (The power of will) George Frideric Handel (23 February 1685– 14 April 1759) was a German- composer who is famous for his opera's oratorios and concertos.

Mozart: The Divine Spark

Wolfgang Amadeus Mozart (27 January 1756–5 December 1791), was a prolific and influential composer of the Classical era.

Beethoven: Ludwig van Beethoven (17 December 1770˙ 26 March 1827) was a German composer and pianist. Beethoven is famous for many works including the ***Pastoral, Awakening of Pleasant Emotions on Arriving in the Country, Scene at the Brook, Merry Peasant Gathering, Thunderstorm, Tempest, Shepherd's Song, Feelings of Joy and Gratitude After the Storm,*** and ***Apotheosis of the Dance.***

My premedical school studies ended any study of music. I know little of Schubert, Weber, Johann, and the Waltzes. I know that the words "Strauss and Vienna Waltz" make up a vision of good gone before the eyes, ears, and feet of those who were a part of it. Mendelssohn, Schumann, Liszt, Chopin, and Johann Brahms were out of my reach. (1949) 61 years later in 2010, I took up where I left off and did a review and gave speeches on, ***"The Musical Brain."***

H. The World

There are 6.6 Billion people in the world.
The top three are:

- China 1.3 billion
- India 1.1 billion
- United States 300 million

Others:

Indonesia 235 Million   **Russia** 141 Million
Brazil 190 Million   **Nigeria** 135 Million
Bangladesh 150 Million   **Japan** 127 Million

There are three Groups that believe in God:
Christians – 2.2 billion or 33%
Muslims – 1.3 billion or 20%
Jews – 1.5 million or 2.3%

There are <u>155 Million atheists</u> in the world or 2.3%.
6.6 billion people in the world
3.5 billion are Christians or Muslims

3.1 billion people are non-Christian
This group includes the:
Hindus
Non-Religious – 872 million
Other Chinese Religions – 785 million
Buddhists – 386 million
Atheists – 153 million

I. The Case for God's Existence

Biblical and Non-Biblical

"It is at a man's own risk what he believes, and he must see for himself that he believes rightly. Belief is a free work, but it can open or shut Heaven or Hell." (***Hibbert Lectures***, 1883)

When one is giving the case for the existence of God the emphasis depends upon the content of the group. If they are all Christians, the emphasis is on the Biblical report that God gave us of Himself. If the groups are pagans, heathens, unbelievers, etc. the emphasis depends on the group's educational level. The scientists get the whole picture (4 pages pp. 9-12) in this report. In other words, the teacher's mentality must adjust to the student's mentality. In any case with the known facts one can destroy the stupid, ignorant, and ungodly, message from the Devil of the "Big Bang" theory with facts. Those who will not hear us or believe us as Jesus said, we are to, "shake the dust off our feet" (Matthew 10:14) and let them go to Hell and proceed with our calling.

"In the beginning God created the heaven and the earth." (Genesis 1:1) (This is the foundation of all foundations.) "These are the generations of the heavens and of the earth when they were created, in the day that the LORD God made the earth and the heavens." (Genesis 2:4) This is the first time LORD GOD is in the Bible. (Yahweh Elohim, "I AM, I AM, Creator.") "This is the book of the generations of Adam. In the day that God created man, in the likeness of God made he him."(Genesis 5:1) And the generations of Noah (6:9), sons of Noah (10:1), Shem (11:10), Terah (11:27) Abraham took Sarah as this wife (11:29) "Now the LORD had said unto Abram, Get thee out of thy country, and from thy kindred, and from thy father's house, unto a land that I will shew thee:"(Genesis 12:1) Thus begins the story of civilization as recorded by Moses as a revelation from God. The Story of the creation by God is evidence of His Divine Nature and Glory. Biblical Christianity is the only truly **creationist** religion. God's past work "all things created" (Colossians 1:16) God's present work "all things consist" (Colossians 1:17) God's future work He completes all things "All things are reconciled to Himself". (Colossians 1:20)

"Now faith is the substance of things hoped for, the evidence of things not seen…Through faith we understand that the worlds were framed by the word of God, so that things which are seen were not made of things which do appear."(Hebrews 11:1, 3) Our faith is the same faith of Abel, Enoch, Noah, Abraham, Sarah, Isaac, Jacob, Joseph, Moses, Rahab, Gideon, Deborah, Barak, Samson, Jephthah, David, Daniel, Samuel and all the prophets. (Hebrews 11:1-40) It is the faith that brought down the walls of Jericho (Joshua 6:20), stopped the mouth of lions (Daniel 6:22, Hebrews 11:33), the woman's dead son raised to life (II Kings 8:5, Hebrews 11:35). One can see that our faith is the same faith that has been present since the creation of man!!!

"The heavens declare the glory of God; and the firmament sheweth his handiwork. Day unto day uttereth speech, and night unto night sheweth knowledge. There is no speech nor language, where their voice is not heard. Their line is gone out through all the earth, and their words to the end of the world. In them hath he set a tabernacle for the sun." (Psalms 19:1-4)

"For the invisible things of him from the creation of the world are **clearly seen,** being understood by the things that are made, even his eternal power and Godhead; so that they are **without excuse:"** (Romans 1:20)

The **everlasting Gospel** as noted from the beginning to the end in the Bible from Genesis to Revelation. "And I saw another angel fly in the midst of heaven, having the **everlasting gospel to preach unto them that dwell on the earth,** and to **every nation,** and **kindred, and tongue, and people,** Saying with a loud voice, Fear God, and give glory to him; for the hour of his judgment is come: and **worship him that made heaven, and earth,** and the sea, and the fountains of waters." (Revelation 14:6-7)

The message is to worship the God who made the heavens and earth.

Our prayer is as the prophets, "Open thou their eyes that they may see." (Psa. 119:18) And Jesus said, **"Blessed are the eyes that see the things that you see."** (Luke 10:23)

Moses asked God, "Who are you? What is your name?" God said, "I AM That I AM." (Exodus 3:13, 14) Man is not certain what that means. No man can know God. Jesus said, *"Before Abraham was, I Am."* (John 8:58)

The way to God: In the Bible God does not question His own existence. God allows man to question Him but sends man to Hell if he does not find Him.

We do not lift up ourselves to God by the weak pinions (shackles) of our own reason that He has given us: If you prove religion by reason you weaken what you want to support. **We must know God by his own methods in the Scriptures.** Our reason gives us an understanding of God in His Word, but **knowledge beyond our reason is by faith.** As our Creator, God is the Father of all men. God is life, light, and love.

The **truth** of Christianity or a belief in God is seen in the fact that men in isolated places around the world have a **revealed innate consciousness of God.** Men who have never in any way communicated with the rest of the world have in their mind a concept of God. **Who put it there? Only God could have put the concept of God in the mind of men.** Man's brain and thoughts are not large enough with their own power to come up with the idea of a perfect and eternal God. **It is God's own revelation to us that He is God.** Those who do not believe God call God a liar. (I John 5:10) **God through revelations and His Word has revealed Himself to us.** The Divine attributes of God and eternity are fixed in our mind by God Himself. God has made Himself known through our human soul, human reason, and reveals an eternity, and a moral conscience. Yet God remains above human thought. Aquinas said God is the Creator, the necessary Bring, the perfect Being, the Cause, the Mover, and the Sustainer of the universe. God is in all things and all things are in Him. (I Corinthians 15:28) **God exists in our minds.**

The truth or proof of Christianity is seen upon some leading facts. Here are a <u>few</u> of these:

1. A Jewish peasant changed the religion of the world, without force, without power, without support, without one natural resource or influence.
2. He was put to death. His followers carried His Word to the known world. The only thing they could expect was danger, insult, and

death! (6 were brothers, 8 were fisherman, 10 died for Him. One traitor committed suicide, and one lived to an old age.)

3. Those who killed him were armed with the power of the country.

4. Their stories never changed.

5. There is no parallel to the story of Jesus and His disciples in the history of the world.

6. The **history** of Jesus, His resurrection, His disciples, and their **miracles** and the **number of witnesses** laid the foundation of our faith. (The Jews who killed Jesus and who argue without facts are less than 1% of the United States or world population. They are no longer loyal to each other; they are dying off because of intermarriage with other races.)

7. **Four separate books** tell the history of Jesus and His disciples. They were written separately and selected among hundreds of books. (These different narratives were then brought together by a special inspired, educated, and religious group 150-200 years later as **Matthew, Mark, Luke,** and **John**. They give the History of the Founder of the largest faith in the world today. The **only faith** in which the Founder was publicly killed, publicly buried, and publicly rose from the dead. **He proved the power over life or death**. The power over death could only be from God. No man can say that this is not strong historical evidence.

From the beginning we have a strong case. Jesus did not leave His truth without witnesses. In Christ the whole law has been fulfilled. Paul said, "We are compassed about with **so great a cloud of witnesses**…let us run the race that is set before us." (Hebrews 12:1)

The death, burial and resurrection of Jesus is the sole proof of our faith in Him. "And declared to be the Son of God with power, according to the spirit of holiness, **by the resurrection from the dead:**" (Romans 1:4) **After His resurrection** He was seen at one time by 500 people, all of the apostles, and by me. (I Corinthians 15:6-8) "This Jesus hath God raised up, whereof **we all are witnesses**…And killed the Prince of life, whom God hath raised from the dead; whereof **we are witnesses**…Him God raised up the third day, and shewed him openly…Not to all the people, but unto witnesses chosen before of God, even to us, who did eat and drink with him after he rose from the dead…But God raised him from the dead…And He was seen many days of them which came up with him from Galilee to Jerusalem, who are his witnesses unto the people… Because he hath appointed a day, in the which he will judge the world in righteousness by that man whom he hath ordained; whereof he hath given assurance unto all men, in that he hath raised him from the dead…And have hope toward God, which they themselves also allow, that there shall be a resurrection of the dead, both of the just and unjust." (Acts 2:32, 3:15, 10:40, 41, 13:30,31, 17:31, 24:15) There is no other name whereby we can be saved. "Neither is there salvation in any other: for there is none other name under Heaven given among men, whereby we must be saved."(Acts 4:12) At the moment of conversion a sinner becomes a saint and free from the death penalty of sin (Ephesians 1:18, Colossians 1:12) The lifelong process of growth is called sanctification, which lasts until we meet Christ. (I Corinthians 1:30, II Thessalonians 2:13, John 17:19, Acts 20:32, Acts 26:18, I Corinthians 1:2) Salvation is a free gift from God that rescues the believer to a holy life, and to a right relationship with God for all eternity. (Hebrews 5:9)

There is a God!

"The fool hath said in his heart, there is no God. They are corrupt, they have done abominable works, there is none that doeth good." (Psalm 14:1) "The way of a fool is right in his own eyes." (Proverbs 12:15) "A reproof entereth more into a wise man than an hundred stripes into a fool." (Proverbs 17:10) "Answer not a fool according to his folly, lest thou also be like unto him." (Proverbs 26:4)

If you answer a fool according to his folly, he with be wise in his own conceit. You make him look better. (See Proverbs 26:5) When one said to Jesus, I have goods laid up for many years. Jesus said to him, *Thou fool, this night thy soul shall be required of thee: then whose shall those things be…?"* (Luke 12:20)

Listen to Paul's Testimony about Jesus and God's Word:
(Keep in mind that Paul was an influential man, a Pharisee, and trained under the all-time great Jewish teacher, Gamaliel. Acts 5:34; 22:3)

Paul said to the Jews, as you are, I am a Jew, an Israelite, and a seed of Abraham. Are they ministers of Christ? I speak as a fool I am more in labors, in stripes, in prison, and in death. The Jews have beaten me five times with 39 stripes, two times with rods; and two times I have been stoned. I have suffered three shipwrecks, been in perils of water, of robbers, my own countrymen (Jews), heathens, city, wilderness, the sea, and false prophets, weariness and painfulness, hunger, thirst, fasting, cold, and nakedness, **and beside these things I have the care of the churches.** (2 Corinthians 11:22-28) However, Jesus said if we call someone a fool we are in "Danger of Hell fire." (Matthew 5:22) The fool who does not believe in the leading truth of God is the sole source of all the wickedness in the world. (Leighton) Sometimes seemingly even the best of men do not collect their thoughts on this subject, even though the whole basis of their souls eternal life depends on it. It is up to us to bring it to their thoughts, which I am trying to do.

There must be a God. It is shocking to think that nothing produced itself out of nothing. That "something" that produced the world out of nothing had to have been uncreated and existed forever. That can only be God. Think of everything in the world and then pick only one thing. Then think of all the things in the universe that lives in harmony with each other. The moon borrows its light from the sun, etc. One cannot think of one or all the things together without thinking that there must be a God. The thing and harmony of the universe is its own evidence. One must ask, "What more does the fool want?" (Miller)

How about man; the noblest of all God's creation. He is God's man on earth to run things for Him. Animated from dirt and God's own breath. (I, for one, do not think that women could have come from a "big blast" or from an octopus with his eight legs with suckers. They could have only come from a man's rib. However, most men I know think that modern woman is not the biblical woman in the garden. I am an exception because

I know that my Cathy could have come only from God.) Without God: every individual of the race owes it's being to another. We were all born from another. Consequently, the whole race would be from itself and at the same time be from another. (Which came first the chicken or the egg?) This makes no sense. There must be a God, because this could not happen.

One cannot put nature in the place of God. When you see nature in all the things, plants that grow, and movements in the universe you are seeing God. They are the same. Your heart may have to be opened for you to see it. "O LORD, how manifold are thy works! in wisdom hast thou made them all: the earth is full of thy riches."(Psalms 104:24) "All thy works shall praise thee, O LORD; and thy saints shall bless thee."(Psalms 145:10) "Before the mountains were brought forth, or ever thou hadst formed the earth and the world, even from everlasting to everlasting, thou art God."(Psalms 90:2) "O LORD, there is none like thee, neither is there any God beside thee, according to all that we have heard with our ears."(1 Chronicles 17:20)

There is the God we worship and love. We cannot express God in words or even in our thoughts conceive Him. The more we try, the more profound is our humility to love Him with the greatest intensity. God has perfect knowledge of all things in general and every single one in particular.

Our Salvation Depends on Jesus' Crucifixion and Resurrection

J. MORE PROOF

The twelve times Jesus was seen after His resurrection:

After Jesus' Resurrection He was seen **twelve times that were recorded.**

Our whole salvation depends on Jesus being raised from the dead. This has never been claimed or recorded by any other religious leader in history. There are numerous verifications of Jesus being witnessed as **RISEN** by early historians other than those recorded in the Bible. There were so many people that saw Jesus after He was risen that the fact is irrefutable. There is not a single witness at the time who has recorded that it was not so. Everyone there knew it. They would have been called "stupid" if they did not know it at the time.

Read the following accounts of the witnesses of Jesus' appearances after His resurrection from the dead. I promise you a blessing if you do. Your mind and heart will swell with a joy and assurance not available from any other fact in history.

In the following statements see if you can find yourself in the crowds that spat on, beat, mocked, placed in chains, and crucified Christ? **You were there!!!**
Jesus was in chains for us!
Jesus carried the cross for us! (You were there!)
Jesus had nails driven in His hands for us (Our sins did it!)
Jesus died on the cross between two thieves for us. (One of them was saved before he died. He believed and asked Jesus for Salvation and received it. Can you see how simple it is? (Can you find yourself at the cross? Look closely, you were there!) Jesus was not held by the cross

Jesus: "**He is Risen**" The tomb is empty. It did not hold Him.

Jesus was with the Apostles by the Sea of Galilee after His resurrection (He cooked bread and fish and ate with them.)

"Then he led them out as far as Bethany and lifting up his hands he blessed them. While he blessed them, he parted from them, and was carried up into heaven. (Luke 24:50-51) The Ascension by Rembrandt (1606-1669) is a famous painting to this day.

    I. Easter Morning (Mark 16:9)
    II. Jesus appears to the women (Matthew 28: 5, 6,7)
    III. Jesus Appears to Peter (I Corinthians 15:5)
    IV. Jesus had supper at a village called Emmaus, with two disciples. (Luke 24: 13, 30, 31)
    V. Jesus appears to ten disciples (Thomas was absent) (John 20: 19,20,21,22)
    VI. Jesus appears to Thomas and eleven disciples (John 20:26,27,28,29)

VII.. Miraculous catch of fish (John 21: 1,5,6,7,9, 10, 11, 12, 14)

VIII. Eleven Apostles (Matthew 28:16-20)

IX. Jesus was seen by 500 brethren

X. Jesus was seen by James

XI. Ascension of Jesus (40 days after Easter) (Luke 24:50-53)

XII. Jesus appears to Paul (Exact place unknown) (I Corinthians 15:8)

Non-Biblical Records of Christ

The First Non-Biblical Records of Christ

Tiberius Caesar (42 B.C.–37 A.D.)

Tertullian: (reference: *Eusebius Ecclesiastical History*, 2006, pp. 37, 38)

Tacitus (60-120 A.D.) *The Annals*:

"Jewish Antiquities" by **Josephus** gives the most important non-Biblical information about the Bible. **He is the only surviving source of most of the available non-Biblical information. Josephus verifies Jesus as having lived, was the Messiah and was raised from the dead.** A reliable witness who knew many witnesses of Jesus and the Apostles and recorded information outside the Bible that cannot be denied.):

Eusebius (260-339 A.D.) The *"Father of Church History,"* was another **non-Biblical witness to Jesus.** One of the most amazing events in Christian history outside the Bible is that Eusebius saw a statue of Jesus and a letter that Jesus wrote and made a copy, which is the only surviving record. Eusebius copied two letters from the archives at Edessa, the royal capitol. They were copied word for word from the Syrian language. Abgar the king of Edessa wrote a letter to Jesus and was also copied by Eusebius. The copy is recorded in Eusebius. (*Eusebius, The Church History,* Paul L. Maier, Kregel Publications, 1999, p.49)

The king had heard about Jesus raising the dead, healing the blind, the lame, lepers, and other chronic diseases.

"When I heard all these things about you, I decided that one of two things are true: either you are God and came down from heaven to do these things or you are God's Son for doing them. I am writing to beg you to take the trouble to come to me and heal my suffering.

I have also heard that the Jews are murmuring against you and plot to harm you."

This letter was delivered to Jesus by a courier by the name of Ananias. I have copied it from Eusebius *"The Church History"* p. 48 and it is as follows:

The same courier delivered *Jesus'* answer to the king.

"Blessed are you who believed in me without seeing me! For it is written that those who have seen me will not believe in me and that those who have not seen me will believe and live. Now regarding your request that I come to you, I must first complete all that I was sent to do here and once that is completed, must be taken up to the One who sent me, When I have been taken up, I will send one of my disciples to heal your suffering and bring life to you and yours."

Further records tell that Thaddeus (One of the seventy apostles) **went to the king and healed him**, his son, (of gout) and many others.

Other non-Biblical Records of Christ:
There are many other historians that verify the existence of Jesus including: Erasmus, Philo, Tertullian, Clement of Alexandria, Origen, Irenaeus, Tatian, and Methodius to name only a few. *Didache* **(*The Teachings of the Apostles*),** which is perhaps the earliest Christian writings. (Even my amateurish reviews of non-biblical church history could fill hundreds of pages of church fathers and writers who believed in Jesus and His resurrection. When I hear someone say they do not believe it, I know they are simply (innocent from ignorance) ignorant in religious history. I never respond since one cannot educate a non-educated person in a few minutes of conversation. A scripture I like, but usually do not quote is: "**Who is a liar, but he that denieth that Jesus is the Christ? He is antichrist, that denieth the Father and Son.**" (1 Jn 2:22) As a faculty member for many years I have learned that there are some people who are not teachable. I can teach the facts of "life and death" as revealed in the Scriptures. I can also teach the facts of "life and death" **as <u>revealed</u>,**

186

witnessed, and **recorded** by some of the world's greatest minds outside the Scriptures. (But some people are not teachable.)

Twelve Men Like You and Me Who Listened to God's Call:

Jesus taught His twelve Apostles so they could teach us. We must study them to learn. They were witnesses to all He said, taught, His crucifixion, and His resurrection. Their dedication could only come from Divine Power.

The Twelve Apostles:

Twelve men who still teach the world, were recruited by Jesus, were taught by Jesus, saw Jesus after He arose from the dead, preached what they had seen, preached what Jesus taught, endured persecution, opposition, and death for Jesus teachings. They began the Christian religion that emerged as the dominant faith of the Roman Empire and is now the largest religion of the world. They called their movement "The Way" to the kingdom of God and were called Nazarenes (followers of Jesus of Nazareth.) We are Nazarenes. The Apostolic Age ended by 70 AD and the second generation of Christians continued in their place. Thousands of Christians were martyred in the next 200 years and Christians continue to be martyred even until this day.

Six Apostles Were Brothers:

James and **John** (sons of Zebedee and Salomi)
Peter and **Andrew** (Son of Jonah, also called Jonas or John)
James the Less (Son of Alphaeus) and **Matthew** whose father was named Alphaeus. They probably were brothers even though the scripture does not refer to them as brothers.
(Jude I refers to Jude as the brother of James.)

How the Disciples Died

Peter: Jesus told Peter he would be martyred. (John 21:18-19) Peter was forced to watch his wife be crucified first. He called to her, "Remember the Lord, Remember the Lord." Peter then asked to be crucified "Upside Down" since he did not feel worthy to be crucified as his Lord. (67 AD)

Andrew was crucified on an X cross-tied by ropes without nails so he would live longer.

James the Greater was the first apostle to be martyred. He was beheaded by King Herod Agrippa by the sword. (Acts 12:2). King Herod died under God's judgment and was eaten by worms. (Acts 12:23) The presumed head of St. James is enclosed in the Cathedral of St. James located in the Old City of Jerusalem.

John, the Apostle "Jesus loved" died a natural death in Ephesus at about age 100 about 100 A.D. and buried in Ephesus.

Philip was beaten with whips and crucified or stoned at Hierapolis in Phrygia. Bartholomew buried Philip. (Asia Minor) (80A.D.)

Bartholomew (Nathaniel) was reported to have had his skin cut from his living body and he was then beheaded in Armenia. His relics are in the church of Saint Bartholomew in Rome.

Thomas was killed by a spear in India and is buried near Madras. A church in India traces its roots to Thomas. (Foxe, p. 34, MacArthur, p. 164)

Matthew was burned at the stake and killed by a sword in Parthia. (60 A.D.)

There are three historical records of the death of **James the Less**: Stoned, beaten with clubs, crucified.

Thaddeus was clubbed to death in Arabia when he would not renounce his faith. (About 100 A.D.) His relics are in Rome.

Judas Iscariot: (The traitor) Hanged himself. (Matt. 27: 5) The limb or rope broke and he fell into the rocks and his entrails (bowels, intestines) gushed out. (Acts 1:18)

Simon the Canaanite (Zealot) was sawed in half while alive in Arabia about 100 A.D.

There was another group of seventy disciples apart from the twelve who became apostles. "The Lord appointed seventy others and sent them two by two before his face into every city and place, whither He Himself would come. Therefore, said He unto them, "The harvest truly is great, but the laborers are few; pray ye therefore the Lord of the harvest, that he would send forth laborers into the harvest. Go your ways: behold, I send you forth as lambs among wolves…and whatsoever house ye enter, first say, Peace be to this house." (Luke 10:1-5)

There is no list of the seventy, but these have been recorded as part of the seventy: Barnabas, Sosthenes, Cephas, Matthias, Barabas, and Thaddaeus.

OTHERS OF NOTE:
John the Baptist: Beheaded by Herod Antipas

Mark: Dragged through the streets and burned. (His bones are in Venice where he is a saint and patron)

Paul: Beheaded by Nero in Rome

Luke: Cause of death is unknown. or Hanged in Greece)

Barnabas: Cause of death is unknown. Stoned to death at Salona.

Matthias replaced Judas Iscariot as number 12. He was stoned and beheaded.

Christ (Son of God) Jesus is alive! Christ (Son of God) is the Messiah (Son of God) Christ (The Son of God) is our Savior. There is no other story like it.

K. Attributes of God

In the Bible God is described as:
There are hundreds of Scriptures: (Listed here are only 49)

God is a Spirit, Our Creator, He gives us access to Him, and Compassion, Life is from God, God is Eternal, is Faithful, is our Father of Glory, has Foreknowledge, is goodness, a God of love, mercy, and grace, is our guide, is our Preserver, our Deliver, Holiness, Perfect, Righteous, Immutable, Impartial, Incomprehensible, Infinite, Invisible, Jealous, Unsearchable, Judge, and Justice, all Knowledge, Long suffering, Loves the Abused, Is Love Exemplified, Omnipotent, Omnipresent, Omniscient, all Power, Providence, Truth, Ubiquitous, Unchangeable, Unique as the only God, has a Voice, all Wisdom, and all things are God's Work.

The most high God, the possessor of heaven and earth. (Genesis 14:22, 24:3, Exodus 8:22, 9:29, 19:5, Deuteronomy 4:39, 10:14, Joshua 2:11, II Kings 19:15, II Chronicles 20:6, Nehemiah 9:6, Job 41:11, Psalms 24:1, 83:18, 89:11, 103:19, 105:7, 113:4, Isaiah 24:23, 37:16, 54:5, Jeremiah 10:10, I Corinthians 10:26, Ephesians 4:6, Revelation 4:11.

When and How Can We Teach or Define Our Faith?

It hurts the case when stupid Christians try to defend or convince someone of our faith. I have been quoted many times in the medical environment by my saying while teaching anatomy, "If you are a Christian and you do not know the Bible, you're a stupid Christian. If you are a surgeon and don't know your anatomy you are a stupid surgeon."

The Basics for Being a Christian?
When Can and How Can We State or Teach Your Faith?

(Our testimony to teaching them the truth, which we cannot do unless we learn how. We are not born with this knowledge.) **"...and take no thought how or what ye shall speak: for it shall be given you what ye shall speak. For it is not ye that speak, but the Spirit of your Father which speaketh in you."** (Matt. 10:17-20) That's what the Bible says about the subject of defending our faith!

"Born-Again". Our deadly sin is not **learning and teaching** the truths of God's Word. The Christian can learn the faith, belief, trust, and obedience for salvation in a few words and still be ignorant of what separates Christianity from the heathen's faith.

(Titus 2:12,13) Looking for "that **blessed hope**" is one of the most famous attributes of a Christian. Our hope is not in this world.

For Those Who Believe:
"Even the righteousness of God which is by **faith** (belief, trust, obedience) of Jesus Christ **unto all and upon all them that believe**: for there is no difference:" (Rom. 3:22)

The death, burial and resurrection of Jesus is the sole proof of our faith in Him. "And declared to be the Son of God with power, according to the spirit of holiness, **by the resurrection from the dead**:" (Rom. 1:4) **After His resurrection** He was seen at one time by 500 people, all the Apostles, and by me. (1 Corinthians 15:6-8) "This Jesus hath God raised up, whereof we all are witnesses…And killed the Prince of life, whom God hath raised from the dead; whereof we are witnesses…Him God raised up the third day, and shewed him openly…Not to all the people, **but unto witnesses chosen before of God, even to us, who did eat and drink with him after he rose from the dead**…But **God raised him from the dead**…And **He was seen many days** of them which came up with him from Galilee to Jerusalem, **who are his witnesses unto the people.**

The Summary of the Christian Faith is Given by Paul:
"Moreover, brethren, I declare unto you the gospel which I preached unto you, which also ye have received, and wherein ye stand; By which also ye are saved, if ye keep in memory what I preached unto you, unless ye have believed in vain. For I delivered unto you first of all that which I also received, how that Christ died for our sins according to the scriptures; And that he was buried, and that he rose again the third day according to the scriptures: And that he was seen of Cephas, then of the twelve: After that, he was seen of above five hundred brethren at once; of whom the greater part remain unto this present, but some are fallen asleep. After that, he was seen of James; then of all the apostles. And last of all he was seen of me also, as of one born out of due time." (1 Cor. 15:1-8) "For therein is the righteousness of God revealed from faith to faith: as it is written, the just shall live by faith." (Rom. 1:17)

God cannot be reached unless Jesus introduces us to Him.
We have been adopted by His blood: By His blood we have become sons
of God:

(Matthew 5:3-12)
Blessed are the poor in spirit: for theirs is the kingdom of heaven.
Blessed are they that mourn: for they shall be comforted.
Blessed are the meek: for they shall inherit the earth.
Blessed are they which do hunger and thirst after righteousness: for
they shall be filled.
Blessed are the merciful: for they shall obtain mercy.
Blessed are the pure in heart: for they shall see God.
Blessed are the peacemakers: for they shall be called the children
of God.
Blessed are they which are persecuted for righteousness' sake: for theirs
is the kingdom of heaven.
Blessed are ye, when men shall revile you, and persecute you, and shall
say all manner of evil against you falsely, for my sake.
Rejoice, and be exceeding glad: for great is your reward in heaven: for
so persecuted they the prophets which were before you.

You face the challenge of an ineffective church organization, an organization
that has become bigger than the churches themselves. (I wrote this 38 years
ago and it is still true.) Instead of the ministers, our spiritual leaders being
called upon to speak out on the issues of the day, this organization has
formed commissions and committees to tell society what the Bible and
Baptists say. You face the challenge of a wasteful church organization. Out
of every dollar you contribute, only 4 to 6 cents (It is only 2 cents today)
goes to foreign missions and 4 to 6 cents to Christian education.

We have not mentioned the challenges of **crime, poverty, starvation,**
drugs, alcohol, sexual problems, inefficiency in justice, the breakdown
of the American home, false leaders, defiance of authority in law, or
the welfare state. (I have watched the church as a whole to continue to
destroy itself by not producing lay leaders. Where are the lay leaders? I

have almost forgotten that there ever was a Laymen's Day at church.) The challenge is great.

Where is wisdom and knowledge to be found? You will find the answer in the Book of Job. "Where shall wisdom be found, and where is the place of understanding"? (Job 28:20) But where is wisdom to be found, and knowledge, where does it abound? "But the wisdom that is from above is first pure, then peaceable, gentle, and easy to be entreated, full of mercy and good fruits, without partiality, and without hypocrisy." (James 3:17)

Wisdom: No vulture knows the path to it; no hawks eye ever spies it; no proud beast ever paces it; no lion moves along it; not a man knows that path; in the land of the living none finds it. No solid gold can purchase wisdom, no silver can be paid for her, there is no price for her in gold or Ophir, in precious beryl or in sapphires. Jewels of gold are no exchange for her. Wisdom is more precious even than rubies. No weight of gold can be paved down for her.

Where is wisdom to be found, and knowledge where does it abound? For she is hidden from every living creature, even from the eyes of a wild bird. Death and the underworld declare, we have only heard of her. God only is aware of her abode, and He declares to man, for you to know Me is your wisdom (Psalms 110:10) The fear of the Lord is wisdom and departing from evil is understanding. (Job 28:28; Proverbs 1:7; 9:10) This will also prolong your days. (Proverbs 9:11)

L. The Islamic Religious War Against America

I recently gave my 95th talk on Polemology (The Study of War) resulting from 40 years of study. The question and answering sessions have been revealing in that most Americans do not understand the religious war being engaged against us.

Medieval wars were carried out for God, personal profit, and honor. War defined the ruling groups of all societies. It was and has been a necessary and pursued status of human condition.

"Death rides astride their camels. Their only refuge is the sword; dumb as the grae, their tongues put forth with the serpent's deadly aim." (Antonio Santosuosso) This is the first time in history that a state was created out of both faith and force of arms.

Why have Muslims won almost half of the world? A study of war suggests: military leadership, religion, and their armies can move from one front to another quickly.

"Allah-a Akbar" (God is great.) This is their battle cry and was used by the shooter at Fort Hood in Texas. The term *"Allah"* is an Arabic word used by Muslims as their name for God. Where they got it is unknown. *"Allah"* is not found in any form in the Bible. It is not biblical. (***Oxford Dictionary***)

Islam itself is in the throes of change and has its own internal struggles for supremacy. Muslims are not nationally oriented. They do not understand patriotism. As fanatics and terrorists, they lay down their lives for what they think is service to God. They see a religion subdivided into nations.

Jihad becomes a personal duty of every Muslim. Jihad lays down an order "to kill Americans and their allies, both civic and military and is an individual duty of every Muslim. This is to "continue until all enemies depart from all the lands of Islam." By relevant verses in the Quran, "by god's word we call on every Muslim to obey gods command to kill Americans and plunder their possessions." "Attack the armies of the American devils who are among the helpers of Satan." This fatwa did not come with the authority of all Muslims. In the Iranian Revolution the late Ayatollah Khomeini called the United States "the Great Satan". Israel is seen as America's agent and "the Little Satan". These terms are one of the battle cries of the Al Qaida. Islamic countries are called "nations of peace", but all the other countries are "nations of war."

In 1818, the Ottoman Empire, with the help of the pasha of Egypt destroyed the Saudi state and decapitated the Saudi Emir. In 1823, the House of Saudi developed as a principality with its capitol in Riyadh. The Wahhabi doctrine of purification and renewal of Islam was adopted. In the 20ᵗʰ century Wahhabism became a major force of the Islamic world. The leader Ibn Sa'ud in 1932 proclaimed a new unitary state to be called the Saudi Arabian Kingdom. The next year Ibn Sa'ud appointed his son heir to the throne.

In 1933, the Saudi Kingdom signed a contract with the Standard Oil Company of California. Saudi politics and Wahhabi doctrines now had a wealthy support. Islam in 1400 years has converted 1.3 billion people or 20% of the world's population. In 2 years, 2020, it is estimated that 1 in 4 people of the world will be Muslims. Christendom, in a longer period, has 2.2 billion people with a great diversity and no recognized spiritual leader. There are now more Muslims than Catholics.

Can you see the psychology of Christians compared to Muslims? The Muslim worldview is Islam only, which is a religion not a country. Due to the more than 1000 Christian denominations without a leader one does not know what **all** Christians believe.

Islam is not only a matter of faith and practice, identity and loyalty, but it also transcends all others.

Islam became the leading intermediate civilization, between the ancient east and modern west in the world with its great, powerful, and rich kingdoms. They are far ahead of Christendom as an intermediate. Religious truth and political power go together supporting each other. Khomeini said, "Islam is politics, or it is nothing." **Islam makes politics, state, country, empire, and religion one community**. Islam Law is considered a holy law. The Quran is the Muslim bible, the mosque is the Muslim church, and the Ulema are the Muslim clergy. The Quran is one book, by one man, and is according to them: eternal, divine, and immutable. The Bible is more complicated as a collection of books over a long period of time but inspired by God. In Islam there is no priesthood, no mediator between God and man, no ordination, no sacrament, and no rituals. Muslims look at the whole Quran as we look at the Ten Commandments.

Islam is not only a theology, but also a culture, a worldview, and a way of life. They feel we are after their souls. There are fifty Muslim governments that cooperate with an identity like no other religion. In 1969 an Islamic conference was held in Rabat, Morocco, where the "Organization of the Islamic Conference" (OIC) was formed in Jeddah, Saudi Arabia. Here was declared the "Islamic Rights of Man".

Sir Steven Runciman, a famous historian of the Crusades said, "It was blood-thirsty Christian fanaticism that recreated the fanaticism of Islam." The Crusades were the Christian's "Holy War." Islamic fundamentalism has replaced Communism as a threat to the West.

According to Islamic law, it is lawful to wage war against infidels, apostates, rebels, and bandits. Only the first two are religious and thus considered Jihad.

In the 20th century Wahhabism became a major force. Wahhabism turns a so-called holy war into unholy terrorism. The Prophet Muhammad said, "There is no obedience in sin and do not obey a creature against his Creator." With the new terrorists the slaughter of innocent civilians is the prime objective. Their objective is to form world opinion, to gain publicity, and to inspire fear. This to them is a psychological victory. They quote Samson as killing innocent people. "The house fell upon the lords, and upon all the peoples that were therein. He slew more at his death than during his life." (Judg. 16:30) The Palestine Liberation Organization (PLO) used this technique. With modern terrorism one cannot tell the terrorists from their sympathizers, or the innocents in their presence. The disregard for human life on a vastly greater scale was seen in the actions in New York and Washington on September 11, 2001. Something new has been added.

The terrorists in the 1960's and 70's generally did not die with their victims but carried out the attacks at a safe distance. In the 1980-1988 War of Iran against Iraq, boy Iranian soldiers walked through minefields armed only with a "passport to paradise", to clear the way for the regular troops. It was said that their youth liked death as we liked life. (The Quran clearly teaches that suicide is a major sin.)

In the Hamas weekly paper on September 13, 2001, it reads, "Allah has answered our prayers." The modern terrorists say those who live under the American evil ways of life, are committing "Crimes or sins." This means to them that there are no "innocent civilians." They say America is the "worst civilization in the history of mankind." A horrible thought from the Muslims is that no one can eradicate Islamic fundamentalism. If one destroys this generation of fundamentalist, they will arise again in a new generation of terrorists.

I hope you can see that this is a fight to victory or death. Show your patriotism. Be a man of prayer for our country and support patriotism in our country. "One for all and all for one. Right for might and might for right." Jesus said, "...**he that hath no sword, let him sell his garment, and buy one.**" (Luke 22:36) Two of the disciples with Jesus when He was arrested had on swords. (Luke 22:38) Peter cut off the priest's servant's ear and Jesus healed it. (Jn 18:10, 26; Luke 22:51)

A dream without a belief is useless. Our dream and belief is in God and country.

Our hope is in the God that created the heavens and the earth. (Gen. 1:1) Yahweh is the one personal name for God in the Old Testament. In English it is LORD GOD (LORD or Yahweh is "I AM" and GOD or Elohim is Creator) and is used 5,311 times in the Old Testament and Elohim is used 2,570 times. It is the name that God gave Himself for all generations to use. (Exod. 3:14,15) Jesus used the term "I AM" for Himself. (Jn 8:58) Our hope is in the God that created the earth and all that is in it. Our God is the only power for life and death.

God Gives us Amour to Fight Spiritual Battles:

1. Helmet of Salvation

2. The Breastplate of Righteousness

3. The Shield of Faith

(Faith = Belief in God, trust that He can and will do what He says, and confirms our commitment to Him.)

4. The Belt of Truth

5. The Sandals of Peace

6. The Sword of the Spirit, which is the Word of God. The Old Testament and New Testament is the Inscription on the Shield.

Ephesians 6:11-18; Genesis 15:1; Exodus 28:29-30; Deuteronomy 33:29; 2 Samuel 22:3, 36; Psalms 3:3; 5:12; 18:35; 28:7; 33:20; 59:11; 84:9, 11; 91:4; 115:9, 10, 11; 119:114; 144:2; Proverbs 30:5; Isaiah 59:17; 61:10; 1 Thessalonians 5:8; Hebrews 4:12

It is not how **long** we are going to live, but **how** we are going to live.

M. There are Three Kinds of Death:

1. Physical death that comes to every man.
2. Spiritual death which is the condition of the lost man.
3. Eternal death, which is the fate of one who dies an unbeliever.

"Behold, **now is the day of salvation**." (2 Cor. 6:2)

The Sin unto Death:

(From my book, *Explore the Brain for the Soul*, 2008, pp.115-119.)
"If any man sees his **brother** sin a sin which is not unto death, he shall ask, and he shall give him life for them that sin not unto death. There is a sin unto death: I do not say that he shall pray for it." (1 Jn 5:16)

"For it is **impossible** for those who were **once enlightened**, and have tasted of the heavenly gift, and were made **partakers of the Holy Ghost, And have tasted the good word of God**, and **the powers of the world to come, If they shall fall away**, to renew them again unto repentance; seeing they crucify to themselves the Son of God afresh, and put him to an open shame." (Heb. 6:4-6)

"For if **we sin willfully after that we have received the knowledge of the truth, there remaineth no more sacrifice for sins**, (Christ will not be crucified again.) But a certain fearful looking for of judgment and fiery indignation, which shall devour the adversaries." (Heb. 10:26-27)

What is the "Presumptuous Sin"?

- "Keep back thy servant also from **presumptuou**s sins; let them not have dominion over me: then shall I be upright, and I shall be innocent from the great transgression." (Psa. 19:13)
- "But chiefly them that walk after the flesh in the lust of uncleanness and despise government. **Presumptuous** are they, **selfwilled, they are not afraid to speak evil of dignities.** (2 Peter 2:10)
- "But the soul that doeth ought **presumptuously**, whether he be born in the land, or a stranger, the same reproacheth the LORD; and that soul shall be cut off (killed) from among his people. (Num. 15:30)

- "So, I spake unto you; and ye would not hear, but **rebelled** against the commandment of the LORD, and went **presumptuously** up into the hill." (Deut. 1:43)
- "And the man that will do **presumptuously and** will **not hearken** unto the priest that standeth to minister there before the **LORD thy God,** or unto the judge, even that man **shall die**: and thou shalt put away the evil from Israel. And all the people shall hear, and fear, and do no more **presumptuously.**" (Deut. 17:12, 13)

N. The Ark of the Covenant

The Ark of the Covenant is one of the most important objects in the Old Testament. It represented the presence of God. It was a sacred object. This was God's special home where they could worship Him and find out His will for them. They needed a special tent to hold the Ark. It was called the "Tabernacle." (Latin for "tent".)

The LORD said thou shall put into the Ark the testimony which I give thee. (Exod. 25:16, 40:20; Deut. 10:5; I Kings 8:9)

As noted, later temples were built for the Ark. This included ones at: Shiloh, Nob, Bethel, Dan, Ephraim, and the most famous Solomon's Temple.

On top of the mercy seat was two angelic gold statues called cherubim at opposite ends. They marked the place of the LORD. In 1 Samuel 4:4 it was referred to as the Ark of the Covenant. God wrote the 10 Commandments on stone. This was the words of the covenant. (Exod. 34:28) "There was nothing in the ark save the two tables of stone, which Moses put there at Horeb, when the LORD made a covenant with the children of Israel, when they came out of the land of Egypt."(1 Kings 8:9, 1 Chr. 5:10) (There should have been a jar of manna. Exodus 16:33-34 and Aaron's rod. Numbers 17:10; Heb. 9:4) The priest, the son of Levi carried the Ark during the wilderness wanderings. (Deut. 31:9) The priest held the Ark into the flooded Jordan River and the waters parted and all the Israelites passed over dry ground. (Joshua 3:17) The Ark, trumpets, people circling the city, and shouting after seven days the walls of Jericho fell down flat. (Joshua 6:20) The Ark was at **Bethel** in Judges 20:27 (Bethel served as a sanctuary during the times of the Patriarchs, Judges and the divided kingdom. It was second only to Jerusalem as a religious center.) The Ark will be seen again when the temple of God is opened in Heaven. (Revelation 11:19, 15:15)

The kingdom split into two kingdoms, Israel and Judah in 931 B.C. Later Israel fell, (722 B.C.) then Judah fell (586 B.C.) and **Israel was no more and does exist today as in the line of David**.

"Ye shall walk in all the ways which the LORD your God hath commanded you, that ye may live, and that it may be well with you, and that ye may prolong your days in the land which ye shall possess." (Deut. 5:32)
THERE IS NO POWER IN CHOICE – THE POWER IS IN OBEDIENCE!!!
This lesson is about obedience and the results of not obeying God! "The understanding of a man is in the candle of the LORD" searching all the inward parts of the belly. (Prov. 20:27)

There Is Loyalty on Loyalty. Within Loyalty Are All Other Virtues.

The Elegy of David as Related to Saul
2 Samuel 1:17-27
(One of the greatest in the entire Bible about the death of loved ones in battle.)
David was mighty with his sword and his pen. He wanted to express a great calamity and to impress our minds and hearts. David shows his passion by lamentations (Mourning aloud.) David wanted this message to not only go far and wide, but from generation to generation. Here David gives his poem as Moses gave his song. Moses commanded that they might hear and learn and fear the LORD. And that their children "who have not known anything" may hear and learn and fear the LORD if they live and that they may be witnesses. Moses' death was approaching. (Deuteronomy 31: 10, 12, 13, 14) There is a deeper sense message in David's poem. The principle is "De mortuis nil nisi borum" (Say nothing but good concerning the dead.)

The Ark in David's Care Was His Joy.
God promised that his name would be great (7:9) as he had promised Abraham. (Genesis 12:2)

The LORD makes Eternal Promises to the House of David. This is the climax of David's life. It is the dramatic and theological center of all the Books of Samuel. **It is the most crucial theological statement in the Old Testament**. It is God's longest speech (197 words) since the time of Moses. The length itself tells us that God put a great importance on His words here. His words show that he is a promise-keeping God. David's family is the only royal family **God would ever sanction to be forever.**

The David Covenant:
The significance of the Davidic Covenant cannot be overemphasized. It becomes the nucleus of the messages of hope to be proclaimed by the future Hebrew prophets to build on for the future generations. It is in preparation for the expectation of the future Messiah. It has been said that these words are the single most significant role of any scripture in the Old Testament in shaping the Christian understanding of Jesus. Nathan's recording God's Words gives us the foundation for the seven Major New Testament teachings about Jesus:

1. The son of David (Matthew 1:1; Acts 13:22-23); Romans 1:3; 2 Timothy 2:8; Revelation 22:16, etc.)
2. One who would rise from the dead (Acts 2:30; 13:23)
3. The builder of the house for God (John 2:19-22; Hebrews 3:3-4, etc.)
4. The possessor of the throne (Hebrews 1:8; Revelation 3:21, etc.)
5. The possessor of an eternal kingdom. (1 Corinthians 15:24-25; Ephesians 5:5; Hebrews 1:8; 2 Peter 1:11, etc.)
6. The Son of God (Mark 1:1; John 20:31; Acts 9:20; Hebrews 4:14; Revelation 2:18, etc.
7. The product of the Immaculate Conception, since He had God as His Father. (Luke 1:32-35)

The David Covenant:
1. God will appoint a place for His people.

(2 Samuel 7:10, 1 Chronicles 17:9; Psalms 132: 13-14)

2. God will arrange the permanence of His people.
(2 Samuel 7:10; 1 Chronicles 17:9; Psalms 132:14)

3. God will prevent oppression from His people's enemies.
(2 Samuel 7:10; 1 Chronicles 17:9; Psalms 132:18)

4. God will set up the Davidic Dynasty, The House of David
(2 Samuel 7:12, 16; 1 Chronicles 17:10, 11; Psalms 132:11,12)

5. God will establish the Davidic Kingdom
(2 Samuel 7:12, 13, 16; 1 Chronicles 17:11; Psalms 132:17)

6. God will ensure the certainty of the Davidic throne
(2 Samuel 7:16. 1 Chronicles 17:12; Psalms 132:11,12)

7:12-16: This describes Jesus as the Messiah. The Pharisees missed this point.

12. And when thy days be fulfilled, and thou shalt sleep with thy fathers, **I will set up thy seed after thee**, which shall proceed out of thy bowels, *(This means out of your body. This links it to the Abraham Covenant.)* and I will establish **his kingdom.** Some people view this verse as proof that Jesus was indeed the Messiah.

13. He (Solomon) shall build an house for My name, *(Solomon built Him a house. Acts 7:47, but God removed the throne from Solomon. 1 Kings 11:31)* and I will establish the throne of **his kingdom** forever. *The Messiah would establish David's kingdom forever. David's successor would be King Jesus.)*

14. **I will be his father, and he shall be My son.** If he commits iniquity, **I will chasten him with the rod of men**, and with the stripes of the children of men: This refers to Jesus the Messiah. "His Father-- My Son" related to Jesus the Messiah. "For unto which of the angels said he at any time, **Thou art my Son**, this day have I begotten thee? And again, **I will be to him a Father**, and **He shall be to Me a Son**? (Hebrews 1:5) In Jewish thought the Son had the full character of the Father. The future seed of David would have the same essence as God. "If he commit iniquity" refers to the intermediate seed until the Messiah's arrival." He shall cry unto Me, Thou

art my Father, my God, and the **rock of my salvation**." (Psalms 89:26) Mary called Jesus her son, "God and Savior". (Luke 1:47)

15. But My mercy shall not depart away from him, as I took it from Saul, whom I put away before thee. This is the unconditional covenant.

16. And thine house and thy kingdom shall be established forever before thee: thy **throne shall be established forever.** (House, kingdom, and throne are fulfilled in Jesus. **Forever**, Christ's Davidic reign will **conclude human history**.)

O. Miscellaneous

1. A Few Scriptures Concerning Righteousness: (There are many.)

- *"Fulfill righteousness"* (Matthew 3:15)
- **"Blessed are they which seek righteousness."** (Matthew 5:6)
- *"Seek righteousness first and all these things shall be added unto you."* (Matthew 6:33)
- "God will judge the world in righteousness." (Acts 17:31)
- "Faith (belief, trust) is counted for righteousness." (Romans 4:5)
- "One cannot establish their own righteousness." (Romans 10:3)
- "Man believes righteousness with his heart and confesses salvation with his mouth." (Romans 10:10)
- "For the kingdom of God is not meat and drink; **but righteousness**, and peace, and joy in the Holy Ghost." (Romans 14:17)
- "Abraham's belief was counted for righteousness." (Genesis 15:6, Galatians 3:6)
- "Put on the breastplate of righteousness." (Ephesians 6:14)
- "Follow after righteousness, godliness, faith (belief, trust), love, patience, meekness." (1 Timothy 6:11)
- "Instructions from Scripture leads to righteousness." (2 Timothy 3:16)
- "God is glad if you love righteousness." (Hebrews 1:9)
- "Nevertheless we, according to his promise, look for new heavens and a new earth, wherein dwelleth righteousness." (2 Peter 3:13)
- "Thus saith the LORD":

"Keep ye judgment and do justice: for my salvation is near to come, and my **righteousness** to be revealed. Blessed is the man that doeth this, and the son of man that layeth hold on it;that keepeth the sabbath from polluting it,and keepeth his hand from doing any evil." (Isa. 56:1, 2)

2. Amen in The Bible

Amen means, "So be it,", "verily", "truly", "I tell you the truth", and amen is sometimes the name for God.

Amen's related to a curse:
Numbers 5:22

And this water that causeth the curse shall go into thy bowels, to make thy belly to swell, and thy thigh to rot: and the woman shall say, **Amen, Amen**. (So be it.)

Deuteronomy:
Chapter 27: 15-26
"Cursed be the man that maketh any graven or molten image, an abomination unto the Lord, the work of the hands of the craftsman, and putteth it in a secret place. And all the people shall answer and say, **Amen**. **Cursed be he that "dishonors" his father or his mother. And all the people shall say, Amen.**_Cursed be he that removeth his neighbour's landmark. And all the people shall say, **Amen**. Cursed be he that maketh the blind to wander out of the way (astray). And all the people shall say, **Amen.** Cursed be he that perverteth the judgment (hold justice from) of the stranger, fatherless, and widow. And all the people shall say, **Amen**. Cursed be he that lieth with his father's wife; because he uncovereth his father's skirt. And all the people shall say, **Amen.** Cursed be he that lieth with any manner of beast. And all the people shall say, **Amen.** Cursed be he that lieth with his sister, the daughter of his father, or the daughter of his mother. And all the people shall say, **Amen.** Cursed be he that lieth with his mother in law. And all the people shall say, **Amen.** Cursed be he that smiteth his neighbour secretly. And all the people shall say, **Amen.** Cursed be he that taketh reward to slay an innocent person. And all the

people shall say, **Amen**. Cursed be he that confirmeth not all the words of this law to do them. And all the people shall say, **Amen.**"

3. What is Truth?

If you do not understand, you are not of the Truth! (John 18:37)

God, Jesus, the Holy Spirit and the Scriptures are Truth. From the study of this one can learn the hundreds of God's truths but can never learn them all.

Jesus did not answer Pilate and Pilate did not wait for an answer because Jesus essentially had said he would not understand. "Pilate therefore said unto him, Art thou a king then? Jesus answered; **Thou sayest that I am a king. To this end was I born, and for this cause came I into the world, that I should bear witness unto the truth. Every one that is of the truth heareth my voice.**" (Jn 18:37) This excluded Pilate and many of those we know.

The study of truth requires a basic knowledge of the scriptures for one to even begin to understand or be able to discuss truth. Jesus answered and said unto them, **"Ye do err, not knowing the scriptures, nor the power of God."** (Matt. 22:29)

The same is true in **teaching the anatomy of the brain**. Here is one example. What is the amygdala? It is a nucleus complex in the brain. (**Truth is in the Bible**.) Where in the brain? In the temporal lobe. (It is the Old Testament) Tell me more about it. It is in the dorsal-medial temporal lobe in the lateral ventricle. (Somewhere in the later part of the Old Testament). (**Unless you know some anatomy you are lost already**). What else? It has 8 nuclei in the complex. These connections go to all parts of the brain. (The truth of the Bible goes to all the Bible). What does it do? It controls our emotions or how we respond to life's experiences. How does it do this? (Again, you are lost because you do not understand the electrical and chemical methods in the brain to conduct our emotions. Just as a study of God's word must be done to understand its truths.) To understand this one must have studied and have a knowledge of how the main areas of the brain function. In the same way in order to understand truth one must have a broad knowledge of the Bible. To say that God is truth, Jesus is truth, the Holy Spirit is truth, is the truth, but it does not answer the question for a non-believer as Pilate was. One must have knowledge of God, of Jesus, of the Holy Spirit and the Bible to understand truth.

Truth is God, Jesus, Holy Spirit, and the sixty-six books of Scriptures as revealed to us through prayer and study, teaches us how to live, but is different from a study of the brain in that it teaches us how not to live or die.

What is Truth?

Truth is God, Truth is Jesus, Truth is the Holy Spirit, Truth is the Scriptures.

What is God? What is Jesus? What is the Holy Spirit? What is the Scriptures: Truth is all the above as noted in the Scriptures. God describes Himself in the Scriptures as "the Truth" is revealed.

The Answer: Truth is God, Jesus and the Holy Spirit, as described in the Scriptures and interpreted after study, prayer, and experiencing God.

The study of truth goes on! The magnitude of this paper is to reveal the magnitude of the question. **"What is Truth?"** (It comes to my mind that no intelligent person would even ask the question except in an environment that would allow a significant amount of time for an explanation.)

Man, as man will never understand all of God's truths. Daniel did not understand his own prophecy that God had given him. When he told God, he did not understand what God had told him. God informed him that he would not understand till the end of time. (Daniel 12: 8,7) Paul said, "the peace of God, which passeth all understanding, shall keep your hearts and minds through Christ Jesus." (Phil. 4:7)

We do not understand this. The message is that we will never understand all of God's truths and we should not speak or act like we do! **We understand that we do not understand it all.**

4. After these many pages do you understand that you do not understand?

If not, read on:

In the Bible there are 3, 294 questions. There are 1,260 promises (do you know them?) 6,468 Commands (do you know them?), 3,268 verses of fulfilled prophesy (do you know them?), 8000 predictions (do you know them?) (**Amazing Bible Timeline, Bible Facts and Statistics, https://amazingbibletimeline.com/blog/q10_bible_facts_statistics/, (Accessed April 29, 2013**)

Therefore, anyone who says they believe or understand everything in the Bible cannot be academically or honestly correct. It is a simply not possible, "to know it all."

What is Truth? Didn't you notice, "Truth is what God says in the Bible."

When I see you Sunday and ask you, "What is truth?" The above answer will get you off the hook", but it does not answer the question.

If you know the whole Bible by memory you can answer it in 70 hours. (The Bible can be read in 70 hours). But, do not be like Pilate and ask a "stupid" question unless you know the anatomy of the brain.

Two Answers to the question: ***"What is Truth?"***

"Truth is what God says in the Bible."
We as Christians already have the "Truth". It is within us. The Holy Spirit is our real teacher.

There are many answers:
God is Love is truth. God is Grace is Truth. God is Mercy is Truth, etc. The name "God" appears 3,358 times in the Bible, each one associated with a truth. The name "Lord" appears 7,736 times in the Bible, each one associated with a truth.

There are at least 30 blessings and miracles received from the first chapter of Mark alone.

Nine Blessings in Mark Chapter 2.

Six Blessings in Mark Chapter 3.

Sixteen Blessings in Mark Chapter 4.

Eleven Blessings in Mark Chapter 5.

Twelve Blessings in Mark Chapter 6.

Eleven Blessings in Mark Chapter 7.

Thirteen Blessings in Mark Chapter 8.

Chapter 8

The Feeding of the 4000

The Unbelieving Pharisees Request a Sign

The Leaven of the Pharisees is Hypocrisy

The Healing of the Blind Man ("I Believe, help my unbelief.")

Peter's Famous Confession ("Thou Art the Christ".)

The First Prediction of Jesus Death and Resurrection

The Cost of Discipleship

Twenty Blessings in Mark Chapter 9.

Eight Blessings in Mark Chapter 10.

Seven Blessings in Mark Chapter 11.

Fourteen Blessings in Mark Chapter 12.

Thirteen Blessings in Mark Chapter 13.

Teaching in the Temple

Mark's Description of the Apocalypse (The Last Things)

The Sorrows (Matthew 24:8)

Persecution, Abomination Spoken of by Daniel (11:31; 12:11)

False Messiahs

The Coming of Jesus (The Rapture)

"My Words Shall Not Pass Away, Watch and Pray, Watch

Thirteen Blessings in Mark Chapter 14.

Chapters 15 and 16

The Trial Before Pilate

The Mockery

The Crucifixion
The Tearing of the Temple Curtain
Jesus Death and Burial
The Empty Tomb, "He is Risen" Go to Galilee, there you will see Him
The Great Commission

And he said unto them, **"Go ye into all the world, and preach the gospel to every creature."** (16:15) "So then after the Lord had spoken unto them, he was received up into heaven, and sat on the right hand of God. And they went forth, and preached everywhere, the Lord working with them, and confirming the word with signs following. Amen." (16: 19, 20)

The Great Commission was given also in the other three gospels, Matthew 28: 19, 20; Luke 24:47; John 20:21; Mark 16:15; Acts 1:8 Hear now the repeated command of Jesus and the Great Commission in 4 more places in the Bible:
Matthew 28: 19, 20
Luke 24: 47-49
John 20: 21, 22, 23
Acts 1:8, 9-15

This was a dangerous mission. They were all killed except John. (This is 11 deaths out of 12. They had replaced Judas with Matthias, which is 92% mortality.) They were going to tell the world about sin and die for doing it. Who was their enemy? Who were they to fight? The same one we fight! The Devil! Do you understand what "liberation theology means"? It is the doctrine that sin was not just a personal problem and that society has to be reformed as well as the person in society. To do this through the ages Christianity had to become a revolutionary force and people died. When Christ comes again it will be as a lion, not as a lamb. For the blessings in Chapters 15 and 16 of Mark Read them for yourself while you are alone.

Mark teaches us about Jesus, His Teachings, His Death, and His Resurrection: Mark challenges us with the cost of discipleship as described by Jesus. The cost for Jesus was death. The cost for us is faith, belief, trust, and commitment. Mark was constantly moving with Jesus and looking up. Are we moving and looking up or are we trying to climb through the "eye of the needle"?

5. War and the Philosophy of War (Polemology)

I have been studying War for 50 years since my return from Vietnam in 1969. I went to Vietnam to learn to do surgery on war injuries to the brain. In the process I began studying the causes of war. My first non-medical book on Biblical Beliefs has 48 pages on Peace and War. (2006) My war course is usually 6 hours. The lecture is usually 40-80 minutes.

To my surprise I learned that a true science of war had never come into being. The term Polemology, the "study of war" only became a word in 1946.

War: (War is as old as Man.)

It takes three things to make war!
MONEY! MONEY! MONEY! (Money is the root of all civilizations.)

There are 25,000 books about the War Between the States (Civil War). These are about battles only. I have studied war like one might study cancer. What are the indications for war? What are the effects and results of war? When is a country ready for war?

6. What About Women in Combat? (See 5 in Book One)

Industrial and military society has changed the place of women in society. Religion has tried to hold them back, calling it "a design of creation." Protestants "abolished nuns and had less plans for women in the ministry." They are now assigning women to submarines.

One of the most famous war historians, who had not done his homework, made a profound personal speculation about women. He said, "Superiority is accorded within humanity not to the sex which gives birth, but to the sex which kills"!! He was referring to male superiority. He did not know about the thousands of Russian women and girls who courageously fought for their motherland. They made up Women's Fighter Regiments, Bomber Regiments, and the famous "Night Witches". Flying low and slow at night they would target the German combat troops when they had pulled back to rest. They cut their engines, glided over the troops, and dropped their bombs. They would restart their engines and return home. The small engines and canvas-covered airplanes were not detectable by radar. The infrared seekers on German airplanes could not see them. The psychological effect was one of terror on the Germans. In one night, they raided the Germans 18 times. They were truly "Night Witches". Sexism was high. Men would not fly as "wingmen" with women and would not even fly airplanes that had been maintained and serviced by women. As a result, all the Women Fighters, Bombers, and Night Bombers ("Night Witches") had women mechanics and ground crews. The Women Fighter Pilots flew more than 4000 sorties each and in 125 battles had 38 confirmed kills. The female pilots won thousands of Russian Orders, Medals, and 29 won the title of Hero of the Soviet Union. (23 of these went to the Night Witches who flew over 24,000 sorties.)

Never, never, never under estimate the genius of women and their desire to defeat men. To combat the "Night Witches" the Germans placed searchlights in a circle. The "Night Witches" usually flew in groups of two. They began going in groups of three. Two would go ahead slowly, low, and fly through the Searchlights. While all the lights were following the two, the third would enter and bomb them. They would regroup with a different two until all three of them had dropped their bombs.

There are many other reports of heroes and successful women in combat. To think otherwise is to be historically ignorant in the story of war. However, the Women Air Force Service Pilots (WASP) was prohibited from flying in combat in WWII.

There are at least three points that must be considered in a study of war:
These three points will be emphasized. They are:
1. Loyalty to country
2. The influence of religion on war
3. Military and civilian discipline

I want to make it clear: I am loyal to my country. I had annual Navy orders in my hand for 62 years. This allowed me to go and lecture or assist on our military bases. I am a Christian. I have taught Sunday school for over 48 years. In this report I am only reporting the results of my scientific study. **Some of it is not good news**.

We all know about war. We are not experts on making war with terrorists.
The Influence of Religion on War:

Christianity and Islam are the only religions that need to be reviewed. None of the other religions have any effect on war. (Religion has moved to philosophy and philosophy has moved our minds from Heaven to earth.):

7. Islam Must be Studied.

The first thing to be noted is that Islam **is not a state**, but a world order. There is no perceptible military objective. There is no country that we can declare war against to defeat Islam. Islam and Terrorists are everywhere, all over the world. According to the Quran, (The most influential book ever written by one man.) the propagation of Islam **by arms is a religious duty**. War is a command from their god. Fortunately for us many Muslims are not good Muslims, just as most Christians are not good Christians and most Jews are not good Jews.

A Brief History of War Between Islam and Christianity:
We now are living in the third time of history when Islam poses a military threat to Christianity. One must keep in mind that the Islamic military threat is primarily against Christians and secondarily against Americans because America is where the Christians are. If we would all convert to Islam, which is their real objective, the war with us would be over. The Muslims say they will be at war until Islam controls the world. It is not personal. No Muslim wants to control the world. They want Islam to control the world. They are not fighting for their freedom. They are fighting for their religion.

It has been said, "**Religion supplies the dynamics of war**." Muslims say, "**Muslim youths love death, as you love life**. We can survive in the desert by drinking water from the bellies of dead camels." Wake up America. Their war cry is as every American heard at Fort Hood, "**Allah akbar**" **Arabic for "God is great."** As noted in the long history of conflicts the only way Christians can relate to Islam is to convert to Islam or go to war.

Religious beliefs do not predispose nations to peace. Even during periods of great faith Christians fought Christians and Muslims fought Muslims far more than they fought each other.

8. Where Does Terrorism Begin?

What makes a suicide bomber?

In Islam countries students spend six hours per day memorizing the Koran. They have no lessons in math, geography, history, or computers. The Koran is "all they need to know" to understand the universe. There are two forces on earth. Muslims and Infidels. All infidels are enemies.

The Saudi leaders control 71,000 mosques and the entire educational system in Saudi Arabia and teach the most radical form of Islam. They have built many more mosques and schools in many countries around the world. Christians have no comparable worldly educational system. They are educating their people into Islam and the Koran and we are not educating our people in religion or the Bible.

The world population is 6.8 billion people. 2.2 billion people are Christians, 1.3 billion are Muslim, and 1.1 billion are Roman Catholics. **An eighth-grade textbook there teaches: "Allah cursed Jews and Christians and turned some of them into apes and pigs."** (This is in the Koran) (Koran 5:60-61) **In the ninth grade**: "Judgment will not come until the Muslims fight the Jews and kill them." **In the tenth grade**: "Be loyal to each other and consider the infidels the enemy. You exist as Muslims respecting Muslim values alone." Saudi textbooks that have been taught **in America** in Arabic teach "A Muslim is automatically a better human being." The Muslims that become citizens must swear allegiance to America, but the

Koran says that if one has to lie to propel Islam it is o.k. **Good Muslims cannot be loyal Americans. Good Muslims must be loyal to Islam,** which is not a country.

The Bible:
The Bible collecting dust on the shelves has been referred to as "gentle prisoners, held in captivity by lazy Christians." **Christians recognize the Bible** as the word of God and must depend on the Bible for all moral decisions.

Moses says in Exodus 15:3 "The LORD (Yahweh Elohim) is a man of war: The LORD is His name."

Both the Bible and the Quran speaks of pacifism as being bad. (Ecclesiastes 10:4; Quran 8:16)

Christ mentioned physical war only two times. The first time *"And ye shall hear of wars and rumors of wars."* (Matthew 24:6) This is the origin or the term "forever wars."

The second time was when He gave a parable of a king going to war. *"Or suppose a king is about to go to war against another king. Will he not first sit down and consider whether he is able with his 10,000 men to oppose the one coming against him with 20,000. If he is not able, he will send a delegation while the other is still a long way off and will ask for terms of peace."* (Luke 14:31, 32) We must assume from the parable that if the king in the parable felt he were able the war would proceed.

Jesus said, *"Render therefore unto Caesar the things which are Caesars and unto God the things that are God's."* (Mark 12:17)

Jesus again said, *"He that hath no sword, let him sell his clothes and go buy one."* (Luke 22:36) Jesus knew that the possibility might arise that the people needed a sword for protection. Barbarians sometimes invaded their villages. This applies today to gun control when many think they are needed for protection. Two of Jesus' Disciples had on a sword when He was arrested. (Luke 22:38) Peter cut off one of the priest's servant's ear. (John 18:10, 26) and Jesus "healed" the ear. (Luke 22:51)

One simply cannot use the Bible as a basis to oppose a just war. That is biblical ignorance! Pacifists are Biblically Illiterate. It just doesn't work when someone is shooting at you!

The Great Commission (Mark 16:15) to Christians from Jesus is to go into all the world and preach the gospel. The Muslim is instructed by Allah to kill anyone who comes in their world and attempts to convert them from Islam to Christianity.

Do you get the idea? It is a "catch 22". The Muslims fight each other and us at the same time.

"Holy Wars" between Christians and Muslims has existed for over 1000 years.

In 2005 there were 660 murders in New York City alone. In three years in New York there will be as many murders as in 911. In 5 years in New York City there have been 5,280 murders since 9/11. This is more than twice as many that died in 9/11. There are 3 million Americans in prison or jail at any one time. **Almost 400,000 are illegal aliens.** (At $50,000 each that relates to 20 billion dollars per year.) There are 600,000 prisoners released each year in the U.S. This is 6 million in 10 years and represents a persistent criminal base. There are 52,000 sex offenders listed in Florida. 800 did not report in and are lost to the police. Last year there were **34 murders of school children in Chicago alone.** In June 2010 in Chicago alone on one weekend there were **ten killed and sixty wounded.** In nine years (1991-2000) there were 290,000 estimated cases of sexual abuse in American **public** schools. There are 32,222 cases of sexual abuse in American public schools each year. (**Newsweek**, April 12, 2010, p. 42) It is dangerous to send our children to some public schools. The police and the F.B.I. have lost control of crime. They just react to it. Academic elites have led the way in devaluing patriotism and American history. Once or twice a year we pledge allegiance to the American flag and our patriotism ends there.

Something new in crime: Crime on military bases. Do you think **thieves**; particularly thieves in the military are going to be loyal to America in a show down? It just won't happen!

Aristotle (384-322 B.C.) "…**good laws, if they are not obeyed, constitute a bad government**."

Immigrants and the Military:
The ability to recruit the needed military men has been stretched. 40% of Air Force active duty enlisted men failed their fitness test. Are they fit to fight? Of course not! As in many historical armies' foreign-born people are being recruited. 63,000 immigrants are now on active duty in U.S. forces. This is 5%. Another 37,250 military immigrants have become U.S. citizens since 2001.

9. What is America's Standing in the World Today?

We all feel and brag that America is the greatest country in the world. I still believe this but look at more facts. Our leadership and perhaps our form of democracy have allowed us to drop behind in many areas.

10. What Are a Countries Standard of Greatness?

- In Exports: We are behind China and Germany
- In Standard of living: We are behind Norway, France, Canada, and Australia
- In Home ownership rate: We are behind Canada, Belgium, Spain, Norway, and Portugal.
- In Affordable higher education: We are 13th. At one time the United States had the highest graduation rate in the world. It is now 10th.
- In 4th grade math. We are 11th.
- In Quality of health care: We are 37th (WHO)
- With 3 million members the Chinese have the world's largest military force.
- By the **usual data**: America cannot claim to be the greatest country in the world over France, Switzerland, China or Russia.

Mercantile wisdom, (Money) is taking over the world!

Why do people want to come here? Get it out of your head it you think they come here for the love of America or freedom. They come because of money. People move to better themselves economically. They come here and get on welfare and Medicaid and make more than they do in Mexico. They send money home to family each month. In one year, they sent 30 billion dollars back to Mexico or Latin America. (Worldwide immigrants send 230 billion dollars home each year.) **There are still great migrations in the world**. Mexicans come to America; the Turks go to Germany, Indians and Pakistani go to Britain, and Arabs to France. **Most of the world is becoming a mixed culture.** This has been called the "science of chaos". **On any one-day about 100 million people are in the process of migration.**

11. Why Do Empires Fail?

I reviewed 18 empires that failed. The major cause of failure in 11 or 61% of the 18 was the major influx of immigrants that changed the character of the country. In the other 7 it included this but also loss of leadership, being invaded by superior military power or Muslims, loss of unity, many wars, famine, plagues, and cruelty with the result of having many enemies. Two examples include: the Mongol Empire (1204-1405) and the Ottoman Empire (1640-1783). The Mongol Empire (1204-1405) of Genghis Kahn was the largest land empire ever created. It contained 100,000,000 (100 million) people and extended from Hungary to Korea. Because of loss of unity and original cultural identity by local uprisings and migration of larger nomadic Turkish population they began losing power. The Mamlukes (slaves who became leaders) defeated the Mongol state in 1260. By 1313 all the Moguls had converted to Islam.

After 600 years the Ottoman (1640-1783) rule came to an end and the Republic of Turkey was founded. They had many internal and external pressures. The "regent mothers" in the sultan's harem became politically powerful. They were known as the "Sultamate of Women." With the accession of Mehment male authority was restored. A religious group, The

Jenissaries, was lazy and parasitic. Mahmut II killed thousands of them and that ended Jainism. The Ottoman attack and defeat at Vienna in 1683 was the last Ottoman assault in Christian Europe. **Crime and bandits were common as the government was unable to maintain order.** They were affected by Britain, France (Napoleons invasion (1805), and Russia (Crimean War 1853-56) and later invasion). **This is the only example of a youth group playing a role in an empire.** They took full control and introduced liberal reform. The "**Young Turks**" took over the weak empire but could not maintain it. They could not defend the country and lost land to Italy and the Balkan Wars (1912-13). In World War I the Ottoman Empire was no more and reduced to Turkey alone. There is talk in America of the young people taking over the political parties and the Southern Baptist Convention in the United States. History reveals that they could not maintain either one.

The **threat of global atomic war has gone down, but the risk of a nuclear attack has gone up.**" A new disorder is seen in **more nations** getting nuclear weapons. America's position is that "as long as these weapons exist, the United States will maintain a safe, secure, and effective arsenal to deter any enemy." Due to "lose" weapons, **nuclear terrorism poses a greater threat than a nuclear war.** Since 1996, a **Comprehensive Nuclear Test Ban Treaty** (CTBT) has not been accomplished.

A long delayed "**Nuclear Posture Review**" is to be released in the near future. (A war scholar is reminded that in the 12th century the pope tried to ban the crossbow. The most ignorant of all peace treaties was the "Pact of Paris" in 1928. This treaty outlawed war for all time. It was the "Day We Outlawed War." The Japanese broke the treaty in two years when they invaded Manchuria in 1931.) There have been hundreds of wars since then.

12. Nine Countries Now Have Nuclear Weapons

- Russia (12,000) (Russia's conventional forces have withered, and they have an increased dependence on nuclear weapons.
- United States (9,400)
- France (300)

- China (240)
- United Kingdom (185)
- Israel (80)
- Pakistan (70-90)
- India (60-80)
- North Korea (<10)

Our isolation has come to an end. The entire Islamic world as well as our allies has seen our vulnerability. The American psychic has changed. There is fear in America. In this type of war civilians will be killed as in all wars. (The number of documented civilian deaths in the Iraq war between 2003 and December 31, 2018, was **205,188**). https://www.statista.com/statistics/269729/documented-civilian-deaths-in-iraq-war-since-2003/ (accessed February 10, 2019

We must remember that God has said, "There will always be wars…" and reason says we should always be ready for war.

War is the people's examination? In war you either fail or pass! It is yet to be determined if we fail or pass with Afghanistan? – You and me the people will either Fail or Pass in this war!

13. What is the Answer to the Declining Parts of America?

Address:
1. Loyalty to country (America!)
2. The influence of religion on war against us. Our country cannot exist without a religious base. Religion is everywhere and always will be. It cannot be ignored. We must take a stand. Is there a God or not? He will not go away.
3. Military and civilian descriptive. The Bible is the number one book in the world. It must be taught, or one becomes illiterate.
4. Immigration must be met, and the effect controlled by education. In 18 great empires that failed the failure in 61% was immigration causing a change in the culture of the nation.
5. Why are we getting behind in the world in: exports, standard of living, home ownership rate, affordable higher education, 4th

grade math, quality, of health care, "China Buys the World and it's China's World, we just live in it," how many military forces are larger than ours and why is France, Switzerland, China, and Russia claiming to be the greatest in the world? These highly publicized problems will not go away on their own.

6. Does the world know that we can respond with a terrorist-like limited nuclear attack? When should we use it to stop the death of Americans dying in wars that seem to come to nothing?

7. How are we addressing the eight new countries that have become independent?

8. 33% of the world's population believes in God and Christ. Why don't we?

9. Does anyone think we are going to be the only country of the world that survives without God? If you do look at the facts in this report.

What Is Loyalty?

The word *"loyalty"* is not in the Bible, but it is clearly covered under the principle of honesty. Be honest and wear your testimony.

Royce first used the term ***"loyal to loyalty"***. Loyalty is the supreme good in life, and **within it is contained all other virtues**. If one tries to get away from loyalty, they fall into disloyalty in many areas. It is wrong to try to destroy the spirit of loyalty. One should seek to associate its fine spirit with a cause worthy of a person's devotion, which is **above themselves** and a **matter of enlightened intelligence**. The *"loyal to loyalty"* and *"loyalty to loyalties"* preserves intact the beautiful spirit of loyalty within each individual. To do otherwise is to injure one's spirit of loyalty.

Billy Graham's Prayer for Our Nation

"Heavenly Father, we come before you today to ask your forgiveness and to seek your direction and guidance. We know Your Word says, 'Woe to those who call evil good,' but that is exactly what we have done. We have lost our spiritual equilibrium and reversed our values. We have **exploited the poor and called it the lottery**. We have **rewarded laziness and called it welfare**. We **have killed our unborn and called it choice**. We have **shot abortionists and called it justifiable.** We have **neglected to discipline our children and called it building self-esteem.** We have **abused power and called it politics.** We have **coveted our neighbor's possessions and called it ambition.** We have **polluted the air with profanity and pornography and called it freedom of expression.** We have **ridiculed the time-honored values of our forefathers and called it enlightenment.** Search us, Oh God, and know our hearts today; cleanse us from every sin and Set us free. Amen!"

Leadership

I have listed my three C's of leadership as **competency**, **confidence**, and **commitment**. In positions of leadership if one is not competent it is recognized early. If one does not have confidence it is recognized under times of stress. If one does not have commitment, then a resignation is forth coming.

- **Aristotle** said, "There exists in nature a principle of leadership and rulership, as also of social union based on justice and expediency." He also said. "The good leader must have ethos, pathos, and logos. The ethos is his moral character, which is his ability to persuade. The pathos is his ability to touch feelings, or to move people emotionally. The Logos is his ability to give solid reasons for an action, and to move people intellectually."

- **Sigmund Freud** said, "That men are divided into leaders and the led, which is an inequality impossible to correct." In this competitive world there is always jealousy around a leader.

- **Lao-Tzu** said, "A sound leader aims to open people's hearts, calms their wills, fills their stomachs, braces their bones, clarifies their thoughts, and cleans their needs."

- **Jane Austen** related the dangers of pride, prejudice, and lack of virtue and emphasized the importance of family and friends.

- **Albert Einstein** said, "Try not to become a man of success, but try to become a man of value."

- **Helen Keller** said, "Your success and happiness lie in you."

- **Voltaire** said, "Work hard and cultivate one's garden". (Cultivate means labor for productivity and, thus, your part of civilization.)

Suicide and Euthanasia:
Suicide: **The word suicide is not in the Bible**. There are no laws related to it. However, human life is sacred since we are made in God's image. (Genesis 1:27) God has the power over all life. "And Job said, Naked came I out of my mother's womb, and naked shall I return thither: the Lord gave, and the Lord hath taken away; blessed be the name of the Lord." (Job 1:21)

The only way to escape from life is to die.

14. The Military Person's Prayer

(The Sailor, Soldier, Marine, Air Force, and Coast Guard's Prayer)

Lord thank you for this day. We know that you are our God and that your love will last a thousand generations. (Deut. 7:9)

We know that you can deliver us from evil; for thine is the kingdom and the power, and the glory forever. (Matt. 6:13)

We know the world is yours and everything in it, and we are yours. (Psalms 24:1) Every heartbeat, every breath, every muscle twitch comes from Thee! Without your love, we are nothing. (I Cor. 13:2)

You have directed us to "Put on the whole armour of God, and take a stand against powers of darkness, and spiritual forces of evil. We thank thee for the helmet of salvation, the breastplate of righteousness, the shield of faith, the belt of truth, the sandals of peace, and the sword of thy word." (Eph. 6:11-17)

Many of your peaceful and innocent people in this county and around the world have been killed by your enemies that follow a false god of hatred and violence. We ask that you bless and comfort all who have lost fathers, mothers, husbands, wives, brothers, sisters and even children. We know you are a Father to the fatherless, a defender of widows, and you relieve loneliness in families. (Psalms 68: 4-6)

You have said in your law, "You shall have no other gods before me." (Exod. 20:3; Deut: 5:7) and the "Joy of the godless last but a moment and they shall perish forever." (Job 20: 5,7) We pray as David prayed, "As smoke is blown away by the wind, may the enemies be blown away." (Psa. 68:2) The godless have declared war on your people. They walk in darkness and their eyes are blinded to You. (1 John 2:11)

Those of us in the military know we have your authority to respond when You said, ***"Give to Caesar what is Caesar's and to God what is God's.*** (Matt. 22:21) According to Your justice we know our godless enemies will be brought down. They are an abomination to You God, Your people, and Your world. (Deut. 18:19)

We ask for strength and wisdom to carry out your will. We remember the past. Now we look to the future. Give our leaders and us the courage to make the hard decisions of war. We know we must go to war, for peace to return to the world. The way of peace the godless do not know. (Romans 3:17) We know many of us may die just as our fathers, grandfathers and great grandfathers died so that we could be free. We are being held hostage by a warring and godless group. Let us die if necessary, so that we can be free again. We commit our lives and souls to thee!

Let the enemy know he has awakened "the sleeping and peaceful giant," that fights under the banner of the true and mighty God. We proceed under your guidance and will "not stop" until the enemy is vanquished. Then Freedom will return to America!

Help us to be strong in Your sight, And America will be strong.

Help us to be "good" in Your sight, And America will be good.

To God be the Glory. (Rom. 11:36. Eph. 3:21, 2 Tim. 4:18, I Peter 4:11, 2 Peter 3:18, Rev. 1:6) Amen! And Amen!

It's not over! Until it's over?

Rear admiral Joseph H. Miller

XIII. Rear Admiral Joseph H. Miller World Experience

Rear Admiral Joseph H. Miller (MC) USNR retired from the Navy in 1986 after 34 years (credited with nine years of active duty) Since retirement with annual Permissive Orders he has had consecutive Navy Orders since 1952 or for 63 years. The Permissive Orders included informal visits to Navy hospitals. RADM Miller completed three years as the first reservist to serve as a Deputy Surgeon General, Pentagon, and concurrently as Commander Naval Reserve Force, Force Medical Officer 1983-1986. On active duty, he served as Chief of Neurosurgery, National Naval Medical Center, and subsequently as Chief of Neurosurgery, US Naval Hospital, Da Nang, Vietnam. As a consultant to the Surgeon General RADM Miller chaired a committee of five prominent civilian leaders of neurosurgery to develop a Navy neurosurgical residency. While in the Pentagon, with Dr. Barry, he wrote and staffed the directive for the establishment of Physician Reservists in Medical Universities and Schools (PRIMUS). RADM Miller has been to Washington, D.C. and Bethesda, Maryland, more than 100 times, Yokosuka, Japan 40 times, San Diego 24 times, Pearl Harbor 22 times, and every other Navy Hospital in the world. (For two months, he personally provided interval neurosurgery coverage at the Tripler Army

Medical Center, Hawaii) He served in the Joint Chiefs of Staff (J4) war planning section as the only Flag officer. Later, at his recommendation, a Flag officer billet was established in J4. The first assignment was a Navy Reserve Flag Officer.

He had duty with the Commander in Chief Central Command, MacDill Air Force Base, December 1982, February 1983, and February 1984. RADM Miller's Military decorations include: Legion of Merit, National Defense Service Medal, Armed Forces Reserve Medal, Navy Unit Commendations, Republic of Vietnam Civil Action Unit Citation, Vietnam Service Medal, Republic of Vietnam Gallantry Cross Unit Citation, Navy Pistol Marksmanship, Meritorious Unit Commendation, Combat Action Ribbon, and Navy Commendation Medal with Combat V.

In civilian life RADM Miller practiced and taught Neurosurgery from 1960 through December 2000. (40 years, 10,000 operations, operated on 1 in 10 patients seen, thus he had 100,000 patients). He served as Chief of Neurosurgery at Methodist University Hospital, Memphis, and Vice-Chairman of the Department of Neurosurgery University of Tennessee and University of Tennessee Training Director in Neurosurgery at the Methodist University Hospital. (1983-2000)

RADM Miller was Founder and Director of the Memphis Neurosciences Center at Methodist Hospital and the University of Tennessee. He developed an international academic interchange in Neurosurgery with 27 countries. He is currently on the Voluntary Faculty of USF Medical School, Tampa, Florida.

He is certified by the American Board of Neurosurgery and his memberships include: The American Association of Neurological Surgeons, The Society of Neurological Surgeons, Congress of Neurological Surgeons, The American College of Surgeons, The Society of Medical Consultants to the Armed Forces. Civilian activities include: Mission Service Corps, **The White House, May 1978**, served on the Boards of Union University, Mars Hill College, Samford University, and Regions Bank. He has researched and lectured on the Philosophy of War more than ninety-six times.

RADM Miller has been a Christian for 77 years, a Southern Baptist Deacon for 67 years, and taught Sunday school for 58 years. He is currently a member of First Baptist Church, Brandon, Florida. He is a 5,258-hour pilot and recently passed the course to be a Coast Guard Captain. He is married to Cathy Miller (40 years) and they live in Apollo Beach, Florida.

He developed 24 Clinical Teaching Systems as a "cerebral computer model". He was an invited medical lecturer 56 times and had numerous Medical Journal publications.

He is a graduate of the Medical College of Georgia with an M.D. degree in 1955 and Mercer University with an AB degree in 1951, Mars Hill college, A.B. 1949. He was also a proud graduate of Ludowici, Georgia High School where they were second place in the state in Basketball in 1947.

Author of 16 Books Since Retirement

Mysteries of the Southern Baptist Beliefs Revealed

You Live! You Die! Who Decides?

Faked Disability: A Shame of America

Explore the Brain for the Soul

Calvin, The Psychopath

The One Love (Cathy Miller, co-author)

Eighty Years Behind the Masts (My Autobiography)

After 400 Years of the King James Bible

The Few

Scriptures for Life

Obedience

Radical Islam Hopes to Take Over Our Country (The Sword of Islam)

Eternal Truth

100-Years First Baptist Church Brandon, Florida, It's Mission and

Vision for the Future (19 December 1915 to 19 December 2015) (Cathy Miller, co-author)

War, 2017, (Cathy Miller, co-author)

Citizen Militia, 2019, (Cathy Miller, co-author)

The author has traveled in many places in the world where Eternal Truth is not known! (My wife, Cathy, has traveled with me on a vast majority of these trips).

He has been a member of eight Southern Baptist Churches and has served on virtually every committee of a Southern Baptist Church. Because of this he can see that the success of First Baptist Church Brandon is due to the long-term ministries and many men and women leaders through all the years among the membership, which are noted in the ***100th Year Anniversary of First Baptist Church*** which he authored and published.

There are three great religions of the world including Christianity, Islam, and Judaism. My recent interest is primarily Islam as an invasive religion with the sword, and Christianity which, is invasive with love. Islam is truly worldwide, and one must have a worldwide vision of it. Islam wants to take over the world. They are an enemy to the Christian world.

The author has traveled to the seven continents of the world. He has studied nations which are mostly Islamic and those that are mostly Christian.

This includes Asia: Iran, Lebanon, Israel, Turkey, India, Thailand, Vietnam, Malaysia, Japan, South Korea, Taiwan, Russia, Philippines, and Indonesia. He has worked with Islamic friends from Pakistan and Bangladesh in the United States.

In Africa: Morocco, (Rabat, Casablanca, Fez, and Marrakesh), Algiers, Tunisia, Libya, and Egypt.

In the Pacific: Australia, (Sydney, Melbourne, Adelaide, Perth, Exmouth), Tasmania, Wake Island, New Caledonia, Fiji (Suva), New Zealand (Auckland, Wellington, Christchurch) and in Hawaii.

All over Europe including Poland, Czech Republic, Hungary, Greece, the Ukraine (Kiev) and Europe, Russia (Moscow, St. Petersburg)

The author has four post-graduate degrees or certificates and has written extensively on academic subjects, the Philosophy of War, (lectured more than 90 plus times on the subject) and theology.

XIV. Experience for Writing the War Book

The author has traveled in many places in the world where Eternal Truth is not known! (My wife, Cathy, has traveled with me on a vast majority of these trips).

He has been a member of eight Southern Baptist Churches and has served on virtually every committee of a Southern Baptist Church. Because of this he can see that the success of First Baptist Church Brandon is due to the long-term ministries and many men and women leaders through all the years among the membership, which are noted in the ***100th Year Anniversary of First Baptist Church*** which he authored and published.

There are three great religions of the world including Christianity, Islam, and Judaism. My recent interest is primarily Islam as an invasive religion with the sword, and Christianity which, is invasive with love. Islam is truly worldwide, and one must have a worldwide vision of it.

The author has traveled to the seven continents of the world. He has studied nations which are mostly Islamic and those that are mostly Christian.

This includes Asia: Iran, Lebanon, Israel, Turkey, India, Thailand, Vietnam, Malaysia, Japan, South Korea, Taiwan, Russia, Philippines, and Indonesia. I have worked with Islamic friends from Pakistan and Bangladesh in the United States.

In Africa: Morocco, (Rabat, Casablanca, Fez, and Marrakesh), Algiers, Tunisia, Libya, and Egypt.

In the Pacific: Australia, (Sydney, Melbourne, Adelaide, Perth, Exmouth), Tasmania, Wake Island, New Caledonia, Fiji (Suva), New Zealand (Auckland, Wellington, Christchurch) and in Hawaii.

All over Europe including Poland, Czech Republic, Hungary, Greece, the Ukraine (Kiev) and Europe, Russia (Moscow, St. Petersburg)

Famous people travel. He has circled the earth seven times, traveled to Japan 40 times, to Pearl Harbor 25 times and has driven thousands of miles in Europe, New Zealand, and Australia. He has studied the world's cultures. One must learn the motto God gave us, "Faith, Hope, and Love."

His life was working and learning. Reading and learning is done without working. Plan your life "NOW". Thirty years in advance he planned for a sabbatical every 10 years. He had three planned concurrent careers: Academic Neurosurgery, United States Naval Reserve, and Founder of a Neurosciences Center with an academic interchange with 25 countries.

After seven days a week for 40 years in neurosurgery he feared retirement. At age 70 he retired to the unknown. He elected a new life. In his 34-foot Sea Ray he and his wife, Cathy, traveled to all 36 yacht clubs in the Florida Council, from Destin to the Keys, and up to Jacksonville. There is much time on a boat, and he used some of this time to memorize the "Teachings on the Mount".

He and Cathy returned to Apollo Beach, Florida. He became busy and coined a new term, "Retirement Career". (Career as in "go at top speed"). He authored 16 books. He is on the voluntary neurosurgical faculty of the USF Medical School. Deacon and teacher at church. Has continued "Permissive Orders" for the Navy. He became the first 80-year-old drilling reservist. He and Cathy have a pool man, yard man, and maids 5 days a week. (Our lot is covered in rocks and palm trees.) His responsibility is to keep the boat dock maintained. Keep the garage in order. Read on and learn what one can do.

XV. To Our Family and Friends that we have sailed and traveled with through the years we have rejoiced. Our worldly things do not sink to sorrow, for things were our servants, not our masters. They represent the cultures of the world and are left to our family each with a message to learn of another people. We leave nothing of note behind that cannot love.

With the constant tailwind of life, we sail out of sight as death pursues us all "Whatsoever of our age is past, death holds it as the ship sails ahead to the "Blessed Hope". (Titus 2:13)

Ignorance has not been our tyrant for our footsteps were ordered by the LORD. (Psalms 37:23) Time has been our friend. Our planned and willed actions of life with thought and imagination has given us a magnanimous memory. Death has no dread, and the grave no fear, for it guides us to endless glory. When the day comes that we drop the heavy and fatal anchor, it will never be weighed again.

XVI. The knowledge of God has given us, wisdom and understanding and has increased our days

with
"80 Years Behind the Masts."
"Give *instruction* to a wise *man*, and he will be yet wiser:
teach a just *man*, and he will increase in learning.
The fear of the LORD *is* the beginning of wisdom:

and the knowledge of the holy *is* understanding.
For by me thy days shall be multiplied,
and the years of thy life shall be increased."
(Proverbs 9: 9, 10, 11)

Mrs. Joseph H. Miller (Cathy) R.N., CNRN

XVII. About the Co-Editor

Cathy graduated from the Methodist Hospital School of Nursing Memphis
Tennessee, in December 1968. She was presented the ***Faculty Award*** for
outstanding achievement in utilizing all aspects of the education program
in the School of Nursing.

In 1980 she lectured to the nurses at the Naval Regional Medical Center,
Naples, Italy.

She was asked to give the Methodist Hospital School of Nursing Address
to the Graduating Class of December 1993.

She was elected President of the Hein Park Garden Club, Memphis, Tennessee, 1987-1988. She spearheaded the research effort and served as the chairman of the committee to put the neighborhood on the National Register of Historic Places. The Park Service officially listed Hein Park as a Historic District on the National Register on November 16, 1988. Hein Park celebrated its new historic status with a Neighborhood Party, May 12, 1989.

In 1995-1996 Cathy served as President of the Memphis and Shelby County Medical Society Alliance. Her emphasis for the year was a program she originated and founded called **Women's Health Partners, "Partnerships in Health for Life"**. The program was designed to improve women's health through a partnership of concern and caring. The health partners were to encourage and support each other to develop and maintain their wellness through preventive medicine. The program was designed to make certain no "partner" fails to receive the motivation and care so vital to a vibrant and healthy life-style.

Cathy served as a Board Member for the Church Health Center, 1997-2000, Christian Mission Concerns of Tennessee Foundation, 1993-1999, Crichton College, 1993-99, and Briarcrest Christian School (1993-1995) in Memphis. She was also a member of the Rhodes College Forum Class of 1991. From 1992-1998 Cathy served as Executive Assistant for the Paul and Katy Piper Foundation, Christ Is Our Salvation (CIOS).

At the time of our retirement in 2000 she was serving as an Executive Board Trustee of the Tennessee Baptist Convention (1997-2000). As a Baptist Children's Homes Trustee (1992-1995) she served as the State-Wide Campaign Chairman of the **"Building on our Tradition of Caring Campaign"** for Tennessee Baptist Children's Homes. Funds were raised statewide for the Boy's Ranch campaign to raise money to build homes for troubled boys. Rear Admiral Joseph and Cathy Miller provided funds to build the Miller-Parker House in honor of their parents, Dr. and Mrs. Joe H. (Elsie) Miller and Mr. and Mrs. Charles (Ernestine) Parker.

At First Baptist Church, Brandon, Florida, Cathy served as a member of the Vision 2010 Team (2004), three terms on the Personnel Committee, (2005-2007) (2009-2010) (2011-2014), and on the First Baptist Church Brandon Foundation. (2011-2015)

XVIII.

"Admirals" Further Experience and Worldly Certifications

Airplane
Private Pilot   19 June 1962
Instrument Pilot   2 December 1975
Citation Jet Pilot Recurrent Course - 28-30 August 1995

Pilot Hours: 5,258

Boats
United States Coast Guard Diploma-   2 May 2002
United States Merchant Marine Officer   15 May 2002

Boat Experience Sea Service
Total Days Operated 368
Offshore 100
Inland Waters 268

Motorcycle
Joseph and Cathy Miller
Jackson State College Rider Course, Jackson, Tennessee
(19 November 2000)

Snowmobiling in the Grand Tetons, 1991
Snow skiing at Crested Butte, Colorado, 1994

Between 1962 and the year 2000 I used eight logbooks.
My first flight was on 17 April 1962
My Last flight was on 16 November 2000
Total flight hours = 5,258

I wrote this while flying East at 30,000 feet in darkness and while watching the sunrise!

Paralleled with the 23rd Psalm
23 March 1996
(While flying Cessna Citation Jet)
Joseph H. Miller, M.D.

The LORD is my shepherd, I shall not want
He makes me to fly up in blue skies
He leadeth me inside the still winds.
He restored my soul:
He leadeth me in the paths of Heaven for His name' sake.
Yea, though I fly through the clouds of death,
I will fear no evil
Thy stars and thy lights protect me.
Thou preparest my head with the beauty of Heaven, my blessings runneth over.
Surely goodness and mercy shall follow me all the days of my life,
and I will dwell in the House of the LORD forever.

This photograph was taken at Hue, Vietnam on 27 July 1969 while I was on a trip reviewing medical facilities. The plane is a Swiss Porter similar to our Otter. It is a short field airplane and it did an excellent job getting us about! Lieutenant Commander Dan Young in the background flew with me. We traveled in pairs.

U.S. Coast Guard Training and Verification
2 May 2002 CFR 10.205 (i) No. 69235
Diploma

Operator of Uninspected Passenger Vessel. Successfully completed the U.S. Coast Guard approved 54-hour Operator of Uninspected passenger vessels (OUPV)
Sea School (the Law School of the Sea)
St. Petersburg. Florida

15 October 2002
License 1068752 Issue Number 1
United Sates Merchant Marine Officer
"Now you can take a 100-ton ship out 100 miles.

Inspiration for Learning to Ride Motorcycles
Every international traveler will tell one of places in the world where riding a motor bike or motorcycle will be the best available transportation to see the area. The accident rate is high among tourists.

Our last three days to be in Memphis we traveled to Jackson, Tennessee, to take the three-day intensive **"Learn to Ride a Motorcycle"** course. It was 20 degrees Fahrenheit and our training motorcycles had no heater. For an individual who for 40 years had spent eight hours a day in the controlled temperature of an operating room this was also an endurance test.

We purchased these two motorcycles new. After one year we decided Florida was not a place for motorcycles. One person each week dies related to a motorcycle accident.

We left Memphis for retirement in Florida on the night of 21 November 2000 after I turned over the chairmanship of the Department of Neurosurgery to Dr. Jon Robertson. I did this at the beginning of the meeting and then left. Cathy was waiting for me at the door. He finished the agenda and his acceptance speech.

XIX. A Thirty-Year Tribute to My Wife Cathy

My Tribute Includes a Trip, Prose and Narrative
13 October 2009

In October 2009 we will have been married thirty years. I am taking you on a trip to the most beautiful places in the world. If we began traveling today, we would not live long enough to go to all the places we have been. We are returning to the beauty and memory of places we want to see again, in the Bavarian Alps of Germany, Austria, Switzerland, and France. We have reservations for our anniversary dinner on October 13th in Interlaken, Switzerland, at the "flashy formal" La Terrasse Restaurant in our hotel the Grand Hotel Victoria-Jungfrau in the Bernese Alps. The three famous mountain peaks; the Jungfrau, Eiger, and Mönch are in view. When asked, "Why do you go to the Alps?" The answer is, "Because they are there!"

We plan to attend church at the (Castle church) founded in 1133 or the Steeple Church founded in 1471. One notes that in the Reformation the mountain people remained Catholic or what they called Christian.

This writing is **Prose** (Words written without a sentence) and it is also *Narrative* (words with a sentence or story). This is not to be just on paper. It is euphony for the ear and euphoria for the mind. (Most of the time words of praise are read at one's funeral. It may be called a reversed eulogy or a panegyric.) I am writing this, and I will read it to you on our anniversary, the good Lord willing, my Cathy, while we are still alive.

To Cathy After 30 Years:

You have made our home better than Eden and more formidable than Rome. You are always there with an inventive innovation deep in wonders. Out of stillness I forever hear, "I Love You." Your reaching hand is invariably looking for my hand. Your snuggle, communicating a mutual tenderness, causes us to be spiritually one person. Your big eyes are my world. Your smile is the world. You are always there and always will be. You are my gift in this life and a miracle that changed darkness into light; the light that beams love known only to a few. The beam brought a spirit and strength, and love that grows and grows and will never wither. The freshness from 30 years ago remains and has become a thousand times over. There is no loss of force or vitality. You will never let me fall. Your objective in life is to be the best wife your husband could ever have.

Your praise is a model.
Your power is simplicity.
Your speech is superior,
Your spirit is pure
Your diction is distinct
Your phrases a melody
Your thoughts are deep
Your hospitality is forever
Your eyes have character and intelligence
Your enthusiasm stimulates the emotion
Your presence is analytical

You exude an innate and intimate dignity and interest as you listen. Your voice is never in a hurry. Calling you on the phone is like calling the angels. The tone of your voice melts the listener. Your good manners are not confused with status of life, as they are the same with the great or the small. To you people are people, all made in God's image, and equal at the foot of the Cross.

You stimulate the intellect
You penetrate the past
You Beautify the future
You define space
You Magnify the present

You awe the academic
You evaporate the pessimist
You see love in every mind
You love the little things as much as the big things
You overcome toils with love and action
You love whatever is your own as provided for you
You love the diversity of beauty loving the smallest flower hidden to others in
the grass

The things in our home seem to love you as you love them. You speak
to them. You constantly roam our house and inspect every big and little
item. When you are not at home, I imagine tears rolling down from the
lamps! You are rarely quiet. Your thoughts are verbal. You speak and hum
to herself and speak and hum to me. You sing to and love your plants. I
see you watering them early in the morning and late at night. Your singing
in church is ordinary but carries the most beautiful angelic harmony
and heavenly message I have ever heard. It lifts me with you to heights
known only to a few. You are constantly conscious of my presence. You
make unconscious sounds of recognition when I turn over or get up early
in the morning. Your brain computes any discomfort I might have. You
are a natural born doctor (Also a registered nurse) and your voice cures
anything I might have.

You are sunshine in the streets
You are the model of love
You are the real value of life
You elevate your husband
You are proud to be his wife
As a wife you are self-cultivated:
A bright light in every dark castle you enter
Envious of the great and small and loved by both
An uncut diamond whose smile reveals a perfect blue-white
All your houses are a castle
Your home is a heaven on earth

(You are the cleanest person I have ever known. You teach the maids how to clean. One can wipe a white handkerchief under our patio furniture, and it will be clean.)

Other wives love you, a great accomplishment in this modern world

Children, Grandchildren, and Great Grandchildren

Migrate to you for love and comfort
Your love breeds a foundation of support
Your interest is in them not to yourself
Your family brings their friends to meet you
Your mother and father were the godliest salt of the earth, loved me from the first minute, and are now shining with God's Light.
(I preformed major surgery on both.)

You will be immortal at least through the next two generations and eternally immortal in heaven.

You rule by your charm. You are a child in disguise. Childlikeness is a beauty in the Kingdom of Heaven. When you say, "Have a good day." You mean, "Go with God".

You are beyond description; one can only feel your presence. A million roses are in your eyes. You have invisible wings like those of a humming bird. You are the vigorous rhythmic flame of a flamingo.

There is a merry laughter and joyous dancing in your heart. You are a maze of flowers and perfumes in the wind. The light within your heart is without a shadow. Your romance is filled with dignity, grandeur, and passion. You are sweeter than any of the passion-flowers in the tropics that climb as a vine producing herbs with showy petals and pulpy edible berries. You are the passion fruit seen in a human personality.

You brighten any shrine of any saint. Your beauty brings a thrill that penetrates the brain, explodes the mind, and brings magic to the evening.

You are the bubble of bubbles, with sweetness and good humor. Bubbles that do not break and gradually fills any space. Your love floats in the air. You lift weights by love that others leave as too heavy.

I remember your first wrinkle by your chin. Two days later you came hurriedly into the room and said, "I have a wrinkle!" I looked and said, "That is the prettiest wrinkle I have ever seen." You said, "Do you like it?" I said, "Yes, I do, it is cute." You said "O.K." and went on about your business. You and I have many wrinkles now and I love each one of yours. They have made you more beautiful. Amazingly you make me love my own because they are a calendar marked by happiness and love. If I drop something on the floor to come back later to pick it up, it will be gone. Anything you see that needs to be done is yours to do.

You are too frugal. Unsuccessfully I have tried at least partially to break you of this. You will not buy anything that is not at least a 50% sale, 2 for 1, or has a coupon. Many of your things you would not buy because they were too expensive. I made you buy them, and you love them no more than the things on sale.

At worship your mind lingers for the sake of your soul and for the souls of all you know. God's message from the pulpit readily penetrates your **open and receptive mind** with a blessing that comes only from God. You carry it like a torchlight to the world. You are like a ribbon that cuts through the air into the heart. On one occasion I asked you to give our blessing prayer before a meal. Your big eyes and excited face looked at me and said, "I am so full of blessing I can hardly pray." Your prayers go directly to Heaven. The moon seems to linger and protects you as you sleep.

The trees are your exquisite towers filled with the musical wind and message from above. You listen, and your religion is the love of God and all His Creation. The music of the world is to you the international language. To you the charging of the bull in a bullfight is breath taking and the ending is a tragedy. It was cruel, but you admired the matador for his skill developed for his role in life. Your manner remained courtly, differential, and modest. In a large church in South Korea we were tossed into the balcony like dry leaves in a storm. As we sat on a promontory you saw God's presence in the crowd and in your heart.

There is always animation in your face. Your mind computes my mind. I have never in thirty years looked at you when I did not receive a smile. This is true even when you were sick or in pain. Your eyes send a message of joy. Your eloquence is natural and not learned from the modern world. You are the balance of all that is good. Your comprehension of life is above that of the greats. Your face is a poet writing God's love from above. One can feel this as a holy twilight in any sunshine. You lead your own crusades with love instead of blood. There are no undercurrents, only what comes from the sky. You were honored and loved as president of the Memphis and Shelby County Medical Society Auxiliary, (the doctor's wives), and president of the Hein Park Garden Club when you had the neighborhood placed on the National Register of Historical Places. As chairman of the Tennessee Baptist fund-raising campaign for the Baptist Children's Homes, you made available the Boy's Ranch in Millington, Tennessee, and also served as a trustee of the Tennessee Baptist Convention. You have been a major part of all that I have done and know.

You beam that we were created in the image of God and are our **"brother's keeper."** God has revealed His will. The practical rules of our lives are to have Faith in God, Believe God, Trust God, Love God, and Obey God. The secret of this balanced existence has given joy, peace, purpose, and freedom from self-deception, confusion, worry, and fear. There have been the usual life's problems, but no worries. I told you before we were married that I would do all the necessary worrying. So far there have been no worries. Throughout your two surgeries and my two surgeries our trust in God eliminated any potential worries. God's word has led to wisdom "more precious that rubies, more important than longevity, riches or honor." He helps in our effort to acquire His righteousness, justice, knowledge, and foresight. God's wisdom, which beams in your heart, has pointed us to "repentance, good deeds, and vision from God's perspective." We have penetrated the mysteries of life. We have accepted its many challenges, our failures, and the rapid changes in our allotted years from birth to death.

Your love is pure. It is not faked love. Others recognize your true love. There is no jealousy in your love or frustration in your life where the objective is from Above. Hate is unknown to you. You have made our life **form** like two chemicals that come together by the catalysis that only love can bring. It came from nowhere. It **formed** just as the earth springs forth its vegetation. My life is yours for a thousand times. You are a ballad to be played until the end. All you love is love. All love is from God. His Love is your glory. When you laugh the stars sparkle brighter overpowering their twinkle. (An Air Force Research Scientist recently proved that the stars do not twinkle. The effect is due to the turbulent winds between them and us. He eliminates the twinkle by a special lens that deletes the winds.) We continue to sing, "Twinkle, twinkle, little star, twinkle, twinkle through the night." (Jane Taylor, London, 1806) A diamond as big as the world would be of less value than that of the head of a pin compared to you.

Your Love:

Bears all things
Begets love
Is beyond this world
Blends into kindness and goodness
Is from eternity to eternity
Conquers all things
Breeds courage and truth
Cures a cloudy day
Defines charity which has no end
Makes labor a joy
Is not seen with the eyes, but with the heart
Is the breath of life, just as the breath is the life of the soul
Is built on beauty and your beauty is built on love
Is glue for all who know it, one cannot separate from it
Is a clear sky and one cannot see above it

Your Love and Heaven are forever.

God (noun) is love (noun). (I John 4:8,16) Love is a subject and substance under the authority of God, it's origin. It also is a subject and substance under the authority to whom God has given it. God's love and your love is **agape** love, meaning others before self.

You have always supported me without a second of hesitation. I could call you and say we are going to the moon in 10 minutes. You would say, "I'll be ready."

You prove that true love is action and cannot be hidden. Your love expands to others. Love is stronger than death because it has no end. My perception of you has no end in time, height, or distance as it is beyond the universe. Our life, love, and perfect marriage are your own tribute. "The fruits of your hands and your works of your love, gives praise at the gates." (Proverbs 31:31) You have made my people your people and our God is the one God. (From Ruth 1:16) You are more Miller than most Millers. I declare you the living spiritual matriarch of our clan.

In the beginning, 30 years ago, our senses were ahead of our intelligence. We had nothing, but courage and a delight in the present and a confidence in the future. The mysteries of that future are now written in the colorfast paint that does not fade. It is recorded in the adoration of an ethereal burning flame in our spiritual, physical, and mental experiences for 30 years. I am ready to do it all over again! You and I are two bodies in one person. The blessings of our thirty years are uncountable, colossal, and so gigantic they could only come from above, (the abode of the Deity) and thus, are immortal producing a happiness that is all magnanimousness.

My life with her has been perfect, but one of confusion. She has confused me as to what are the big things? And what are the little things? I am still learning the difference. Big and Little Things seem to be the same for Cathy.

XX. Our Thoughts Have Been Worldly

Now I Leave Eternal Thoughts for Ourselves and Country
A. Overcome the World
B. You Live, You Die, Who Decides?
C. Eternal Truth is Enlightenment

A. The Way to Overcome the World

This hopes to: clear the mind, get rid of presuppositions and prejudices, awaken the soul, prove that God exists, and learn that soul growth is the goal. This is the way to overcome the world.

The brain functions much like a group of computers, but a computer does not have feelings, nor does it know right from wrong. All morality and ethics are revealed in God's word.

The greatest tragedy and failure of the religious leaders of the last fifty years is that of widespread Biblical Illiteracy. We are now beyond post-modernism. The secular world has pushed us in a counter-counter reformation. The swords of religious liberty are used by non-religious minds against religion. (They support immoral religious leadership, pornography, abortion for all, homosexuality, non-baptized babies go to Hell and even worse, Biblical Illiteracy.)

Our leaders who have abandoned the proper teaching of the Scriptures have led us into a **world of unbelief**. One has to know the Scriptures in order to believe them. Vandals publicize more on walls than we do in church. The concept of God's righteousness has become man's ignorance. With ignorance of a subject, there is no way to defend that subject. Ignorance produces more ignorance. It grows like a fungus. The problem is no longer disbelief but is **no belief**. Our leaders preach to one another and by so doing support the concept of "Let's just love one another and let the world go to hell." Every leader now knows about Biblical Illiteracy, but it must be at the bottom of their priorities.

When Biblical ignorance occurs, we become infiltrated with corrupted and heretical beliefs. The way to heaven is to be good-looking and rich. Alcoholism is a disease. Women can't be ministers, but men ministers can be immoral, and on and on and on

Heresy and ignorance crowds out the eternal. Many people check the questionnaire that they believe in God, but do not know the Biblical God. Understanding the God that described Himself in Exodus 3:14,15 is central to understanding the Christian beliefs. The Bible is not a record of God's Word. **It is God's word**. The best proof of God is revealed. One cannot prove God by words or things; if they try, they make God a thing. Dead souls don't produce. With widespread Biblical Illiteracy among Christians there are dead souls somewhere in the process of education. Part of man goes to heaven and part does not. Be blessed in the search for the soul and thus overcome the world.

B. You Live, You Die, Who Decides?

Not even science knows much about death and it is rolling in our direction at a high rate of speed. We all need to learn as much as we can about it. No earthly person has ever returned from the trip, but we can prepare for it in several ways. The first obstacle to overcome in our minds about death is the universal tendency to deny it will happen, to ignore it, and to not prepare for it. If one has no faith, no religion, or no belief in God and this is one's firm, fixed and final decision then eat, drink, and be merry and let it happen. There are no reasonable solutions for that position. For the Christian the issue is settled, and no further comment is needed.

Extensive studies are needed regarding the almost universal ignorance related to death. This involves the Grey areas of Life, Life and Death Ethics, the Code of Medical Ethics, Bioethics, Anatomical and Physiological Studies of the Brain, Physiological Basis of Consciousness, Euthanasia and the desire for Death, 30-year Experience with Euthanasia and Assisted Suicide in The Netherlands, Death and the Bible, Death and the Desire for Death in the Bible, and Humanism.

One needs to be educated in the events leading up to death for you and your family. This requires knowledge of the 12 Levels of Life from Normal to Death. Only then can one place a value on the quality of life at each of these levels. One must also be able to separate out the clinical levels of Consciousnesses, as we know them from alert, to alert and confused, drowsiness, stuporous, deep stupor, coma and deep coma. A review is also included of the various memory deficits including amnesia.

The Science and Legality of death is reviewed by describing Brain Death, the Persistent Vegetative State, the Florida law, Living wills and Terminal Care, and the role of Ethics Committees.

After education one must then decide if they are capable of making Life and Death decisions. The truth is that some people cannot.

In order to develop an action that will change the shameful condition of death decisions in America education is needed describing the needs necessary for action. This includes Leadership, Salvation, and the reversal of the widespread Biblical Illiteracy Among Christians.

With knowledge Congress should be able to develop a law or laws of the people instead of having the courts with ordinary men and their prejudices making them.

C. Eternal Truth is Enlightenment

Man is master of his Fate, but he must seek the Truth.

We must discover the real world. All generations are struggling for the truth! Truth is our heritage and gift to the next-generation, so we must support education for all people. Some generations have essentially halted progress, and others are making progress, only because of a few.

In our world, we must proclaim religious freedom and free speech. The concept of human liberty is more than 4,000 years old and is repeated by Christ Himself.

We must dare to read, think, speak, and write the truth. Truth is not only violated by falsehood, but also by silence. Ignorance produces the work of monsters. Ignorance is not bliss; it is oblivion. Ignorance is sin, not innocence.

Man is what he believes, coated by either truth or ignorance. Truth demands a basic standard of living for the masses to ensure security and freedom for their development. Man is master of his fate, but he must seek the truth. Truth is on the march, and nothing can stop it!

References

1. ***Columbia Encyclopedia***, (Sixth Edition), editor Paul Lagasse, Columbia University Press. 1893-2000)

2. ***Encyclopedia of World History***, William L. Langer, Harrap/Galley Press, 1940-1989

3. ***The Art of War***, (1521) Niccolo Machiavelli, Introduction by Neal Wood, a Da Capo Paperback, (1965), 1469-1527. Art of War (1965)

4. ***Dictionary of the Bible***, Herbert Lockyer, Sr., Editor, with F.F. Bruce and R.K. Harrison, Thomas Nelson Publishers, 1986.

5. **The Economists**, *"Staying Alive"*, Leaders, November 24, 2018.

6. **World History**, Philip Parker, Metro Books, New York, 2010.

7. *"In the Shadow of the Sword",* Tom Holland. Anchor Books, Random House. Inc. New York, 2013.

8. ***War, History and Philosophy of War,*** RAdm Joseph H. Miller and Cathy Miller, AuthorHouse, 2017

9. ***Smithsonian***, Vol. 49, No. 09, January-February 2019, Smithsonian.com.

10. ***1776,*** David McCullough, Simon-Schuster, New York, 2005.

11. ***The Spiritual Brain***, Mario Beauregard and Denyse O'Leary (***A Neuroscientists Case for the Existence of the Soul***), HarperCollins Publishers, 2007)

12. ***Explore the Brain for the Soul and Overcome the World***, Rear Admiral Joseph H. Miller, AuthorHouse, 2008.

13. ***You Live, You Die, Who Decides?*** Rear Admiral Joseph H. Miller, AuthorHouse, 2008.

14. ***Eternal Truth, Eternal Truth is Enlightenment***, Rear Admiral Joseph H. Miller, Westbow Press, 2015.

Good References, but not noted in this book:

1. The Heritage Foundation, James Carafano, January 17, 2019
2. Militia, United States Wikipedia, 1/19/2019 The Militia Act of 1903 included **Organized militia, Unorganized militia, and a state defense force as authorized by state and federal laws.**
3. Chief Kessler's Constitutional security Force 2/26/2013 – this Civilian Militia Expands to 38 States to Protect the Constitution, by James Dean

Printed in the United States
By Bookmasters